MANAGEMENT 101

MATTHEW J. CULLIGAN

PRENTICE HALL
Englewood Cliffs, New Jersey 07632

M000035075

Prentice-Hall International (UK) Limited, *London*
Prentice-Hall of Australia Pty. Limited, *Sydney*
Prentice-Hall Canada, Inc., *Toronto*
Prentice-Hall Hispanoamericana, S.A., *Mexico*
Prentice-Hall of India Private Limited, *New Delhi*
Prentice-Hall of Japan, Inc., *Tokyo*
Simon & Schuster Asia Pte. Ltd., *Singapore*
Editora Prentice-Hall do Brasil, Ltda., *Rio de Janeiro*

10 9 8 7 6 5 4 3 2 1

Library of Congress Cataloging-in-Publication Data

Culligan, Matthew J.
    Management 101 : the best of Joe Culligan's back-
to-basics techniques / Matthew J. Culligan.—1st ed.
    p. cm.
    Includes index.
    ISBN 0-13-512112-4
    1. Management. 2. Strategic planning. 3. Sales
management. 4. Public relations. 5. Business
communication. III. Title: Management one hundred
and one.
HD31.C822 1993   93-4451
658—dc20   CIP

ISBN 0-13-512112-4

PRENTICE HALL
Career & Personal Development
Englewood Cliffs, NJ 07632

Simon & Schuster, A Paramount Communications Company

Printed in the United States of America

To the inspirational and incomparable
Betty Harper Fussell

CONTENTS

v

GUIDE TO LISTS

CHAPTER 1

CHAPTER 2

CHAPTER 7

CHAPTER 8

CHAPTER 9

CHAPTER 10

CHAPTER 12

CHAPTER 13

Using the Telephone

CHAPTER 14

CHAPTER 15

CHAPTER 16

CHAPTER 17

CHAPTER 18

CHAPTER 19

CHAPTER 20

CHAPTER 22

CHAPTER 23

CHAPTER 24

CHAPTER 26

ABOUT THE AUTHOR

Matthew J. Culligan has, during four decades in business, demonstrated a rare combination of creative and administrative abilities. After service in World War II and retirement for battlefield wounds, he entered the magazine business as a space salesman. Rapid promotions followed with greater opportunities in other corporations in the field of his choice, commercial communications. He managed small departments, regional divisions, national marketing organizations, and, finally, entire corporations. The corporations included National Broadcasting Company (television and radio networks), Interpublic, Inc., Curtis Publishing Company, Mutual Broadcasting and Teletape Corporation.

He advocated good corporate citizenship and raised record amounts of money for The Boy Scouts of America, the United Jewish Appeal, and served on presidential commissions during the Kennedy and Johnson administrations, including becoming a public member of the State Department during the Johnson administration, traveling extensively in the East Pacific and Pacific Latin America.

The editors of *The New York Times* named him "One of the Men Who Shaped U.S. Business" during the 1960s. *Time* magazine described Culligan as "one of America's greatest marketing experts." He won the Silver Anvil Award of the Public Relations Society of America for his revitalization of the Curtis Publishing Company. A national survey by *The Gallagher Report* cited him as "The Man Who Did Most for Magazines" and "The Man Who Did Most for Advertising."

After retirement from business he opted for a new career in writing. His published works are: *The Curtis-Culligan Story, How to Be a Billion-Dollar Persuader, Back-To-Basics Selling, Back-to-Basics Public Relations and Publicity, Back-to-Basics Management, Back-to-Basics Planning, How to Avoid Stress Before It Kills You, The 70 Million Dollar Decimal,* and *Horrid Horoscopes.*

He created two television documentaries, *Norman Rockwell's American Experiences* and *History's Odd Couple.*

A dedicated environmentalist, he founded The Environmental Monitor, a not-for-profit foundation which will link the outstanding computer data bases on environmental protection.

INTRODUCTION

The basics series of books I have written during the 1980s "grew like Topsy" rather than as a well-planned program. The first was about the gentle art of persuasion, the skill of getting what you want (maybe even deserve) by speech, text, and body language. A good friend, suitably gruff, complained that that book, entitled *How to Be a Billion-Dollar Persuader* was too general. "Why don't you get back to the basics of selling?" he asked. *Back-to-Basics Selling* was my response. It was published by the unforgettable Nat Wartels, the founder of Crown Publishing. When it succeeded, Nat suggested that I do the same for public relations and publicity, a BTB approach. When that book, *The Basics of Public Relations,* succeeded, the momentum carried me logically to overall management. *Back-to-Basics Management* was an immediate success and was acquired by publishers in Scandinavia, in Spain for Latin America, and in Portugal for that country and Brazil. More exciting was the publishing of *Back-to-Basics Management* in Japan where print orders are huge compared to those in the United States.

The mosaic was completed with *Back-to-Basics Planning,* which included considerable input marketing.

In 1990 an editor at Prentice Hall who had heard me make the commencement address at his university asked if I had considered an amalgamation of the individual books into a kind of monitor of the basics of management in the broadest sense. This book is the answer. It is a distillation of nearly 2,000 pages, a BTB concoction presented almost conversationally, as though I had the opportunity to talk to you personally.

The 1980s were not, repeat not, glorious years for the American business community. There were self-inflicted wounds as a result of elitism, cronyism, laziness, and greed.

Because the economy expanded dramatically with greatly lessened government regulations, clever, often unprincipled individuals took outrageous advantage and introduced into the U.S. business system a new concept—that debt was a very minor problem. If the U.S. government could increase its debt by trillions, why should not business conglomerates? Junk bonds were the visible result. Corporate mergers and hostile and "friendly" takeovers became routine. The foundations of many fine businesses were shaken, loyalty of company to personnel and personnel to company became antique. If the historians of the twenty-first century do give a title to the 1980s, it may well be "The Decade of the Cash In." This was the decade in which top management of countless corporations "cashed in" with stock deals, option deals and "golden parachutes" with little regard for the millions of loyal employees who were outside that magic circle and long-suffering stockholders.

Can the 1990s be very different? Perhaps, though human nature changes at a glacial pace. It can only be hoped that human nature will change for the better during the next decade and thereon.

Now, about this book. It does violate some of the standard rules relating to uniformity. Some sections have few chapters, other sections have many. I followed my own advice about management by objective (Chapter 2) by determining that my goal is *maximum effectiveness.* I concluded that some concise chapters suited my purposes best and, in other cases, because subtopics are so closely related, breaking a section into multiple chapters would be too choppy.

Throughout the book I have relied heavily on the use of lists to present key points and summaries of information. I favor this approach because it makes the material immediately accessible. Because these lists serve as a handy summary of the contents of each chapter, I have included after the Table of Contents a section entitled "Guide to Lists," which catalogs by brief description and page number the lists presented in each chapter.

It is my fondest hope that readers of this book will use it as a handbook, perhaps even removing some of the lists of "do's and don'ts" for easy reference and travel companions on business trips.

My intent in this introduction is to describe the book from a vantage point. *Management* is the senior art/science of business and industry, the umbrella. The fabric of the umbrella is *Communications;* it covers all. *Planning* is the mechanism of the umbrella. *Marketing, Selling, Public Relations* and *Publicity* are the spokes of the umbrella. Each of those elements is a *section,* divided as mentioned, into a varying number of *chapters.* The tone of the book is as close to conversational as I could make it.

So, on to *Management 101* with my wishes in an ancient toast: May you have your heart's desire.

SECTION 1

MANAGEMENT

CHAPTER 1

Back to Basics Management

Today's business requires more than knowledge of techniques and technology. It demands that the managers understand the human aspect of management. Foundation block number one in back-to-basics management is:

News + information + comment = knowledge

Knowledge + thinking + feedback = understanding

Understanding + commitment + discipline = back-to-basics
management

It is important for the back-to-basics manager to understand that knowledge is not enough for successful management in today's world, that this whole formula must be used for a completed cycle of success.

Foundation block number two is:

Effective communication. We can store and pass on information through the use of computers, but it is talking and listening to one another that is important. This communication must take place within a higher and more pragmatic area of management.

Foundation block number three is:

Interpersonal relationships. For this communication to be effective and management to be successful, the human aspect of interpersonal relations must be taken into consideration.

Consider these criteria for back-to-basics management and managers:

Back-to-basics management:

1. Recognizes natural talent.
2. Is antibureaucratic.
3. Disdains fear and greed as motivators in business.
4. Puts heavy emphasis on learned skills.
5. Recognizes the need for both instinct and nonconformity in thinking.
6. Subscribes to a compassionate person-to-person management style.
7. Is the perfect strategy for today's manager, who must use the new technologies with time-tested management principles.

Back-to-basics managers:

1. Know themselves.
2. Are experts at getting things done.
3. Are skilled in time management and self-organization.
4. Use communication as their prime management tool.
5. Are big on people skills.
6. Are creative and innovative and know how to motivate and use the creative output of their people.
7. Know how to delegate work successfully.
8. Are effective supervisors.
9. Recognize signs of distress.

▪ CREATIVE LISTENING

Listening is one of the more important skills a back-to-basics manager can learn. Forty-five percent of the time he spends in communication is spent listening. Without good listening habits, a manager's effectiveness in using what he hears can drop below 25 percent. Listening is more than hearing words. It is understanding what is being said, what is not being said, and what our motivation for listening is. Our motivation and emotions greatly influence our listening effectiveness.

The five blocks to effective listening are:

1. Attempting to extract only the facts from a message.
2. Allowing certain words to affect us emotionally.
3. Rejecting what is being said because of our predisposition to the subject.
4. Looking and acting as if we are listening when we are not.
5. Criticizing what is being said because we dislike the speaker or his or her mannerisms.

Here's how to increase your listening effectiveness:

- Prepare yourself to listen.
- Listen to the speaker from his or her point of view.
- Concentrate on the major points, not on the statistics. Keep looking for information you can use.
- Build defense mechanisms against words that have emotionally laden meanings for you.
- Learn to keep an open mind. Look for the positive aspects of what is being said.
- Pay attention. Note how the talk is organized.
- Keep your mind on the speaker.
- Listen between the lines for information and ideas that may not have been put into words.

- Try to anticipate points and ideas.
- Review and weigh what you are hearing. This will help keep your mind from wandering.
- Withhold judgment, evaluation, and decision making until the speaker has finished.
- Ask silent mental questions about what is being said.
- Actively seek areas of interest for yourself in what is being said.
- Don't let note taking be a distraction.
- Adjust to distractions; don't just tolerate them.
- Exercise your mind. Learn to listen to technical information and expository material.
- Keep eye contact with the speaker (especially on a one-to-one basis).
- Listen with your whole person.

■ DECISION MAKING

Decision making is the fundamental activity of managers. Even when managers feel they do not have enough facts, they must act. Managers are constantly being presented with facts and information stated in words (verbal maps) on which they must base their decisions; managers must make sure that these "verbal maps" fit the actual territory or reality they are describing. A manager must always remember that people describe circumstances and events according to how they interact with the situation. As a result, the "facts" may not always be an accurate and adequate description of what is really going on.

A manager's judgmental thinking can be helped by remembering:

1. You can't possibly know everything about everything. Develop the habit of open-mindedness. Learn to use the phrase "as far as I know" in your thinking.

2. Learn to think in terms of degrees by silently adding the phrase "up to a point." This will help do away with either/or type of thinking.

3. Be analytical and honest. Try not to select things that prove only your point of view.

4. We see things not as they are, but as we are. When we speak in terms of good, large, and other subjective adjectives we are not describing qualities, but our personal reaction to the subject. Learn to incorporate the silent phrases "to me," "to him," "to her," "to them" in your thinking.

5. Be careful in using common nouns such as house, dog, or manager. No two things are exactly alike. Oversimplified labels can lead us to erroneous conclusions.

6. Make sure you have the authority to make the needed decision.

7. A decision should be made by people as close as possible to the function it affects.

8. It is important that you train those you supervise in the art of making decisions. You should demand that they offer a partial solution, if not a full one, when they bring you a problem.

9. All decisions carry a risk factor.

10. All decisions bring changes you must be prepared to handle.

11. Don't spend time making decisions that you don't intend to carry out.

12. Before implementing decisions, gather as much information as practical about the circumstances surrounding the decision.

13. When planning your implementation of the decision, make sure you have included all elements that may have to be handled.

14. In your planning, make sure you have set alternative courses of action in case of obstacles or problems.

15. In communicating your decision, remember the phrase "people are a resource" is a working reality for the back-to-basics manager.

16. Communicate your ideas, decisions, policy, and values in such a manner that they elicit support and motivate.

17. Communicate decisions to those you report to first.

18. Plan your communication to your superior in such a manner that you totally inform him or her of all the surrounding facts and circumstances and elicit his or her support.

19. Make sure you communicate with other departments that may be affected by your decision.

20. Try to include the employees whose work will be affected in both the decision-making and implementation plans.

21. Write, speak, and communicate in language that motivates employees.

22. Show employees how the decisions will be to their benefit and why their participation is needed.

▪ MANAGING CHANGE

Change is vital to the continuing growth of our society. One of your prime functions as a back-to-basics manager is to manage change and prepare your people for change. Most people see change as a fearsome proposition; they see it as instability.

However, people adjust to change more easily when they feel they have been instrumental in either the decision-making or the implementation process. Change is vital to the continuing growth of any organization. Because of this, it is important to understand that change is what gives your company a competitive edge.

Keys to managing and understanding change are:

1. Understanding that the more ingrained the routine or habit, the harder it will be to change it.

2. Maintaining consistency in your attitude about fundamentals, which will help your people during times of change.

3. Setting boundaries, which will help minimize feelings of instability during times of change.

4. Remaining reliable in the eyes of your people during change, and explaining the why's and wherefore's of a change.

5. Being comfortable with change yourself.

6. Before initiating any change, exploring your own reactions to the changing situation.

7. Recognizing that routines and sameness (not systems) can cut down on productivity, you must examine these areas for possible change.

8. Remembering that each action you take in making a change will bring a reaction of some sort.

9. To the best of your ability, knowing the reactions of all those who will be affected by change.

10. Being sure to consider the reactions of others to change when doing your implementation planning. (Don't forget to allow extra time for these reactions.)

11. Making sure you have provided for alternative courses of action in planning for change.

You should make a change when:

1. It will give you an edge over the competition.

2. The change will be truly beneficial.

3. You feel that the ensuing reactions can be handled and will be beneficial.

Initiating a successful change requires these six steps:

1. Make a critical judgment and decision.

2. Motivate your people and all those involved.

3. Produce an action.

4. Find possible alternatives in case of problems.

5. Make sure your people learn how to relate to the new situation.

6. Be prepared to handle unforeseen consequences.

■ MANAGING MOTIVATION

A back-to-basics manager-leader must be able to show others how to meet their goals and needs in a work situation. Motivation is the inner drive of the individual that moves him to action to meet goals and needs. To manage motivation, you must understand the how and why of human interaction. By understanding human interaction, you will be able to form (and change) attitudes and opinion, stimulate creativity, help your people learn and develop, manage conflict productively, and master a host of other topics that are needed for effective human interaction and leadership. In back-to-basics management leadership, the individual is preeminent and not the task. As a manager, your performance will be judged by the performance and productivity of others. Your goal is to free yourself from detail and task-defined roles so that you can move up to the real challenge of leadership—managing and motivating people as individuals and in groups.

In understanding motivation it is important to remember that the reason anyone wants to accomplish anything is the benefit or the reward for completion of the task.

In managing motivation these points will help you:

1. The desire for the result of behavior is the driving force that produces behavior.

2. A benefit must be a benefit to the employee (not to the manager alone) to produce results.

3. A benefit or reward must tie in with a person's tangible and intangible needs.

4. Tangible needs are the substantive payoffs the person doing the job wants from the job.

5. Intangible needs are the reason why a person wants what she wants from the job.

6. Business job goals are specific and measurable and deal with objective matters.

7. Behavioral job goals are less measurable and involve changes in behavior or interpersonal skills that will help achieve a business goal.

8. We are all motivated all the time, because we tend to do those things we find rewarding.

9. Each of us tends to think of rewards in a different light. Thus, it is your job to make the reward fit the individual to accomplish the task.

10. When you link goals with needs, you provide rewards that produce job commitment.

11. Employees' needs (tangible and intangible) can be identified through their behavior and statements about career goals.

12. Employees' statements about their tangible needs give you clues to their intangible needs.

13. A performance appraisal conversation about every six months will keep you up to date on the changing motivational needs of your employees.

14. Because we cannot always meet an employee's tangible needs, it is important to try to meet his intangible needs.

15. Intangible need motivation achieves the same level of motivation as tangible need motivation.

16. When talking to your employees, speak the language of motivation; use such words as "participation," "opportunity," "involvement," and "meaningfulness."

17. Always speak in terms of benefits to those you are trying to motivate.

18. To communicate and motivate, you must have a two-way dialogue.

19. Both you and your employee must be in the right receptive mood for a two-way dialogue to occur.

20. The back-to-basics manager-leader gets his or her employees involved strategically with decisions, delegates in a planned, purposeful manner, ties employees' needs to company goals and quotas, and encourages analysis and criticism of what's going on.

CHAPTER 2

Management by Objective

■ REQUIREMENTS FOR USEFUL AND PRODUCTIVE MANAGEMENT

There are three basic premises upon which all useful and productive management by objective programs are based: involvement, participation, and autonomy.

❏ Involvement

From design of the job description to performance review and reward, the employee is completely involved in the job to be done: *what* is to be done, *how* it is to be done, authority for doing it, and responsibility (for better or worse) in accounting for its execution. The involvement is complete. That is, the manager does not write the job description and ask the employee to "sign off" on it; the employee writes the job description, using standard guidelines provided by the company, and the manager and the employee rework it until both are satisfied that it is accurate. This same mutuality of effort is apparent in every aspect of the employee's work. Just as the arrows in the pyramid don't go in only one direction (down from on high), so the communication and involvement flow both ways, commencing from the bottom.

❏ Participation

Between departments and among people within any given department, there is a need for constant communication to resolve conflicts and elicit mutual consent for all the activities crucial to each person and group. This participation is fundamental to the MBO concept.

❏ Autonomy

Under MBO the employee has both responsibility and authority to succeed or fail. The employee meets with the manager for advice, training, and guidance, but they usually communicate only at the end of a performance cycle, when the task(s) are completed. This, logically, gives the manager more time to manage, to think, and to plan rather than hover over employees monitoring their every move.

It is important to remember that you should avoid superficial and nonconnected programs. Doing something just for show or setting up an isolated project as a kind of prototype in limbo is not a satisfactory way of launching MBO programs. MBO organization planning coupled with a back-to-basics business plan with objectives and strategies is the best way of guaranteeing a payoff. And the payoff—rewards, satisfaction, feedback, seeing results—is what the working environment should be all about.

■ WHAT IS MBO WORTH?

Why should you even bother with all this? MBO sounds like a lot of work; what's the payoff? Thousands of companies have instituted MBO since the 1950s. They continue to use it. The reasons why can be summed up as follows:

- MBO provides the greatest flexibility in managing and directing people in an enterprise, allowing a venture to remain highly competitive in a constantly changing world.

- It is a system that permits a manager to become more involved and committed to the enterprise; it allows managers to manage and all employees to feel themselves a part of the process.

- Everyone is a part of the organization, its goals, its purposes, under MBO. Their commitment and devotion are based on something besides payday.

- If everyone is an important part of the process of a venture, and they know that they are, they have a greater stake in its success and profitability. Books such as *In Search of Excellence*[1] deal with companies that are successful because they create a certain atmosphere and standard of excellence; those companies have very highly evolved, long-term organization and personnel planning processes that have contributed mightily to their success and profitability.

❑ Payoff

The payoff occurs when the personnel policies and procedures interconnect directly with our organization planning. There is no organization without people; people function within an organization, either by design or by improvisation; function is the fundamental definition of a business. Ergo, your personnel planning cannot be done without organization planning, and both organization planning and function rely upon your personnel policies and procedures.

❑ What Types of People Can Slow You Down?

What kinds of people can be stumbling blocks to a successful MBO program? We touched on this topic earlier when we talked about

---

[1] Thomas J. Peters and Robert H. Waterman, *In Search of Excellence* (New York, Harper & Row, 1982).

instituting a partial MBO program rather than abandoning the idea altogether in firms that aren't yet ready for a companywide program.

- *Too busy.* We all know these people; they're too busy to start anything new. (They are also usually too busy to get their current work done.)

- *Go on without me.* These folks are happy to see us try to make something work, but don't count on their cooperation. Progress is particularly difficult if these people are managers.

- *Perfectionists.* They will rework the nitpicking fine points of the program until it dies of overpolishing, overmodification, and excessive detail the first time around.

- *Cast in stone.* Once a plan is written, say these recalcitrants, never change it, never modify it, never be flexible. Of course, no improvement is possible under such conditions.

- *Copycats.* They copy, right down to the last detail, the plans of some other department or company, so, of course, their plan bears no relation to the needs of this particular department or company.

- *I've always done it that way.* People of this mind-set see no need for change because the old ways are the best ways. Sometimes that's true, but they'll never give anything new a chance.

- *Tell me again.* These folks need everything explained and explained and explained. By the time the explanations are exhausted, it's too late to implement the plan.

- *I don't understand.* These people will get hung up on clarifying or tinkering with some particular part of the plan and remain hanging there forever. They'll never see the whole picture.

❑ Avoid the Pitfalls

Don't let people and problems get in the way of launching the MBO project. Be forewarned and be prepared. Here are some useful strategies:

- Check the progress of your plan on a regular basis, paying particular attention to those people (or types) who can create pitfalls. Be alert for them and look specifically for any signs of problems.

- Define the problem (or person) and analyze the source. Be objective and thorough.

- Look at your options. What are your limitations? What are the opportunities to remove those limitations? Is the problem incurable, or can you devise some training strategies?

- Initiate an alternate plan to bring the recalcitrants aboard or start over with a new tack or a fresh approach.

▪ CHECKLIST FOR THE ORGANIZATION PLAN

"Form follows function."
The development of an organization that best serves the tasks to be performed is the primary objective in organization planning. The best back-to-basics planners and managers strive for flexibility, autonomy, and participation among all employees in the organization. Here are some reminders on how to achieve those goals:

- Most American businesses are organized like the military. Your objective should be to tap all that human potential, not draw little boxes on an organization chart.

- "Quality circles" allocate human resources by task, not by department. Problem solving in that kind of environment involves utilizing many skills from many sources. The whole is often stronger than the sum of its parts.

- Flexibility in an organization, the ability to function effectively in a changing world, is a good beginning for management by objectives.

- Since "form follows function," tasks should dictate the type of people and their mode of interrelationship in an enterprise.

- Management by objective fundamentally involves the management of people.

- MBO defines the goals and the methods of reaching them and establishes qualitative measurement of the progress toward achieving them.

- MBO can be instituted in three ways:

  Set objectives above what is currently done.

  Incorporate personnel goals with corporate goals on an annual basis.

  Integrate MBO into your long-range strategic planning.

- Everyone manages something: people, money, resources, assets, departments.

- Analyze your management style: Are you "X" or "Y"? Do you direct or delegate?

- MBO can be threatening to people who do not welcome responsibility for their own actions.

- Why use MBO?

  It allows the greater flexibility in managing people.

  It enables a manager to manage and permits all employees to feel themselves a part of the process.

  Therefore, everyone plays a meaningful role in the enterprise.

  With everyone a part of the process, all are dedicated to achieving a venture's goals.

- The future is now. How will we work in the last years of the twentieth century?

  We work in teams, interdependently.

  We must learn to manage changing life-styles.

  There are more large-scale enterprises—conglomerates.

  We are a young working nation (50 percent of the work force is under age 30) and there are more workers over age 65. This demographic change alters a whole range of key business factors, from employee benefits to marketing.

  We are a more educated society, seeking more challenges.

People seek greater involvement, participation, and autonomy in their work.

- Other people can slow you down, as the "doubting Thomases" look for reasons not to implement fully your MBO program.
- Avoid the pitfalls:

  Check the progress of your plan on a regular basis.

  Define the problems and analyze their source.

  Look at your options: what can you change?

  Initiate an alternate plan to bring others aboard.
- Avoid superficial and nonconnected programs. Programs must make sense to all and have a payoff to be effective.
- Your personnel policies and procedures provide the payoff for your back-to-basics organization plan.
- What are the functions of management under MBO?

  Planning

  Organizing

  Performing

  Controlling

  Reviewing
- Managing people is like managing a company: process and purpose are interconnected.
- Instead of managers constantly questioning employees, managers should also question themselves.
- Whether your problem as a manager is high employee turnover, lack of in-job growth, unmet goals, or management overload, the one universally applicable solution is training your employees.
- Take fundamental human needs and motivators into account in designing your MBO plan. Once the physical, safety, and social needs are fulfilled, employees want more: they want self-esteem and, ultimately, self-actualization (a maximization of their ability and potential).

- Translate employee needs into management functions:

  Prepare job descriptions so employees will know their duties.

  Ask employees to help set goals.

  Evaluate results so employees will know how they're doing.

  Advise, guide, counsel, and train to supply the help employees need.

  Reward good results.

- Monitor the performance of your employees by:

  Identifying key job duties.

  Indicating the expected results.

  Identifying which results to measure.

  Determining ways of measuring the results.

  Measuring achievement as prescribed times.

  Rewarding good results.

  Listing areas to be improved.

  Starting the monitoring process over again.

- An individual's personal objectives and life goals must somehow relate to the organization's goals and standards. Personal values cannot be in conflict with company values.

- Don't be afraid to use consultants to help implement MBO; maybe you can avoid "reinventing the wheel."

- The steps for personnel planning are:

  Define the work to be done in terms of skill, time, and number of people.

  Identify company resources: revenues, costs, expected profits.

  Analyze your people costs in terms of number and kinds of jobs, competitive rates, benefits packages, and incentives.

  Write the job descriptions.

  Set work goals, action plans, and a time frame.

  Establish a review process.

Set up training and guidance programs.

Establish salary/grade levels with review and increase guidelines.

Devise a review process for reviewing the success of your own back-to-basics planning and management, so that you stay competitive.

Develop guidelines for problems and problem people.

Set up equitable payoffs and incentives.

■ Always remember the word *justification* when preparing a personnel plan.

While there is no such thing as a *perfect* or *absolute* organization tool, management by objectives is the most logical choice for a company or enterprise that wishes to run its operation based on sound business practices and good business planning.

Management by objectives is the management of people. MBO helps define where all of you want to go (the goal) and how you can get there (the strategies), and it provides a quantitative measurement of the target and your progress in reaching it.

You can't plan a company's goals without people, and you can't manage and inspire people without involving them in the company's goals. MBO is a circle (albeit perhaps not a quality circle): form follows function, people make a company, companies give people purpose.

If you plan to institute management by objectives as your company's method of organization and personnel planning, there are three ways you can go about it:

■ *Objectives.* In this approach you work with your managers to set objectives over and above what they currently do. You use this approach to stretch the managers (and their departments' contribution) in an orderly and targeted way.

■ *Total planning process.* Here you incorporate personnel goals with corporate goals; the organizational structure becomes part of the business planning process of the organization on a year-to-year basis.

▪ *Completely new way of looking at your organization.* In this approach, MBO goes beyond the annual business planning process and addresses the future of the organization, its purpose, its people, its training; MBO becomes an integral part of the strategic planning of an operation and truly takes the ebb and flow of that anthill and turns it into the ebb and flow of the tides themselves. It assumes complete reorientation of company procedures, it makes a different set of assumptions about the nature of people in an organization and how they are to be utilized, and it assures a change in the delegation of responsibility.

Let us say right now that there is no "correct" choice among the foregoing three options. The fact that you think of your venture, its position in the competitive world today, the composition of your work force, and your commitment to business planning as an orderly process will all dictate the choice you make as to which of the three ways you will go. You know best whether your company is ready for the third option. You may want to begin with the first approach, to stretch your people and prepare them for the future. You may be far enough along in orderly business planning to go with the second approach and incorporate your human resources goals into your business planning goals on an annual basis. This chapter makes no assumptions about which way you will choose to go. But we would like to share with you some of the procedures and processes that will help you make the choices.

▪ ALLOCATION OF MANAGEMENT TIME

Everyone is involved in management—of people, of money, of resources, of departments. We have great respect for both presidents and telephone operators, sales managers and typists. They *all* manage something. As the first exercise in MBO, it is necessary to analyze (together!) how much time is spent managing and how much time is spent doing.

We are always fearful of generic charts; they tend to simplify complicated functions and minimize human potential. But they can help us organize our thoughts about what we're *supposed* to be doing (as opposed to what we are *probably* doing). The only thing that everyone in the world shares is time. The rational and effective allocation of our time for business, for family, for society, and for ourselves is our major goal in life. By looking at Figure 2.1, you can tell (in general terms) whether or not you are channeling your business time in a meaningful and effective way, both for yourself and for your company. It is the first step in the long process of defining the objectives of management and of each employee in an MBO program.

■ **FIGURE 2.1**

The Allocation of Time at Various Organizational Levels

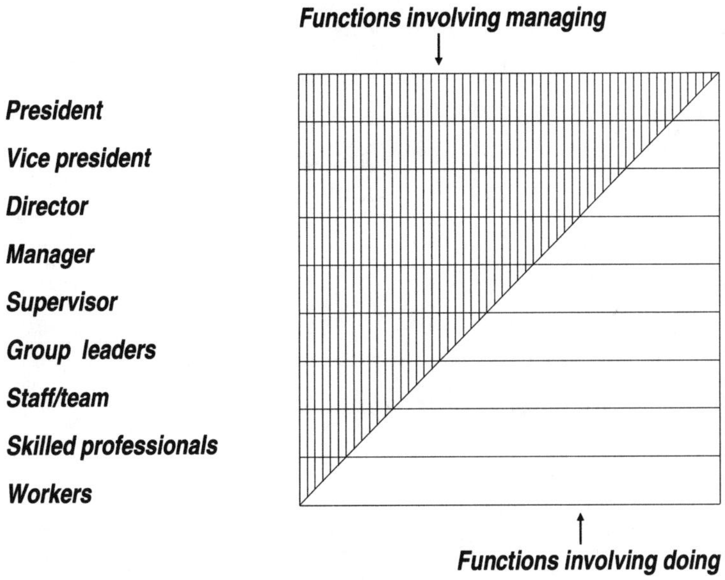

Functions involving managing

President
Vice president
Director
Manager
Supervisor
Group leaders
Staff/team
Skilled professionals
Workers

Functions involving doing

■ **QUESTIONS FOR MANAGERS**

As the overall company planning process, organization planning works only if everyone is involved, participating and exercising control over their functions (having autonomy). Just as you analyzed your management *style* earlier in the chapter, your function as a manager must involve constant review—of yourself. In a sense, the new ways seem a mirror image of the old. Instead of a manager constantly questioning an employee about the job function, that manager must constantly question himself or herself.

The following questions are only a partial list of the behavior you should monitor in yourself. As you get more and more involved in the process (and the success) of formal organization planning, you will add to the list yourself.

- Do I ask employees to participate and contribute so that they can shape their own work, or do I use their ideas myself?

- Do I give them a chance to change or modify their objectives/goals?

- Do I ask them for ideas about the total department/company?

- Do I "stay off their backs" and not hover over them, allowing them to organize their own work?

- Do I let them seek help when they need it and not volunteer to "take over" when they get into trouble?

- Can they judge when their work is complete, or do they have to wait for me to say so?

- Do I ask them to point out "pitfalls" voluntarily when they see them, so we can work together on them in advance?

- Do I have an "open door" to informal communication, or am I "too busy"?

■ TIPS FOR MANAGERS WITH PROBLEMS

James F. Evered, in his *Shirt-Sleeves Management,*[2] provides a series of lists of hard-nosed tips for managers who find themselves in certain problem situations. These tips are compatible with MBO

---

[2] James F. Evered, *Shirt-Sleeves Management* (New York, AMACOM, a division of American Management Assn., 1981).

process and fit in very nicely with the managers' plans for alternative actions when the unexpected occurs or when the back-to-basics organization/personnel plan needs modification to adapt to changing situations. Perhaps you will find them helpful.

❑ High Employee Turnover

1. "Plan ahead for human resources needs" (fundamental to MBO).
2. "Match job/people specifications" (ditto).
3. "Select above-average people" (the need for criteria is obvious).
4. "Train people thoroughly."
5. "Provide continuous coaching and ongoing training."
6. "Provide full-spectrum management of people" (involvement, participation, autonomy).
7. "Keep employees fully informed at all times."

❑ Lack of In-Job Growth

1. "Provide challenging opportunities" (temporary assignments, task forces).
2. "Recognize achievement" (the payoff).
3. "Delegate to the maximum." (Yes!)
4. "Provide training for growth." (Are you listening?)
5. "Give constant encouragement" (feedback, reward).
6. "Maintain high expectations" (and satisfy them).
7. "Develop 'stretching' goals" (the first approach to implementing MBO).

❑ Goals Not Being Met

1. "Encourage employee participation in goal setting" (fundamental).
2. "Give necessary training and coaching." (Got it?)

3. "Solicit employee suggestions." (This is the heart of the process.)

4. "Give plenty of feedback" (as we said).

5. "Provide positive reinforcement" (as opposed to management by terror).

6. "Keep all goals realistic" (and attainable).

7. "Set a personal example" (don't expect more of others than you're willing to give/do yourself).

❏ Possible Union Organization

(The following criteria should apply in all business relationships.)

1. "Provide good working conditions."

2. "Provide adequate income."

3. "Listen to employees and respond to them."

4. "Maintain an open-door policy."

5. "Provide in-job growth."

6. "Treat people as valuable human beings."

❏ Manager's Job Overloaded

(With proper back-to-basics organization planning, the following reminders will at least be a part of your plan; they may even be unnecessary because they have become a part of your very fiber.)

1. Select above-average people.

2. Train all employees.

3. Delegate to the maximum.

4. Maintain high expectations.

5. Recognize achievement.

6. Allow maximum free rein.

7. Use participative management.

8. Display trust and faith in people.

▪ THE HUMAN FACTOR IN ORGANIZATION PLANNING

It should be obvious by now that the fundamental thrust of good, back-to-basics organization planning emphasizes the human factor. In the last half of the twentieth century, most of the seminal writing, much of the reorganization of companies, and many of the touted success stories have concentrated on human wants and needs, and human satisfaction, for in that realm the ultimate success of the business can be assured.

Many writers have dealt with the human being's *fundamental needs*, or "maintenance factors," and with the motivators, or "achievement factors." Figure 2.2 illustrates the hierarchy of human wants and needs and how they pay off for the company employer.

▪ FIGURE 2.2

The Hierarchy of Human Wants and Needs

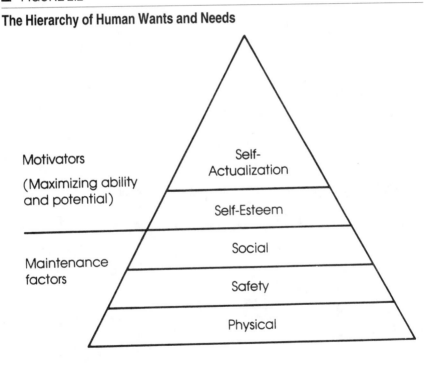

Physical

It should be obvious that these needs operate on the personal as well as the business level and that enlightened managements prosper when they create an environment and process in which these needs can be respected and satisfied.

■ TRANSLATING HUMAN WANTS AND NEEDS INTO MANAGEMENT PROCEDURES

There is no mystery to translating employee wants and needs into management functions. It is an orderly process, summarized in Table 2.3. From the table, it is apparent that specific *policies* and *procedures* can be created based on the requirements of the manager and the employees. *Monitoring* employee performance may then be done with the following steps:

1. List key job duties.
2. Agree upon expected results.
3. Decide what to measure.
4. Decide how to measure.
5. Discuss and record achievement.
6. Establish improvement objectives.
7. Start the process over again.

❑ TABLE 2.3

Translating Employee Needs into Management Functions

Employee Needs	*Manager Should*
To know specific duties	Prepare job description
To participate in setting goals	Ask employee to help set goals
To know how he or she is doing	Evaluate results with employee

(continued on next page)

❏ TABLE 2.3 *(continued)*

Employee Needs	Manager Should
To enlist manager's help	Advise/guide, counsel/train
To receive recognition for good results	Reward for good results

Before we go into the technicalities of developing personnel policies and procedures and a back-to-basics personnel plan, we would like to share a personal credo about this process:

An individual's personal objectives and life goals must somehow relate to the organization's goals and standards. Personal values cannot be in conflict with company values.

This is important to remember as an employee, as a manager, as the president-owner of a company. No explanation is required; the reasons are self-evident, both from a personal point of view and from a company point of view.

❏ Managing Time

The back-to-basics manager has a grasp of the psychological function of time and how to use it. Time has a direct relationship to productivity. The back-to-basics manager is conscious of the use of time and the quality of time spent. By upgrading and understanding your attitude toward time, you can become more efficient.

Traditional time management tells us we must first:

1. Be selective and set priorities for our work.
2. Delegate and eliminate all the tasks we possibly can.

If you have done this and you still do not have time to produce as you should, then you must increase your capacity to discriminate and refine your tasks so that you can increase your output.

You can do this by forming very clear mental pictures of a situation. The clearer the picture, the faster you can take action. The clearer the picture, the more decisively and efficiently you can act with full energy.

Increase the clarity of your mental pictures by:

1. Increasing your alertness.
2. Increasing your available energy.
3. Increasing your knowledge and experience.

You can manage time more effectively by:

1. Being single-minded, keeping your attention on the task at hand.
2. Not allowing yourself to become preoccupied.
3. Remaining alert; not doing things habitually.
4. Changing routines and habits in order to stay alert.
5. Giving your mind challenges on a daily basis.
6. Learning new skills.
7. Taking 3 minutes out of every hour to refresh your mind and reset priorities.
8. Reviewing your day each night, looking for those times when you were not alert.
9. Setting specific times for daydreaming.
10. Being positive in your thinking and attitudes. Positive attitudes produce energy; negative attitudes reduce energy.
11. Learning to turn negative energy into positive energy in group meetings and individual encounters.
12. Ridding yourself of anxieties, fears, doubts, and uncertainties, all of which use up your energy.
13. Learning to rid yourself of inner dialogues and "battles" that use up your energy.
14. Remembering that relaxation and receptivity increase alertness and energy.

15. Learning to rid yourself of stress and tension.

16. Allowing plenty of time for rest.

17. Exercising and keeping yourself physically fit.

18. Learning to see things in a different manner than you have in the past.

19. Knowing when to start and stop projects.

20. Learning to set priorities and delegate.

21. Learning to communicate effectively so that time is not wasted.

22. Learning to listen.

23. Learning to say no.

24. Learning how to handle interruptions so that they are not the main thrust of the day.

25. Learning when your best decision times, working times, and creative times are.

26. Learning how to take time off.

27. Learning to make a time plan, with daily agendas, monthly calendars.

28. Learning to make a yearly plan and a five-year plan.

29. Remembering that attention and effort give projects and ideas value.

30. Knowing where and how you spend your time.

31. Doing the right things right.

32. Working smarter, not harder.

33. Always making sure you are solving the right problem.

❑ Managing Delegation

Delegating is the art of being able to hand someone else a job you can do perfectly well. To be efficient, a manager must decentralize his job through delegation. A manager's job is to supervise—not to do—the tasks. Research shows that the most successful managers are those who continue to manage during times of crisis, rather than folding up their sleeves and doing the work themselves. As a back-to-basics manager you must make a conscious effort to select those tasks that you alone must do. Many managers have trouble delegating because of their internal feelings about delegation. They feel they may lose something, such as power or authority. To delegate efficiently, you must gain control of these inner feelings and doubts.

When you delegate you:

1. Free up your available time.
2. Multiply your energy.
3. Let those under you develop their skills.
4. Make time for leadership development.
5. Make time for innovative ideas that keep you ahead of the competition.
6. Find out whom you can trust to carry out projects.

To delegate successfully, you must:

1. State policy clearly and explicitly.
2. Define the tasks to be delegated precisely.
3. Have job descriptions for employees.
4. Communicate the task so that the employees understand how it fits in with their job description.
5. Set goals and objectives for each task.
6. Make sure employees understand how it fits in with their job description.
7. Set controls so that you know the task is being completed.
8. Let the employees do the things their own way, in a manner that is comfortable to them.
9. Make a plan for each task that can and should be delegated.
10. Look at each task as if you were unfamiliar with it.
11. Encourage employees to make decisions and solve problems.

12. Ask employees to suggest solutions (even if the solutions won't work) whenever they present a problem.

13. Set up checkpoints so that major pitfalls can be avoided.

14. Review each uncompleted task, looking for the causes of the breakdown in the system. Take this information into consideration when delegating the next task.

15. Make sure that both you and your employees can see and understand the results of the tasks which have been delegated.

16. Learn to use planning tools, daily agendas, and tickler files; encourage employees to do the same.

17. Remember that your managerial success depends on your ability to direct others.

❏ Becoming a Leader

You can be given the title of manager, but you cannot be given leadership. To be a leader, you must demonstrate your leadership ability to those you are leading and managing. You must be willing to accept and use the power that comes with a leadership role. To be successful, you must show employees how to achieve what they want. Leadership is a matter of degrees. It does not happen all at once, and many of the successful leadership characteristics are learned ones. As a leader you will have the power to shape and mold the present and future through the cooperation of a group. You will act as a role model to those in the group.

To be a leader, you must:

1. Have a voluntary following.

2. Demonstrate to your following that you can help them achieve their goals and are the best person available for this task.

3. Understand the weaknesses and strengths of yourself and your following.

4. Accept responsibility.

5. Be willing to accept power without undue reluctance or zeal.

6. Use power without abusing it.

7. Have the ability to motivate others.

8. Have the ability to achieve your own goals.

9. Form premises that lead to useful conclusions.

10. Continue learning and growing in your own skills as a leader.

11. Delegate successfully.

12. Help your people to participate in decisions that affect them.

13. Be nonpunitive.

14. Communicate and encourage two-way communications.

15. Show pride in your people and their performance to maintain high morale.

16. Be able to plan both short- and long-term projects successfully.

17. Be able to sustain your leadership role in times of crisis.

18. Recognize distress and take positive action.

19. Know that each individual counts and that each one can, if properly motivated, make a specific contribution.

❏ Body Language

It is the person receiving your communication who makes what you say or do valuable. Without a receiver you are only uttering sounds. When you communicate, you are always dealing with a perception of each individual. Because of this what is not said and what we do with gestures, tone of voice, and entire environment must be thought of as part of the communication process.

To understand this process better:

1. Learn to read the body language of yourself and others.

2. Know that body gestures and language should reinforce each other.

3. Learn to listen and observe others.

4. When observing others, keep in mind their body gestures, eye motions, skin/touch sensations: How does their hand feel when you shake it? How do they deal with the space around them?

5. Learn to process all the signals from the silent languages to get an accurate reading.

6. Remember that some signals may have more than one meaning. It is the entire picture that gives a true reading.

7. Remember that we give different signals in different settings.

8. Remember that a signal may change its meaning according to the setting.

9. Learn body language at a conscious level.

❑ Managerial Coaching and Training

Coaching and training are a never-ending process for the back-to-basics manager. Whether you are conducting a formal training course or explaining a task one-on-one to an employee, you must have knowledge of how to train. In learning to train others you must start by understanding how people learn and how the mind works. No matter what the training or coaching situation, the following must be understood for you to be successful at this task:

1. We learn by two main methods: rote memory and experience/association.

2. Experience/association has been found to be more effective.

3. A person must participate in the activity in order to learn.

4. We must be able to articulate and relate knowledge in a pragmatic sense in order to retain or use it effectively.

5. The mind works in an orderly fashion when gaining and relating information.

6. The mind works in three steps: (I) it gathers facts and experiences, (II) it relates and associates this information to previous information, (III) it draws a working conclusion on which action is based.

7. If, in step I, the facts and experiences are erroneous in nature, the conclusion will be erroneous.

8. Once you accomplish steps I and II, the mind will inevitably reach a conclusion.

9. Keep your statement of facts short and to the point and introduce only one fact at a time.

10. Your association statement should show how information is to be used.

11. Have employees verbalize their conclusions.

12. Be aware of learning blocks in employees.

13. Try to state information in such a way that you help employees draw mental pictures.

14. Try to present information so that it relates to the current work situation.

15. Remember that 80 percent of our learning is visual.

16. Use universal analogies and metaphors.

17. Find common points of understanding.

18. Try not to speak in terms of good or bad; avoid judgment blocks that lead employees to fear making mistakes.

19. Keep the atmosphere open and relaxed.

20. Use circles and horseshoe sitting arrangements when training a group.

21. Come from behind your desk in a one-on-one basis.

22. Remember that the normal attention span is very limited.

23. Speak clearly and use voice modulation and body gestures to help make points.

24. Encourage trial-and-error conversation.

25. When counseling and coaching, reinforce effective behavior by helping employees be aware of their strengths.

26. Let employees know where improvement is needed and show them how you can help them.

27. Help employees see the relationship between their needs and those of the company.

❑ Communications Skills

Effective communication is central to everything a back-to-basics manager does. Human interaction succeeds or fails as a direct result of our ability to communicate. Communication is a process composed of five things: Who? Says what? To whom? Through what medium? With what effect? Communication is inseparable from your total behavior as a manager.

❑ Managerial Goal Setting

Goals are internalized dreams; plans and objectives are means to accomplish goals. The back-to-basic manager must know how to set goals for himself and for his employees and how to make appropriate plans to reach those goals and objectives. Research shows that you must have a clear picture in your mind of what you want to achieve and that both goals and plans must be written out to be carried out successfully. Most managers understand the importance of planning but a lack of organization keeps them from doing the extensive planning that would give them a competitive edge.

In setting goals and planning your first step is to become organized:

1. Make sure you have formal job descriptions for yourself and for your employees.

2. Identify every task, function, and time-consuming act.

3. Become aware of what must be done on a daily, biweekly, weekly, bimonthly, monthly, quarterly, semiannual, and annual basis.

4. Establish how long each task takes to complete without interruptions.

5. Remember that being organized is a learned skill that takes self-discipline and the breaking of old habits.

6. Clean house, making sure your whole office is well organized from the files to the top of your desk.

7. Write down each task you are responsible for in a yearly planning calendar on the date it is due—plus the date it should be started to be completed on time.

8. When handling interruptions and emergencies, do not deviate too long from your plan.

9. Leave your work area clean whenever you will be out of the office and urge that employees do the same.

10. Insist that all files, equipment, and other items be put in their proper place immediately after use.

11. Twice a month, check to make sure all files and information are where they should be.

12. It takes 21 days to break or make habits and may take you as long as 6 months to become truly organized.

13. Make sure your personal life is in order.

14. Learn to say no and explain why if you are asked to take on tasks outside of your normal duties.

15. Remember, at any time, anyone should be able to step into your job without confusion. Business cannot afford to keep people who make themselves indispensable.

Once you are organized, your next step is to start setting goals and objectives and making plans to carry them out:

1. Take a good look at your personal goals and business goals. Do they mesh?

2. Form a mental picture of where you would like to be at retirement, both personally and financially.

3. Set goals and objectives within specific time frames.

4. Make a list of what must be done to achieve each goal and objective.

5. Remember the more detail you give your planning, the easier it will be to achieve the goal.

6. Make sure you have a starting date and a completion date in your plan for each step necessary to complete goals and objectives.

7. At the end of each day fill out a list of what must be done for the coming day.

8. Make a notation on each item that can be delegated and to whom it should go.

9. Leave nothing to memory in your daily planning.

10. Check your list the first thing in the morning before leaving for the office.

11. Take 3 to 5 minutes each hour to clear your head and check off your list. Reset priorities if necessary, based on finished projects and incoming information.

12. Make sure you can easily identify long-term projects on your daily list.

13. Make a monthly plan and agenda.

14. Add at least 3 hours a week for exercise (not weekend time) to your weekly planning schedule.

If you are having difficulty reaching goals and objectives, are you:

1. Making your daily agenda too long and impossible to complete?

2. Not setting priorities or seeing too many areas as priorities?

3. Experiencing the noncompletion syndrome, not being able to finish even small tasks? Start with a small area and force yourself to finish it. Work up if necessary.

4. Unable to visualize yourself finishing a task or completing your goals?

5. Experiencing a lack of self-esteem, self-confidence, self-motivation, self-discipline?

6. Experiencing a fear of success?

Make sure you see failure in degrees and point out your successes.

To make your goals work:

1. Form success habits by openly acknowledging the completion of even minor goals.
2. Learn to visualize yourself completing your objectives each day.
3. Speak in positive and decisive terms about your goals and objectives.
4. Project positive self-control by preparation and affirmative action steps.
5. Focus on the rewards of success. Be sure to define the benefit you will get by completing a goal.
6. Talk of goals and objectives in vivid and pictorial terms.
7. Think and act like a winner.
8. Dedicate yourself to carrying out your plans and goals 1 day at a time for 2 weeks, then go all out for a month.

Let us summarize the fundamental qualities of the back-to-basics manager:

- Recognizes the essential humanity of everyone with whom he is associated—accepting them as warm, feeling, caring human beings
- Believes and trusts people—and tells them his or her own feelings toward them
- Expects employees to become all they are capable of—and is ready to help them on the way
- Works with employees to establish sound goals and convert their ideas into reality
- Helps employees to use time efficiently
- Points out what the organization expects from people through clear statements of company policy
- Helps people develop the self-discipline needed to identify and achieve their potential

- Understands that effective communication is motivation; keeps the communication network open at all times
- Delegates responsibility
- Supports his or her people in their decisions
- Praises good performance and helps people correct their mistakes by working with them on a one-to-one basis
- Responds to people's needs
- Understands that the optimal use of his or her managerial skills fulfills his or her economic responsibility to the company
- Is fully cognizant of today's business ethics and understands the need for all participants to gain some good from every business relationship

To sum up, the back-to-basics manager has an optimistic view of people. She builds on cooperation rather than competition. She deals with all aspects of business in ways that reflect appreciation for people. She understands and appreciates the human relationships among her organization, its people, and the outside world.

We think the lessons to be learned are not only "basic" but absolutely essential. We feel back-to-basics management fits right into current business practice, and certainly into the evolving role of the American corporation.

Organizations are only what people make them. Remember that, and the author will feel he has achieved his objective. And you will be better equipped to achieve your personal objectives in management.

❏ Some "Do's" and "Don'ts" on Delegating Authority

When you delegate authority, you are giving the individual the right to do it his way. You will dampen his enthusiasm and feelings of accomplishment if you insist that it be done only your way. For example, if you give your secretary the authority to answer repetitive inquiries—by letter or memo for your signature perhaps—when the letter or memo comes across your desk, don't change it. As long as the substance is correct, what matter does it make if the style is not yours? It can be a real growth experience for the person involved.

❏ Planning Delegation

Saying you need to delegate more is easy. But planning and deciding on what should be delegated becomes more difficult. As a rule of thumb, those tasks that you do well and can train someone else to do should be considered. The first part of planning should be to list tasks that can be delegated. Here's how to go about it:

- List all the tasks you are responsible for.
- Keep a running list of all you do during the day for two weeks (even answering the phone during lunch break).
- Keep a time sheet or estimate the time needed for each task.
- Make a list of the qualities and/or skills needed for each task.
- Review your personnel and their skills and attributes.
- Place the name of a staff member by each task, matching skills and attributes with the need of each task.
- Make a list of all the details and instructions an employee will need to accomplish each task.
- Decide on checkpoints and balances for each task.
- Decide on alternative time plans for each task (in case the job needs to be redone or is not finished).
- Review in your mind all tasks that you have previously delegated. Examine the causes of failures as well as successes.

If you are not used to delegating or have been delegating very little, pick two assignments that would cause the least amount of upset (and time, on your part) if they are not finished or need to be redone.

- When delegating a task for the first time, have checkpoints set up so major problems can be avoided.

❑ Setting Up Checks and Balances

Checks and balances in delegation allow you to retain control. Since ultimately you are the one responsible for the work, you must have ways of seeing that work is done according to your instructions and standards. The system that you develop needs to let you know:

1. If the task was done.
2. What the results of the task are.
3. If any complications or problems occur.
4. What are any short- or long-range effects on business.
5. If any new ideas or ways of proceeding have been developed.
6. Whether the employee feels he can handle a similar task again.

Not every task needs a verbal discussion. Nor do employees need to be praised or criticized in person for their performance on every task. In setting up systems you should keep in mind:

- Verbal interruptions take up valuable time.
- Not all tasks are of equal importance.
- Written reports and reporting systems allow you to review performance and evaluate at your own convenience.
- Specific methods for reporting help employees gather and have all needed data and cuts time lost in rambling meetings.
- Letting the employee know that you are aware the task has been completed is essential.
- Organization and attention to detail is a must.

❑ Tools

In back-to-basics management and leadership of all kinds it is important that your mind be as free as possible from any kind of detail that is readily available; for example, keeping phone numbers at the forefront of your mind uses up valuable thinking space. Here are a few tools that can help:

- *Tickler files:* allows you to keep track of the dates that assignments are due.

- *Desk and calendar planners:* allow long-range planning and easy to follow agendas at a glance.

The back-to-basics manager and leader:

- Avoids trespassing on authority once it is given.

- Periodically checks performance.

- Encourages her people to make decisions.

- Defines jobs for her people so they are provided with the greatest challenge and opportunity.

- Inspires her people with the will to work toward objectives and goals.

- Makes full use of the skills and abilities of her people.

- Has her people participate in setting work objectives and schedules.

- Gets group reaction before going ahead with projects.

- Generates a sense of belonging.

- Encourages cooperation with others.

- Goes to bat for her people.

❑ Delegation Review

Not every task that is delegated gets done or is done correctly. When reviewing a poorly or unfinished task that has been delegated, make sure all the steps have been included. One of the biggest problems in communicating a task that is to be delegated is our intimate awareness of the task, which is not usually shared by subordinates. Thus, much usable knowledge and information that should be passed on with the assignment often is not. This breakdown in communication can be avoided by:

- Addressing the tasks as if you know nothing about it so you include all the steps no matter how obvious.

- Making sure you give a full set of instructions, including warnings about unseen pitfalls.

- Seeking feedback, that is, having the employee repeat her understanding of the task and all the elements in her own words; you may then see if she does understand the task and directions.

- Getting the employee involved, asking for any suggestions she may have on accomplishing the task—or how she feels she can best do it.

- Developing daily, weekly, and monthly agendas: keeps your mind moving and allows you to keep track of your work flow.

- Developing employee agendas: allows you to keep track of their work flow so you can see at a glance what assignments are being completed.

- Holding weekly staff or employee meetings (with an agenda): helps you to discover any operating problems and to check up on assigned tasks.

- Instituting a system of reporting: this will allow both the employee and you to follow the work flow. Include a check-off list for easy reading and filling out.

Any one of these may suffice for your needs, and you may find that a combination will be very useful.

Without delegation you as a manager will be frantic and your effectiveness will be greatly diluted. Your outlook will be subjective. The other skills required of you will go unused. Delegation is necessary to ensure the continuity of any company. It is through delegation that employees grow, become familiar with policy, and learn how to handle authority and leadership. Delegation increases your effectiveness as a back-to-basics manager and leader.

SECTION 2
COMMUNICATIONS

CHAPTER 3

Personal Communication in Business

■ PERSONAL COMMUNICATION BY SPEECH

Generally, far too much talking occurs in business. This is partly because many people are fond of the sound of their own voices, and partly because emotional considerations intrude when they are not wanted.

The objective of verbal communication is only in part to convey information. The other part of this objective is to give emotional satisfaction, or the contrary, to one or both parties to a transaction. In many transactions, such as those between people who are bound to one another in various ways, and principally by marriage or parental ties, the emotional element can be vastly more important than the informational one—to the extent that an objective analysis of it by someone not emotionally involved would often rate this informational content as unimportant if not nonsense.

49

Companies are set up, and people and/or companies cooperate with one another on a business footing, in order to be able to do things they could not do by themselves. This involves the pooling of information, skills, and resources to achieve a common end, which is the financial gain of the people concerned. Emotional considerations are an impediment to attaining this goal efficiently.

And yet, of course, they do come up in business. And how. They do so for a number of reasons:

First, although business ties between people are much looser and more temporary than marriage or parental ties, they nevertheless exist. When business partners cease to cooperate effectively, or incompatibility develops in the manager-employee equivalent of the parent-child situation, a surgical solution, consisting of moving one of the parties to another department or requesting his resignation or dismissal, is vastly easier than in a family context. But dismissal at least is still generally considered as something to be avoided if possible, as it may create unpleasantness and upheaval, and is likely to be preceded by traumatic and emotion-laden transactions between the people concerned over a considerable period.

Second, because people in business are often not only cooperating but also competing, they are concerned with promoting their own careers, using methods that involve varying degrees of ruthlessness and lack of consideration for other people. Ambition may manifest itself in cool-headed and unemotional moves to further one's own interests or in cruder attempts to ingratiate oneself with one's superiors and to denigrate persons who get in our way. All this comes under the general heading of "office politics."

Third, there is plenty of scope for straightforward ego gratification in business. Quite apart from any considered attempt to promote their own careers, people in business, as in any other branch of life where they come into contact with others, are always seeking some degree of ego gratification, usually unconsciously. If they are psychologically well balanced and have normal self-confidence, it is unobtrusive and unobjectionable to colleagues.

If they have psychological problems and lack self-confidence, they will often feel the need to compensate for this by showing off, and the less they have to show off about, the more they will feel impelled to do so. This can be very tiresome for people who have to deal with them continuously in business just as in social situations. But there are also people of high talent who are nevertheless unsure of themselves and may compensate by excessive ego gratification or other emotional tantrums. Yet their talent may be of such value to the company that everyone else has to put up with them in the general interest.

All this leads to a great deal of talking in business situations that has little to do with the general object of the firm: its business success and, consequently, the financial success of its stockholders, managers, and employees. Clearly, it is impossible to eliminate it completely, and maybe a firm in which no one ever talked about anything except strictly business subjects would be so boring to work in that it would not attract people of talent. But it has to be kept under wise control, and this is one of the main objects of personnel management.

Sensible personnel management will attain this object, first, by selecting staff who not only have the required skills but also are psychologically well balanced and are likely to get on well with the other people in the firm and, second, by providing opportunities for advancement and personal success that minimize the motivation for them to achieve this at the *expense* of their colleagues. Obviously, some people have to be promoted and others are not suitable for promotion. The latter have to be made to understand that the company, and with it they themselves, will in the long run benefit if someone else and not they is promoted. The so-called "Peter principle" applies here. This states that people who are performing effectively in a given job tend to be promoted out of it into another in which they do not perform effectively. The most obvious example of this is when someone who has shown himself outstanding in a specific skill is promoted to manage others doing the same job, and he has no talent for management. Management implies authority over others, and because it is the managers who fix the terms of employment and rewards of those they manage, they tend to value their own skill, that of management, more highly and pay it more. Consequently, management jobs are sought after. This is not necessarily justified. A brilliant specialist who would be a hopeless manager may be worth far more to a company than his department head and should have much greater rewards. Wise personnel management will provide for this and create an atmosphere in which it is recognized by all that the management function per se is not the only one that leads to personal success. It will encourage any kind of talent that is useful to the company and reward it accordingly, not only in money, but also in perks, status, and psychological gratification.

The result of such policies, if they are successfully applied—and heaven knows it is not easy—is that everyone feels useful and adequately rewarded in relation to the others, and much less time and energy are wasted in communication, chiefly oral, that is not relevant to the business of the company and may be actively destructive of that business.

The techniques of oral communication in business concern first its content and second its manner.

There is little specific to say here about content. It is just a question of having something interesting and useful to communicate, and of formulating it in a way that avoids the five main obstacles to effective communication discussed in Chapter 4.

A person's oral communication is closely tied up with her psychological equilibrium and self-confidence, which, as we have seen, are in a business context themselves dependent on the extent to which she feels herself valued and making a useful contribution to the success of her firm. Some people communicate better orally, and some feel happier in written communication. The wise man and woman, recognizing the preference, will try to put important communications in the form in which they feel more comfortable.

If you have difficulty, through nervousness, in expressing yourself effectively in speech, for instance in business meetings and discussions, here are a few tips:

1. Don't be in a hurry: let the others talk first. Your intervention will probably be more effective when they have had their say.

2. Prepare your contribution by noting key words and phrases on a piece of paper. Also put down reminders, as others speak, of points made that you wish to contest or enlarge on. There is no shame in speaking from notes: on the contrary, it can give an impression of seriousness.

3. While the others are talking, practice physical and mental relaxation. Sit comfortably, and consciously relax all your muscles from the feet up, excepting your neck (otherwise your head will flop over!). Cultivate mental calm by breathing slowly and regularly. Avoid outward manifestations of stress like fiddling with things, lighting cigarettes and puffing nervously at them, crossing and recrossing your legs, adjusting your tie or dress or smoothing your hair, or coughing unnecessarily. Concentrate on such nervous signs in other people, and allow yourself to feel superior because you can do without them. If it helps you to relax to doodle on your writing pad, do so.

4. When you feel it is time to speak, watch your timing and then do so decisively. Don't try to cut in on someone else: first, it is rude, and second, you may not succeed, in which case you will feel frustrated and tense. Choose a gap in the conversation and catch the eye of the chairperson, official or unofficial, of the discussion, and then start off, if possible, with some statement that creates attention and interest. Then you will have everyone listening to you. Make your points firmly and clearly, and don't go on talking unnecessarily. Use the lower end of your voice register: high-pitched voices sound nervous and unconvincing.

As soon as you start it will be much easier. And because you are relaxed, you will have no trouble in finding the words you need to make your points.

Practice and experience will give you increasing confidence, and you will gradually become used to the sound of your own voice.

Everybody, whether naturally nervous or not, should cultivate speaking without the "er's" and "um's" and other interjections that are so common in spoken communication, and should complete their sentence. You have only to listen to a recording of an ordinary conversation between people who are not trained in speaking to notice how inconsequential so much of it is. Sentences are started and not finished; they go off at a tangent and are peppered with "I mean's," "you know's," "sort of's," and other redundant fillers. Many people also mumble and speak too fast to be readily understood. Practice avoiding these faults. One thing that can help is to have someone record you without your immediate knowledge. Lis-

tening to the recording will help you realize what you do wrong—
without actually hearing your voice in this way, it is very hard to be
objectively critical of it—and then consciously cultivate avoidance
of the faults you pick up.

Much of this also applies to speaking on the telephone, and in
fact many nervous people find this much easier as they are not
visually exposed as they are in face-to-face conversation. The need
to speak clearly and slowly is even more important here, and of
course you have to convey your full meaning without the help of
expression and gesture. Don't just say "Hello" when you pick up the
telephone. Identify yourself, or your department, or company as
appropriate. This will save time and sound more efficient. In this
way, and by enunciating clearly so that you do not have to repeat
yourself, you can considerably reduce the cost of long-distance
telephone communication. Remember, too, that when you are talking international long-distance by satellite, there is a noticeable delay
between your voice and the reply that comes back. Frequently one
tends to think that the person has gone off the line and says "Hello?"
just as he is beginning to speak. So you have to start all over again,
with expensive seconds ticking away.

It applies also, only more so, to appearances on TV or radio. No
doubt you will get help from the producer, especially if you are
inexperienced. While you are waiting to be brought into the conversation, if it is a talk show, practice the relaxation techniques described earlier. And when you do speak (on TV) look the MC or the
person you are answering straight in the eye, or if you are told to
look at the camera do that straight in the eye, too. TV is rather
merciless to diffident interviewees. Fortunately, nearly everything
is pretaped these days, which makes it much easier to be relaxed than
when you are on live.

A last tip if you are faced in a meeting with one of those selfish
people who keeps trying to interrupt and won't let you finish what
you have to say. This technique is supposed in England to be
common practice among Oxford University dons. It consists in
pausing for breath, not at the logical place at the end of the sentence,
but somewhere in the middle—and then carrying right on with the
next sentence without stopping. If you make a habit of this, it is very

difficult for someone to interrupt you, as the person is caught unawares when you make your breathing space. Try it sometime.

■ **PERSONAL AND MASS COMMUNICATION IN WRITING**

In business context, personal communication in writing uses the media of letters, memoranda, reports of meetings, departmental instructions, telexes, and so on. By "personal" we mean here communication to groups of people who are all known to the writer, at least by name; this is opposed to "mass" communications, using the public information media, with the audience of which the writer is not personally acquainted.

In all cases, the object is to leave the reader or listener more favorably disposed to a point of view, which in the commercial context is usually that the expenditure of money on the product or service in question, rather than another, would be advantageous or otherwise gratifying to him or her. In the case of mass-consumer advertising, it is generally "her," as the decisions on purchases of such products are mainly made by women.

To achieve this end, the persuader has to secure the attention and interest of the persuadee and not lose them until he has fully exposed his arguments and inducements. This may be relatively easy, when he has a "captive" audience; in other words, when the persuadee is physically or morally compelled to read them or listen to them. This is the case, in extreme instances, with army trainees who will be punished if they cut the class or go to sleep in it and in less extreme cases when it would be bad manners to get up and leave in the middle of a presentation to which you have been invited; or again when the prestige and personality of the persuader, such as the president of the United States when he has taken TV time to expose a new and important departure in policy, commands the attention and respect of the persuadee. Or it may be extremely difficult, as in print advertising: the reader is in no way compelled to pay any attention to your message, is looking at the medium because he is interested in something else, that is, the editorial material, and is well aware that you are only after his money anyhow.

Even so, both the Army lecturer and the president will get better results if they behave as if the audience is not captive—if they strive to gain and hold its voluntary interest and attention in a way that is relevant to the point they are making.

In print advertising, which is perhaps the most difficult case, various devices are used to secure attention. They usually involve a combination of words and pictures that is in itself gratifying or promises the satisfaction of some important human urge: ego enhancement, sex, appetite, status, money, success. The problem is that this gratification has to be linked to the product or service in some way. If this can be done directly, so much the better.

If not, a more or less tortuous process has to follow, by which the subject is brought round to the product or service being advertised, and this is invariably less interesting. At this point there is a strong probability that the reader will get bored and turn the page. You will have achieved something: you will have reminded the reader of the product name, and it is just possible that he or she will associate it with the irrelevant gratification you have offered, and this may favorably tip the scale in the split-second decision-making process that happens when he or she is confronted with a range of competing products on the supermarket shelf. But you may cause irritation, because the reader may rightly feel that his or her attention and cupidity have been stimulated under false pretenses, and so may have been made *less* favorably disposed to the product or service than he or she was before. But advertisers trade on the perversity of human nature: they know, and the research they have carried out for them usually confirms this, that, even when a reader is irritated by the persuasive techniques she is aware are being used on her, she will often buy the product or service by which she has been irritated—just because she remembers the name.

The manufacturers of soap and detergents, which are among the biggest spenders on advertising, have few illusions on the amount of conviction created by their advertisements. The technology of washing has hardly evolved at all in decades, and the results obtained with one product are likely to be objectively indistinguishable from those of its competitors. But, to maintain sales, manufacturers hammer away with advertising that is repetitive to the point of nausea, boring, and an insult to the intelligence and discrimination of their buyers. Unfortunately, this policy seems to work. Although objectively they know that, when mythical housewife A in the commercial is moved to ecstasy with the new whiteness she gets when mythical housewife B gets her to try product X, it is all a load of rubbish, there is something that sticks, and this keeps the product selling. The housewife buys it because she knows from experience (probably having tried them all) that this product works no less well than the others and because she likes some detail that may be quite unconnected with washing—the colors on the pack, the smell of the product, the hairstyle of one of the actresses in the commercial, or some other fragment of communication that strikes some chord that the other commercials do not.

Fortunately for the peace of mind of the copywriter with a conscience, it is not inevitable that advertising should insult the intelligence of the people to whom it is addressed, or cause them to feel deceived as soon as the product name is mentioned.

Some advertising specialists believe it is always possible to find something interesting to say directly about the product or service, so that the reader or viewer does not feel that his attention has been obtained on false pretenses. It is at any rate worth devoting a great deal of effort to looking for such a something.

One of the world's most famous copywriters was David Ogilvy, an Englishman who came to America after World War II and set up an agency to produce advertising based on this principle. His advertisements were all designed on similar lines: they were like newspaper articles about the product, usually illustrated by photography of very high standard, and they were written with meticulous craftsmanship and obvious sincerity. The product name was always in the headline, so that the reader knew where he was right from the beginning. There was no trickery, and there were none of the usual attention-getting gimmicks, such as fancy typography, cutout photographs, funny drawings, and triple exclamation marks.

Some of these advertisements became very well known. The most famous of all, perhaps, was "The man in the Hathaway shirt," which was nothing but a portrait of a distinguished-looking man wearing a shirt, with quite a lot of copy saying how excellent the shirt was. There was just one seemingly minor detail: the man in the picture was wearing a patch over one eye. This patch was never explained. But it was enough to create intrigue. Who was this man; was he a real personality? Why was he chosen to advertise this shirt? There was nothing dishonest about this. There is no reason why an advertiser should not use a one-eyed model. Its very simplicity, and this one unusual feature, made this advertisement stand out, and made very large numbers of people read it.

Ogilvy's ads, and those of another agency called Doyle, Dane, Bernbach—which was famous originally for its Volkswagen advertisements that deliberately flouted the Detroit stereotype ("Think small," said the headline of the best known of these, which showed a tiny picture of a VW Beetle in a lot of white space)—stood out like healthy thumbs in a mass of sore ones from the mass of magazine pages, in those days before communication was dominated by TV. They were honest and unconventional. But other advertising specialists could answer, and often did, that this kind of approach worked only because it was used for products in which there was direct interest to be exploited—because these products were unusual, luxury items, or expensive. And what would happen to the readership figures if every advertisement was like them?

Be this as it may, the principle remains. In every kind of persuasive writing, you must do your damnedest to secure attention by a headline, headline/picture combination, title, opening shot, or gambit that creates interest directly about your proposition, and so does not get attention on false pretenses.

The word "proposition" has been used very deliberately here. For every piece of persuasive writing, advertisement, political statement, or whatever, must have a proposition. You cannot persuade unless you yourself have worked out exactly what you want to persuade about, and then can communicate this to the persuadee, so that she knows in what way you are suggesting that she should change her mind. If you are in a competitive situation—if other people are also trying to put a proposition to the same audience—it is important that yours should be different and distinctive.

This principle was formulated by another guru of the advertising business in the postwar period—Rosser Reeves of the Ted Bates agency—in his concept of the unique selling proposition, the USP. It is a principle that nearly everyone in the business accepts today, though some would argue that a nonunique proposition, if presented in a unique way, becomes unique in itself. The fact remains, and this applies not only to advertising but to every use of words for persuasive purposes, that you must first get it very clear in your mind what it is that you are going to propose to your audience, viewers, or readers. The more exclusive you can make this proposition, the better. If it is genuinely unique, your speech, presentation, or advertisement will more or less write itself. If you have to *contrive* to make it unique, be careful. Your effort of contrivance may make your proposition seem bogus, especially if you claim that your product "is the only one that contains wonder-working X," when it is easy to guess that X is a proprietary name for a familiar substance, dressed up for the occasion. It is better, if you cannot find something genuinely unique, to rely on uniqueness of presentation, provided this remains relevant.

After having secured attention for your proposition, you must develop it, in logical order, in words that your readers, viewers, or listeners can understand without effort, which sustain their interest, and which do not give any cause or excuse for disbelief. The way you do this depends on the medium you are using. It is obviously very different if you were writing a small newspaper ad or a 15-second TV commercial. But the principle is the same.

The argument must lead inexorably to the conclusion that your proposition should be adopted, and moreover that all others put forward by your competitors should be rejected. Naturally you have to be careful about how openly you say this: in advertising, there are rules that prevent you from denigrating a rival product, unless you can prove what you are saying. In politics they are not so squeamish about matters of this kind. Your argument should in any case justify your proposition—show why it is correct and so make it easy for your readers or audience to accept it.

As with all writing, be simple where you can. Avoid using long words if short ones will do. Put as much meaning as you can into verbs. Keep your listener, viewer, or reader awake by using slightly unexpected vocabulary. Use paradox and metaphor when these are appropriate.

And you must never give your readers, listeners, or viewers the chance to say "My eye!" We happen personally to think that this is done all the time in TV commercials. One housewife, for instance, recites a lot of phony sales talk, which only an inexpert salesman would normally use, to another housewife, who is converted on the spot like Saul on the road to Tarsus and rushes out to buy the product. No one ever behaves like either of them. Such sales arguments can only be honestly spoken (phrased more subtly) by the advertiser himself or his representative. Such commercials make us squirm, because they insult the "housewife" by making her look a perfect idiot. But they are so common they must work to some extent.

And the whole should end up with action you want people to take—action made as simple as possible, whether it is "Vote for me," "Fill in and mail this coupon," or "Step round to your nearest dealer." It is quite useless to be persuasive if the persuadee does not know what to do about his new-found conviction.

All this applies to the 10,000 words of a political exposition, to the 1,500 words of a business presentation, to the 500 words of a longish press advertisement, to the 30 words of a short TV commercial, or the 5 to 10 words on a poster. All that changes is the amount of detail and the contribution of the visual element.

Much of it also applies to word-of-mouth persuasion, usually called salesmanship. And a good deal of it also to journalism.

Journalism is commercial writing (i.e., writing for which you get paid), which is not normally designed to persuade, but to describe, entertain, or inform. The subject matter is interesting in itself. But there is still a requirement to capture attention and sustain it and to tell the story in a clear, logical, and interesting way. Usually journalists have to do this very fast, against a deadline, and to write well in these conditions takes experience and unusual fluency with words. Journalists, of course, have to have other skills, commonly summarized in the phrase "a nose for news." They have to be able to find stories, and for this they have to be determined, resourceful, and sometimes a little unscrupulous. But good journalistic writing follows the same rules as any other kind.

To be a more effective communicator:

1. Create a climate in which you have a strong relationship with your employees.

2. Make building this climate one of your primary responsibilities.

3. Avoid the tendency to communicate because of your title.

4. Try to adopt the employee's frame of reference.

5. Be mindful of other points of view.

6. Remember that you are trying to develop a team that will achieve mutual goals.

7. Remember that the listener decides if he or she wants to listen, read, or be motivated; shape your communication accordingly.

8. Use words to transmit ideas and information. People give meaning to the words.

9. Remember that no two people ever grasp a meaning in exactly the same way.

10. Ask these six questions before each communication:

    a. What do I intend to communicate?

    b. What will I actually communicate?

    c. What do I really mean, and what will be the emotional impact of the communication?

    d. What does the receiver of the communication expect to hear?

    e. What might he hear, despite what is being said?

    f. How will he feel about what he hears?

11. Remember that communication is a two-way process.

12. To communicate effectively, not only must you be understood, but you must also have generated a desired action.

13. Present one idea at a time, make the statement, develop the idea, restate the idea, call to action.

14. Say what you have to say simply.

15. Make your statements brief.

16. Use words that draw mental pictures for those listening and reading.

17. Get acceptance of one idea before moving on to the next.

18. As a listener, be responsive to emotions, encourage expression, sympathize and empathize, and give of yourself to the speaker.

19. In written communication, command the attention of the reader.

20. Think of your reading audience as one person, to achieve a more personal touch.

21. In writing memos, try the direct-mail formula:

    a. Promise a benefit.

    b. Enlarge on the benefit.

    c. Tell the reader specifically what he will get.

    d. Go into detail, backing up your promises with proof.

    e. Tell the reader what he might lose if he doesn't act now.

    f. Rephrase your reader benefit.

    g. Incite to action now!

22. Make sure your ideas are in logical order.

23. Use copywriters' attention-getting devices:

    a. <u>Underline</u>.

    b. CAPITALIZE.

    c. Indent imaginatively.

    d. Use exclamation points for extra emphasis!

24. Before sending a letter ask yourself:

    a. Is it reader oriented?

    b. Is it tactful?

    c. Is it clear and concise?

d. Is it conversational?

e. Is it helpful?

f. Have you created good will?

If the answer to each question is yes, send the letter.

25. When running a meeting, remember that it gives participants a chance to develop into a team.

26. Have a specific purpose in mind when calling a meeting.

27. Don't call a meeting if the matter can be handled in some other way.

28. Make the purpose of the meeting known beforehand.

29. Invite only those who are needed in the meeting.

30. Start at the time announced.

31. Stop when the purpose of the meeting has been achieved.

32. Prepare your agenda in advance.

33. Keep to your agenda.

34. Schedule far enough in advance so everyone can think about the purpose.

35. Ask questions—that's the easiest way to get a discussion going.

36. Learn to handle members who dominate a meeting by fielding questions to others in the group.

37. Ask members who do not participate direct, specific questions.

38. Bring the discussion back to the point with questions.

39. Do not take sides when conflict occurs.

40. Remind the group during conflict that intelligent people have different opinions.

41. Use humor to relieve tensions.

42. When you make a mistake, admit it and laugh at yourself, ask the group for help, and try something else.

43. Use Robert's "Rules of Order" to reach a conclusion.

44. Listen better than anyone else.

45. Adjourn on time.

CHAPTER 4

The Five Main Obstacles to Effective Communications

■ 1. IMPROPER ORGANIZATION OF THOUGHTS

You cannot communicate effectively if you haven't sorted out properly in your mind what it is you want to communicate and determined whether your argument is valid.

There are two main logical processes: deduction and induction. Deduction is when you move from the *general* to the *particular.* Induction is when you work the other way around, from the *particular* to the *general.* You can only plan intelligently if you have a clear idea of which of your conclusions are deductions, and therefore certain, if the proposition on which they are based are certain.

Incidentally, all market surveys and opinion polls draw conclusions that are based on *induction,* and usually two stages of induction. The first stage assumes that the behavior of a sample of people is representative of that of all such people, at a given moment. The second stage assumes that such people will continue to behave in the same way in the future. There is an important element of probability assessment in both these stages, and this is basically what the job of being a statistician is all about. He knows from his training and experience (again an inductive process) how to construct a sample that will be representative of a population with a sufficient degree of probability this behavior will continue in the future.

But pollsters sometimes read the wrong conclusion, and this is usually because something unforeseen or not sufficiently foreseen happens, and falsifies the second stage of induction.

You must develop a rational sequence of thought in what you want to communicate. You must avoid woolly statements, because you are clear about what is certain, what is highly probable, and what is only faintly probable. If you are making a sales pitch or a presentation, you will not make statements that can easily be refuted, and you will build up your argument logically and convincingly. When you are thoroughly clear about what you want to say or write, and have confidence in it, you are already half-way to effective communication.

▪ 2. A FEAR OF BEING PRECISE

You cannot communicate effectively if you are afraid to make precise statements (in case someone should pick you up on them), ones that you are prepared to substantiate.

Some people are obtuse with their facts because they have not done their homework properly (and are not sure of their facts). The result is again ineffective communication.

The conclusion is obvious. To communicate effectively you have to know your facts and not be afraid of committing yourself to them. This usually means a good deal of hard work, reading and checking the source material, getting information from people. It also means being clear about your motives.

▪ 3. THE USE OF LANGUAGE THEIR AUDIENCE DOES NOT UNDERSTAND

You cannot communicate effectively if there is not a fully common basis of language between you and your audience. When you are communicating, whether orally or in writing, you must make a conscious effort to picture to whom you are talking or writing. Try to establish a clear idea of what these people are like: their background, their interests, their level of education, their hopes and fears.

Be sure the communication is in words the typical reader or listener will easily understand. If you are a mathematician or a physicist, decide, for instance, whether your audience knows what a vector, a parameter, or an abscissa is before using such words. You can easily imagine other examples for other specialties.

Many engineers and scientists working in advanced areas of technology are inventing words all the time. They discover new concepts, and they give names to them. But often they become so familiar with these concepts that they forget they mean nothing to nonspecialists. Sometimes different words are used for the same thing in different companies, and so they are not even readily understood by other engineers in the same business. In-house jargon is especially apparent in data processing and electronics. Be careful, too, of abbreviation. Advertising men are always talking about OTS and POS material, but there is no reason that anyone else should know these acronyms mean "opportunities to see" and "point-of-sale" material. Ensure that the beginning of your communication arrests the attention of your listeners or readers. Having obtained attention, you have to keep it. You will do this if you think about what your communication must sound like on the receiving end.

■ 4. YOU CANNOT COMMUNICATE SUCCESSFULLY IF YOU DO NOT HAVE SUFFICIENT MASTERY OF THE TOOLS OF THE TRADE

These tools are, basically, your use of the English language and the concrete forms of its expression.

English is a very rich language: it has evolved over the centuries from the primitive tongue, now lost, spoken by a tribe that probably lived in southern Russia some 3,000 years ago. This tongue evolved and changed with the migrations of its speakers and gave rise to most of the languages now spoken in the Western world. English is so rich because it has a heritage from both the two major families of languages: those that descended through primitive German and those that came down through Latin. It has received inputs, at different periods of history, from many other tongues: the Anglo-Saxon spoken by King Alfred had received a few words from the original Celts and more from the Roman colonists. After the fall of the Roman Empire, the language received more inputs from Scandinavia and then, with the Norman invasion, from French. With the Renaissance, there was more influence from Latin and also Greek, and some from Italian. And with the British colonization of many parts of the world, and the American spread westward in contact with American Indians and Spaniards, a whole new lot of words was absorbed. Finally, English speakers, and in particular Americans, have always been very ready to invent new forms of speech, which start as slang and later become respectable. This is not the case with all languages: in some countries, the citizens do not like imports from abroad, especially from English, as they are afraid that their language will become "impure" and in the end cease to be spoken at all with the inexorable spread of English.

Something else of importance has also happened to English: in the fifteenth and sixteenth centuries, its grammar became very much simpler—before it had been highly complicated, more so than modern German or Russian, and on a par with Lithuanian or Icelandic. But in this short space of time, it shed a whole lot of unnecessary word endings and forms, as you can easily see if you compare a page of Chaucer with one of Shakespeare, who lived about 200 years later. Of the other Western languages, basically only the Scandinavian ones have become similarly simplified. If we are going to write clearly and persuasively, it is important that we should have a rich and extensive vocabulary and that we should not take too many liberties with grammar.

So we cannot give a final answer to the question: "What is good English?" It depends on your generation, whether you are speaking or writing, and on the degree of formality of the context.

The best yardstick is whether your statement is simple and clear and whether, if it breaks the conventions of "normal" English grammar and syntax, there is a good reason for this.

Always look for the simplest way of expressing your thoughts. Don't use a long word if a short one will do. There is nothing wrong with long words if they are necessary, but so often they are not. For instance, why say "obligate" when "oblige" is just as good? or "utilization" instead of "use"?

As well as short words, use short sentences. Research has proved that long, complicated sentences are much more difficult to understand. Rather than writing a string of subordinate clauses, break up your thought into short sentences.

It is a good idea to go over the first draft of anything you write and see whether any abstract nouns can be usefully changed into verbs in this way. Your writing will nearly always end up clearer and more direct.

Another questionable development in modern English writing, especially by scientists and engineers, is the practice of using nouns as adjectives. This can be useful and save space, if it is done with discretion.

Another mark of competent writing is the avoidance of "buzzwords," or currently fashionable phrases, for which there is a good equivalent in normal English. Here are some examples of buzzwords: interface, parameter, syndrome, synergy, symbiotic, ambivalent, viable, posture, stance. They are all good words when used precisely. A similar misuse of language is overplay with imagery. In ordinary light conversation, words like "fabulous," "terrific," "overwhelmingly" are normal, and no one means them literally. In business or technical writing, they should be used with care and only when the heavy emphasis they imply is needed.

When words and phrases are overworked, the meaning falls out of them and they become clichés. They were once fresh and imaginative, but now they are tired out. Examples are "exploring every avenue," "leaving no stone unturned," "crying all the way to the bank." When writers use them, it makes their prose stale and hackneyed and suggests they have taken the easy way out.

Another sign of sloppy language is the mixed metaphor. A metaphor is a phrase that has a literal meaning. For instance, you might say "inflation is crippling us." Inflation means blowing air into something, and this is not an obvious way of crippling someone. So this is really a mixed metaphor, but it is an extreme example to which not many people would object. In fact, "inflation" has become what is called a dead metaphor, which means that you no longer think of the original and literal meaning when you use the word. This original meaning subsists only when you are talking about balloons or tires.

But if in conversation you were to say, "his business is all washed up, but he is hoping to get it off the ground again," you would be mixing a metaphor of jetsam on the beach with one of aeronautics. As conversation, this would be acceptable. But in good business English it is not. Emotion, or feeling, is an important part of communication. The tone of voice we use and the expressions and gestures that accompany what we say usually add nothing to the bare facts of our communication, but they color them. They add nonverbal to verbal messages. When the communication is written, the same process takes place by the use of imaginative language, which in the extreme case turns into poetry. In such writing, the facts may be much less important than the emotional coloring.

But emotion must be kept strictly under control in business communication. In business, and also in politics, it can have either a positive or a negative effect. The effect can be positive when a speaker uses charm or the force of her personality to bring off a sale or to spur her staff on to greater efforts. It can be negative when a speaker allows contempt, dislike, fear, spite, revenge, or anger to dominate the objective content of what she has to say. These effects can also manifest themselves in written communication, especially letters. A hasty, emotion-laden letter or memo can be even more destructive than its oral equivalent, because while you are talking to someone, anger can pass and you can apologize for or otherwise correct your misplaced emotion; when you have written it down it stays on the record.

▪ 5. NOT KNOWING THE CULTURAL DIFFERENCES

Americans tend to be more informal than most other nationalities. Maybe this is because the great majority of them or their ancestors (apart from those who were brought across the Atlantic against their will as slaves) came to the country at some point in history to start a new life in which only their own talent, hard work, and initiative would count, unimpeded by the conventions and hierarchies of older, more formal societies. Also, compared with individual European peoples, they are very numerous and live in a large country without a great deal of contact with foreigners; consequently, except in certain strata of the more cosmopolitan cities, they do not often meet people with radically different values, and when they do they tend to treat them as *similar strangers.*

After the initial contact, communication exchanges between similar strangers, unless they are very insensitive, usually contain a great deal of probing for common ground. They put up signals and look for responses, or they respond when they recognize signals. They ask and answer questions that can lead to shared interests and experiences, or mutual acquaintances. The signals can be the use of certain words, jargon, or slang phrases or the reference to certain persons or special knowledge, which all indicate membership of business, technical, cultural or interest groups. It is almost like the freemason's special handshake. There is also accent, less important and decisive these days, but which can still indicate geographical and ethnic origin, social background, and life-style.

After the process of identification as similar strangers, a period of limited acceptance follows, if both parties feel there is any point in pursuing the relationship. Testing goes on, to check the limits of common experience and trust, and to assess the potential of the other person as a friend, sexual partner or lover, or as someone to do business with, to employ or be employed by, or possibly to exploit.

Handshaking served a similar purpose originally. By putting your hand into that of a stranger, you show him that you are not preparing to draw a sword or some other offensive weapon, and you are at the same time assured he is not contemplating such action either.

CHAPTER 5

Writing for Exactness— Contracts and Technical Exposition

In certain written documents, precision is essential. These are generally of a legal nature or records of agreements. Lawyers are trained in this sort of writing, and when important contracts are involved, it is clearly desirable that they should be drafted by a lawyer, especially as they will be read and picked over by other lawyers. However, it is very useful for the business executive to know how to draft an agreement.

There are four and sometimes five parts to a contract:

1. The statement of the parties to the agreement
2. (Sometimes) The definition of the terms used
3. The "recital" or preamble
4. The body of the agreement
5. The signatures

The first part states the names and addresses of the companies or persons who are parties to the agreement. There are generally two parties, but sometimes there are more; some may intervene in only a part of the contract. Each party may comprise more than one person or company. For instance, an agreement signed by the seller and the purchaser to purchase a company might also include the participation of a bank which guarantees the payment of the funds. Or there may be three or more companies that have gotten together to set up a joint venture. It is necessary to state unambiguously who is involved, and this ideally means, for legal exactness, giving the name of the company, the state in which it is registered, the address of the registered office, its legal form, the amount of its registered capital, and the person authorized to represent it, with the basis of his authorization. If some of this information is missing, except perhaps the last item, the contract may still be valid, provided there is no possibility of confusion. As company names are often frequently repeated in the body of the contract, it is usual to specify an abbreviation, either by saying something like "hereinafter described as . . .", or just putting it in brackets. If the party is a physical person, his full name and address are given.

Thus, a typical agreement might start as follows:

AGREEMENT

Between:

The Wonderbrush Cleaning Company, incorporated in the State of New York, having its registered office at _____, with registered capital of $_____, represented herein by Mr. _____ by virtue of a decision of the Board of Directors dated _____ hereinafter described as "Wonderbrush,"

Of the first part (or on the one hand)

The Hirise Property Company, incorporated in the State of Connecticut, having its registered office at _____, with registered capital of $_____, represented herein by Mr. _____, its President, hereinafter described as "Hirise,"

Of the second part (or on the other hand)

To simplify the subsequent wording, complicated contracts at this point include a list of definitions. These set out the special sense in which certain words or phrases are used in the contract. For example, "The Property" would probably mean a particular piece of property being sold, as described in detail elsewhere in the agreement; "The Bank" might mean a particular bank providing a loan, defined here. In the body of the contract, these words and phrases are conventionally written with initial capitals to indicate that they are being used in this restrictive way.

The "recital" or preamble states the background to the contract, that is, the situation that has led up to the agreement between the parties. It usually starts with the word "Whereas." A typical simple example might be: "Whereas the Property has been offered for sale by the Party of the First Part, and whereas the Party of the Second Part has expressed the desire to purchase the same, now the parties have agreed as follows . . . ."

There then follows the body of the agreement itself, sometimes starting with the heading "Witnesseth." It is divided up into articles or clauses (unless it is so short and simple that there is only one clause). These are set out in logical order. Typically, they begin with a definitive description of the object of the contract (the property, loan, equipment being sold or leased, for instance), followed by the "consideration," which means the price payable for the product or service, then by the manner of payment, the duration of the agreement, the procedure for its early termination, the circumstances in which one of the parties would be considered in default, the consequences of such default, the arrangements for arbitration in the event of disagreement on the interpretation of the contract, the body of law under which it is to be interpreted, and also perhaps the methods by which the parties may communicate on matters concerning the agreement.

The document concludes with the signatures, usually witnessed to ensure that the persons signing are indeed the persons they claim to be.

The overriding priority for the language used in drafting documents of this nature is that it should be unambiguous. This does not necessarily mean that it should be clear, though this is obviously an advantage for laypersons who have to read and understand it. Many legal documents are hopelessly unclear, and one has a sneaking suspicion that this is sometimes partly, if unconsciously, intentional—to keep the whole business on a technical and professional level and ensure that a lawyer has to be used to interpret them. There is undoubtedly a "gamesmanship" aspect to the drafting of legal documents, and indeed to much else that goes on in legal procedures: the language used is often quite unnecessarily archaic.

But absence of ambiguity is clearly essential. Each word and sentence must mean one thing and one thing only. This goal is not always attained: if it were, there would be a great deal less litigation.

British legal documents normally have no punctuation. This is, paradoxically, to ensure that they are not ambiguous. It is held that precision of meaning should not depend on whether commas, colons, and so on are correctly placed, but should be achieved through the words alone. This is a valid argument, and it was even more so before the era of the typewriter when documents were copied out by hand: then, a splutter of ink from a scratchy quill pen might have been interpreted as punctuation and held to alter the sense of a crucial passage. But the result today is a form of text that is even more specifically "legal," and even more obscure to people who are not familiar with this kind of writing.

Elegance of style clearly has to take second place in the priorities. For instance, in normal writing, one tries to avoid close repetition of prominent words in the same or successive sentences, unless a specific emphasis is intended. The writer will look for a synonym or will say "it," "he" "she," or "the latter," referring back to the thing or person previously mentioned. Legal writing will tend to avoid this, because the synonym may not be an exact one (very few are) and will use "it" or a similar word only if there is no other person or thing to which or whom it could conceivably refer. Despite all this, legal documents often have an elegance all their own, partly through the use of archaic words and expressions. Lawyers are not insensitive to style, though it cannot be their first priority, and logical exposition and precision can create their own elegance.

Most writing for exactness that you will have to do, assuming that you are not a practicing lawyer, will not be legal contracts, but letters setting out your terms for a sale or job, instructions to subordinates, or memoranda to superiors setting out the conditions for the feasibility of a project, as you see them, and so on. Again, the first priority is that what you say should be unambiguous, but here this is closely followed by one of clarity: that the document, whatever it is, should be readily understandable to the person or persons for whom it is intended.

If you are not a lawyer, and especially if the addressee is not a lawyer either, avoid using technical legal language, even if you think you are familiar with it. You may not use it correctly, and this may lead to unnecessary complications. And you may not be understood. If you do use a word that has specific legal meaning, make it clear whether this or the everyday sense is intended. For instance, in legal language the "term" of a contract is the end of its period of validity, and this can be confused with "term" in the ordinary sense of a name or word. "Determine" is sometimes used by lawyers to mean to bring a contract to an end. And "consideration," in legal writing, is the material equivalent given in exchange for something. Try to be precise and clear in ordinary language, and if necessary give a definition of what you mean.

Another form of writing in which both precision and clarity are required is a technical exposition. Many scientists and engineers have to write papers about work they have done, and often they make a hopeless mess of it. They break all the rules in this book, and in particular they use terms that are not universally understood. Many engineers who have specialized in a particular branch use their own names for parts or elements with which they are very familiar, and are not consciously aware that these terms are not employed in the same way by other engineers. This may be because these parts or elements are so specialized that they are not used at all in other branches, and it was necessary to invent new terms for them. This is happening all the time in electronics and data processing, where the technology is constantly changing. For example, who knew what a "byte" was 20 years ago? Other terms are invented because they shortcut a longer one previously used. An example of this that has gone into ordinary language is "outage," which has not been in the dictionary very long and was invented to mean a period of unserviceability, for instance, of a power plant, but many other such new terms are used by technical people that are not yet in current use and need explanation or paraphrase. Or a word that is generally used with a given meaning may be employed in a particular context with a special one. Computer people, for example, use the word "architecture" to mean the technical design of some piece of "hardware"—itself a term that has now passed into ordinary language and means the physical elements of date processing equipment, as opposed to the "software," which designates the intangible elements, the programs exploited by the equipment. Again, initials or acronyms of words are sometimes used instead of the full phrase by engineers who assume that everyone understands them. BFO and SSB are familiar to radio people and mean beat-frequency oscillator and single-sideband (transmission), but radio engineers often forget that ordinary mortals have no idea what they mean. Many other acronyms you use all the time may be totally mysterious to someone who is not in your specialty. And last, you may cause ambiguity by shortening a composite term, when the shortened version has its own meaning in a different context. An oversimplified example, again in radio, is to say "carrier" instead of "carrier wave"; obviously "carrier" has its own different meaning in a different or nontechnical context, and especially an airline one.

The point, of course, is not that you should never use such terms when you are writing for exactness. That would be absurd, when you are writing for other people who share the same vocabulary. It is that when you do so you must make sure that this is the case and that your readers will understand you without difficulty either because the context rules out all ambiguity or because your readers are specialists in the same field as you are and use terms in exactly the same way.

There are two particular cases where exact writing is more than ever necessary. One is the writing up of descriptions of processes or equipment for patent applications; the other is the preparation of technical manuals.

In patent applications, both legal and technical precision is required. There are, of course, lawyers who specialize in preparing patent applications, but when the process or equipment is highly technical, they must depend on an engineer or scientist for a clear explanation of what is to be patented. If a breach-of-patent case arises, the other side will do its best to demolish this explanation; so it is most important that it should be completely unambiguous, using terms that can mean only what they are intended to mean. Otherwise, your firm can get into some very expensive trouble.

In the writing of technical manuals, the requirement of clarity is just as important as that of unambiguity. Their purpose is to tell other people how to use a particular piece of equipment. So again:

1. Choose terms that are in general use, if possible, and if not, define them, making maximum use of illustration, exploded or otherwise.

2. Write simply, using short sentences. Try out your manual on someone who is not familiar with the equipment, to isolate points on which you have not made yourself crystal clear. For anything but the simplest of manuals, word processing equipment is an enormous help in writing such material, if for no other reason than that these devices make it very easy to revise and update: you must revisualize the memorized material and make the necessary alterations; then you press the print key, and out comes a complete updated version. The writing of technical manuals is a specialized profession, and those who practice it are skilled in sorting out the information it is necessary to communicate, putting it in logical order, and writing it up in a simple language. Large companies who market advanced technology equipment often farm out the whole process to specialized service firms, which have the technical writers, illustrators, and photographers, together with the appropriate computerized equipment. They can do the job more competently and economically than the client company, especially when, as is the case with complicated machinery, the technical manual may run into thousands of pages and the technology may be changing all the time.

SECTION 3
PLANNING

CHAPTER 6

The Basics
of Planning

The difference between adequate individuals and organizations and great ones is *values*.

When considered in order of importance, the primary value is *philosophy*. What do individuals regard as their role in life? What is the basis of corporate missions?

Next on the list of values is *planning*. How do individuals realize their role in life? How do corporations realize their missions?

The purpose of this section is to get back to the basics of planning.

Technological change has speeded up so significantly and affected every business so completely that to launch a business venture without adequate knowledge both of what is and of what will be is foolhardy.

The *complexity* of our environment—in terms of political, cultural, societal, demographic, and legal changes—dictates that a wealth of specialized knowledge be applied to ensure the success of any venture. The need for the so-called Renaissance man or woman in this society may be diminishing; the generalist may have become an endangered species. However, it is our contention that those generalists will ultimately make the best managers, the best CEOs, the best visionaries because they can see the whole picture, pull it together, articulate it and emerge as the consummate planners of the future.

Ultimately, then, the orderly back-to-basics planning process allows the planner-manager to look at a problem/opportunity from a broader perspective. Lawyers, accountants, engineers, or designers will inevitably look at the world from their particular perspectives—not wrong, but specialized. Good planners examine many facets of the situation and see the venture in a more all-inclusive manner.

■ "WHAT GOES UP MUST COME DOWN"

A good manager in the planning process always facilitates a continuing dialogue among departments and all levels of management. Check the comparison between the planning process and the communications flow shown in Figure 6.1 on page 85. As noted earlier, the planning process (represented in the figure by the larger arrows) moves upward through the blocks (the departments) for a viable plan to be developed. However, when we look at those same departmental blocks from a communications standpoint, the communications flow (represented by the smaller arrows) must move downward and laterally as well as upward. That is, people should be encouraged to communicate with their peers, their superiors, and their subordinates.

■ STRATEGIC PLANNING: SEVEN MAJOR STRATEGIC AREAS

Large-scale planning is fundamental to the success of any company. And the major strategies that give a firm its direction fall into seven areas. Success lies in all these areas, not just a select few.

■ FIGURE 6.1

The Planning Process Compared to the Communications Flow

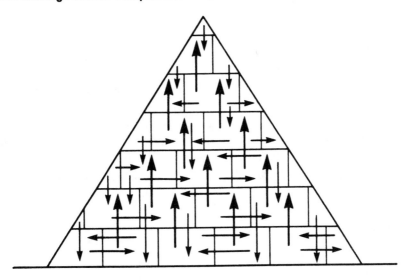

The arrows from the broad base *up* represent the planning process.
The smaller arrows represent the interplay between departments
and people on a continuing communications flow.

❑ New or Changed Products

A business exists to furnish products or services. The profits that
result mean many things to many people, but mostly, they are a very
important measure of how well an enterprise serves its customers.

The fundamental questions are: Do we serve our customers
well? Are changes needed in our product(s)? Are we lagging behind
competition? Does a need exist that we are eminently qualified to
satisfy? If so, should we develop a product/service to meet that need?

❑ Marketing

Remember the words of Nietzsche: "The greatest stupidity is to lose
sight of what one is trying to do." Marketing strategies are designed

to guide the planning process in getting a product or service to a user. All else is frill.

❑ Growth

Growth strategies are the company's answer to such questions as: How much growth? How fast? How soon? Must we preserve capital or invest it? Are we prepared to serve our customers if we spark growth now? (The nightmare of any planner must be to get the public interested in buying a product, only to have them find that it is not yet on the shelf—for whatever reason: shortage of raw materials, inadequate delivery systems, lack of sufficient personnel, etc.) They say bigger is better. But is that true in your own particular venture?

❑ Financial

Every business must have a clear strategy for financing its operations. Depending only on profits produced, hoping the banks will refinance a loser, trusting that advertising and public relations will salvage a damaged product/service reputation, and all the other errors we read of daily can never take the place of sound financial planning, both for the present and for the foreseeable future.

❑ Organizational

What type of organization is best for your business? The classic pyramid hierarchy may be right for one firm, while the "quality circle" may be better for another. (Apple Computers is not structured like IBM, but both make pretty good computers.) How centralized should the firm be? What kinds of departmental structures and interfacing are required? What positions and job ladders are most suitable? Are the divisions responsible for profits? How should staffs be designed, recruited, trained, and organized?

❑ Personnel

Major strategies in the area of human resources give direction to the composition of the enterprise itself. They vary widely and involve such issues as unions, compensation, selection, recruitment, training, and appraisal. The bottom line is: What kind of people do we want to be?

❑ Public Relations/Advertising

These functions are not independent from the main business but rather must support all other major strategies. They are designed to illuminate a company's business to a variety of publics: customers, government(s), shareholders, suppliers.

■ DEVELOPING MAJOR STRATEGIES

In developing major strategies of any kind, you should perform a corporate self-appraisal, analyze the consistency of your strategies, and develop strategies to meet unforeseen contingencies.

❑ Corporate Self-Appraisal

What is our business? It is surprising how many companies don't really know what business they are in. The classic case is, of course, the railroads in America, which for too long overlooked the fact they were in the *transportation* business, not in railroading. And as we know, bye-bye railroads.

In the go-go 1980s when mergers were the quickest way to an improved balance sheet and a higher stock price, many companies got into businesses they knew nothing about and in which they had no experience and, in many cases, no real interest.

❑ Assuring Consistency of Strategies

Establishing consistency between departments, between divisions, between companies, striving for a common goal is the hardest task in appraising plans. In launching a totally new manufacturing division (computers), RCA may have made a classic error in taking on IBM across the board, in all sizes. If the object of a conglomerate is to make all divisions profitable, then consistency would have dictated carving out a share of the computer marketplace and building on that success. Other similar examples will cross your path every day. Never lose sight of the word *consistency.*

❏ Developing Contingency Strategies

What do you do when things go wrong? After the plan has been written and evaluated, and after it has been adjudged both sound (in light of your corporate self-appraisal) and consistent, then what do you do if the world (either internal or external) changes under your feet? We have heard planning described as the process you go through to take care of the "known" so that you'll have time to take care of the unexpected when it occurs. (And it will!) *Reappraisal, monitoring,* and *reviewing* on a regular basis are a must for management to ensure that the contingency strategies are continually updated.

■ RULES FOR IMPLEMENTING STRATEGIES

And, finally, in implementing strategies, some cardinal rules must be followed:

- Strategies should be communicated to *all* key decision-making managers. Remember the pyramid: that which goes up should come down. We assume that the subordinate managers were part of the analysis and planning process; now they should know the results and the company's goals.

- All premises (assumptions) critical to the planning process must be developed and *communicated* to all managers. What is our collective view of the environment in which we will be functioning?

- *Action plans* must contribute to and impact upon major objectives and strategies. These are tactical programs for getting it done. Who, when, how, for how much?

- Strategies should be *reviewed* regularly. Monitor, monitor, monitor. Status reports are crucial.

- Develop *contingency* plans for all objectives and strategies.

- Make your *organization* fit your plans. It must be designed to support the accomplishment of goals. The refrain "This is the way we've always done it" should be banned from your premises. While wholesale housecleaning is not a planning device, the proper allocation of human resources to those areas in which they can perform best is not a hit-or-miss proposition. It is a fundamental process in accomplishing goals.

- Continue to *teach* planning and strategy implementation in your organization. Lip service to planning by chief executives is a surefire guarantee of its failure. When the person at the top *believes* in back-to-basics planning and strategy implementation, and the employees know that he or she believes in it, they will believe in it. Furthermore, a chief executive who is committed will see to it that all the training necessary to make a strategy work will find its way into the company budget.

The following techniques should be utilized to make planning a part of the firm's everyday operation:

Practice management by objectives.

Conduct formal reviews (not hit or miss).

Budget reviews (how're we doing?).

Be result oriented (reward for achievement).

Establish ongoing training programs (learn while you earn).

Integrate long- and short-range plans.

❏ Strategic Planning

Strategic planning can be made to have bottom-line impact. Effective top managers can guarantee its success if they carefully develop strategies and take the proper steps to ensure their implementation.

In fact, if your organization is to be successful over a period of time, it really has *no other alternative.* Remember, the future is always now.

❑ Checklist for Strategic Planning

"Where do we go from here?"

- Do we need new or changed products to meet our competition?
- Do our marketing strategies get our products/services to the customer efficiently?
- Have we analyzed our growth in light of our future needs?
- Do we have a clear strategy for financing the present and future?
- Does "form follow function" in our organization planning?
- Does our personnel plan meet the needs of our company's objectives and strategies?
- Do our public relations and advertising plans support all our major strategies?
- Do we know our corporate destiny? What is our real business?
- Are we consistent in all our strategies? Have we removed all the conflicts?
- Do we have contingency strategies in place, through reappraisal, monitoring, and reviewing?
- Are our strategies communicated to all our key decision-making managers?
- Are our assumptions (premises) communicated to all our managers?
- Have we all agreed on action plans, and are they in place?
- Do we teach the planning principles on a regular basis to all our supervisory and managerial staff?
- Are we result oriented? Do we reward achievement?

In the past 50 years there has been enormous change in the way organizations are run, with the people in the little boxes being allowed much more flexibility and greater participation. For instance, the change of "personnel departments" to "human resource departments" involves more than semantics. It is a recognition of human needs and a sign of flexibility in business in the twentieth century. But despite the change in the manner in which organizations are run, the structure of those organizations, as reflected by the organization charts (see Figure 6.2), remains fixed in a form that West Point would admire.

■ FIGURE 6.2

Military-Corporate Organizational Structure

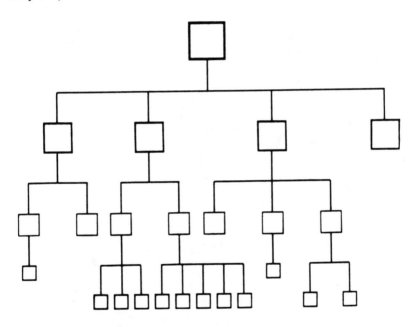

The U.S. Navy was described as "designed by geniuses to be run by idiots." The command structure was straight down, rigid and largely uncompromising. Such organizational structures can still be useful for administrative, record keeping, and payroll activities. They are hopelessly outdated in modern business and industry.

In business we deal with human beings, not robots. Some fine people who worked for me resented "being put in boxes." Figure 6.3 could be entitled "The Communications Structure." If you must have an organization structure chart, you should accompany it with a communications structure chart to break the "little boxes" pattern of thinking and action engendered by rigidity of organizational structure charts.

■ FIGURE 6.3

The Quality Circles Structure

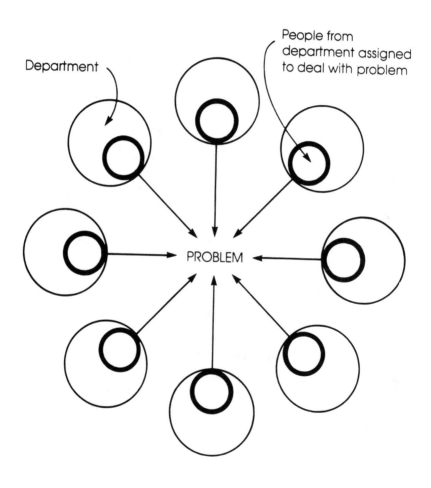

I would like to share a personal credo about this process:

An individual's personal objectives and life goals must somehow relate to the organization's goals and standards. Personal values cannot be in conflict with company values.

This is important to remember as an employee, as a manager, as the president-owner of a company. No explanation is required; the reasons are self-evident, both from a personal point of view and from a company point of view.

■ THE BACK-TO-BASICS ORGANIZATION PLANNING PROCESS

What follows is an overview of the steps to follow in implementing organization planning. But first, a further word about implementing a new process: don't be afraid to use a consultant. Although times change, and sometimes consultants are looked upon as a waste or an unnecessary addition to the process, they can make significant contributions in areas such as this. They have years of experience in the organization planning process as well as its pitfalls and can become that good "right arm" during the analysis and preparation work involved in instituting a new methodology. The good consultants will involve all your people from the beginning and work together with you to make it your plan. This is a prime example of "not reinventing the wheel." Ultimately, the time and money saved on research, the pitfalls avoided, and the speed of implementation will be worth the cost and efforts of using a consultant. If done properly, all your employees will make the plan their own and have a vested interest in making it work.

■ ORGANIZATIONAL PLANNING STEPS

1. Define the work to be done, the tasks, the departments. (You might find yourself reorganizing your company when you define the work by tasks rather than by people.)

Define the skills to do each job.

Define the time to do each job.

This defines the human factor—the people to do the work (types, training, number).

2. Write the job description. Extensive guidelines have been published on what job descriptions are, what they should include, how they should be evaluated, and how they should relate to each other. Writing the job description is initially the work of manager *and* employee. Evaluation could use outside help. Defining relationships requires much management time and input.

3. Employee and manager set work goals, develop action plans, and agree on the method and time frame for their implementation.

4. Set up a process, both written and in person, for the orderly review of these work goals. Recent studies indicate that performance reviews are more beneficial if they are performed more than once a year and if they are *not* necessarily related to merit increases, bonuses, and so forth.

5. Set up an orderly and companywide training and guidance program. This can range from training the secretarial staff in word processing equipment to initiating support of continuing education in job-related and/or stretching programs. Training and guidance keep your employees on the cutting edge of change, not running behind the rest of the pack.

6. Establish salary grade levels, promotion flexibility, transfer flexibility, promotion incentives, and salary increase incentives that are competitive within your own industry and with related industries.

7. Create an orderly review process for your job descriptions, salary grade levels, promotion, and salary increase guidelines so that you know you maintain a competitive edge.

8. Set up procedures for reviewing not only progress but dealing with problem people; this means itemizing, in detailed person-

nel policies and procedures, the methods you wish your managers to use, and to use consistently and equitably.

9. Reward your employees consistently and fairly for work well done. Set up additional incentive rewards for the super-achievers. These can range from family vacation for the super-salesperson and incentive bonuses for surpassing a goal to restricted stock plans and company ownership awards.

■ THE PERSONNEL PLAN

The personnel plan is a fundamental part of the process of preparing your back-to-basics plan. The organization planning that we have reviewed is the bedrock on which your personnel plan is built, but now you must concern yourself more with numbers than with processes. Those numbers will be derived from all the work you have previously done. The following are the steps in the process of personnel analysis by which you prepare your personnel plan:

1. Identify the resources of the company (what are the sales projections, what is your expected profit margin, etc.?).

   a. What are your expected revenues?

   b. What are your fixed costs (other than people)?

   c. What are the department's/company's required profits (or acceptable losses)?

   d. What are your relative costs (not people-related costs, but those costs related to production)?

2. Analyze your people costs.

   a. List the number and kinds of jobs. Can you use more or fewer people, or different kinds of people, based on the needs indicated in your business plan?

   b. Analyze your union requirements. Can you cut, or must you expand? When is the next contract up for renewal? How do you expect it to go?

c. Are your salaries competitive? Will you have turnover? Do you overpay?

d. Build in incentives for overachievers.

These exercises will prepare you to fill out the financial and personnel sections of your back-to-basics business plan. Remember one word as you embark on the process of back-to-basics business planning: *justification*. If you have trouble justifying all the requests in that plan, perhaps you should take another good, hard look at it before you pass it along to upper management. If you can justify the requests, then you have done your management job well, and both your staff and your superiors will be happy with you.

■ QUALITATIVE AND QUANTITATIVE STANDARDS

All planning decisions take into account at least two kinds of standards: qualitative and quantitative. Among the fundamental qualitative standards in the business planning field are:

- *Management development.* Who is in the slot? What if a truck hit the boss tomorrow? Must we go out and buy talent, or are we growing it here?

- *Image.* How do I want this company to be perceived? By the public? (Which public?) The stockholders? The employees? The government(s)?

- *Contribution to the community.* What do we owe to our community? What can we give to it? What will we get back?

- *Talent development.* What about our future? Who are our thinkers and creators? Is a competitor getting ahead of us?

- *Technical advancement.* What's going on that will affect us? Can we afford to wait? What are the risks? What are the advantages?

- *Political-social influence.* What is our balance with production partners? With trading partners? Does a government agency present looming problems? Should we take a stand? Should we be out in front, leading our industry toward new horizons?

Quantitative standards are those that ask the question, "How much?" These are the familiar names that often appear in financial statements:

Budgets	Customers	Assets
Costs	Share	Liabilities
Revenues	Profits	Profit margins
Volume	Losses	

CHAPTER 7

The Elements of Strategic Planning

The strategic planning cycle is the greatest opportunity a business will have in getting its people to talk to each other, to share with each other, to work off each other. It is the opportune moment for people to come out of their departmental isolation and share their vision, their dreams, their problems, their ideas about the company and its future.

The buck must stop somewhere. And once the plans of departments and divisions are articulated, executive decision making takes over. The final decisions will be made in light of the overall needs of the company, which we will discuss later. But a fundamental back-to-basics strategic planning principle is cooperative activity under inspirational leadership.

■ ORDERLY MONITORING OF THE STRATEGIC PLAN

All this structured creativity is most powerful when there is a formalized way to monitor the *progress* of the plan. Summary reports, performance data, revised estimates, reaffirmations, updates—all must become a part of the ongoing life not only of the plan but of the business itself. Later we deal with the use of *action plans* to direct and monitor the implementation of the strategic plan.

▪ ## THE ROLE OF MANAGEMENT IN THE PLANNING PROCESS

Good management, when most successful, is like two sides of a coin: it must combine *fiscal responsibility* and *integrity* with *creativity* and *vision*. Just as it is impossible to separate the two sides of a coin, so it is impossible to separate these elements of good management. In the back-to-basics planning process, executive management must:

- Balance the requests and goals of the various departmental and divisional plans.

- Review and give realistic appraisals. Provide feedback.

- Resolve conflicts and trade-offs.

- Be the final arbiter of profits, growth, image.

- Be an effective presenter of the company's goals to its many publics.

In summary, what are the most valuable assets executive management can marshall in this highly competitive world? *Honesty, integrity* and *credibility* are worth their weight in gold. In the long run these traits win out over all others. The back-to-basics planning process, when done in an orderly, open, cooperative manner, paves the way for that kind of management and that kind of business practice.

Thus, planning is a generic function of management. It is a fundamental, organic part of the day-to-day operation.

■ CHECKLIST FOR THE PLANNING PHILOSOPHY

"The longest journey begins with (thinking about taking) a single step."

With apologies to Lao Tzu, this quote is a reminder for the journey you will begin: planning the future—of your department, your venture, your life.

The planning philosophy is no more and no less basic than brushing your teeth every morning and evening. For the planning philosophy, which starts as a conscious thought process, can evolve into a habit that soon becomes second nature to the back-to-basics planner. A careful review of the following fundamental principles of the back-to-basics planning philosophy can help you form your own ingrained planning habit:

- Identify sound business practices for your venture.

- Determine your company's philosophy; simply stated, what is your nature and function?

- Remain flexible in a changing environment.

- Implement an ongoing program of personnel development and training to ensure the growth of your people.

- Formalize the planning process, remembering that it is organic and must be monitored.

- Don't lose sight of your objective. You are planning for long-term growth.

- Remember the pyramid. Build from the bottom up, block by block.

- Recognize that people have a vested interest in the success of a plan if they participate in the planning process.

- Develop a plan that is total and comprehensive, relate each aspect with all others, and involve everyone in formulating its objectives and strategies.

- Provide open and continuing dialogue between all departments and all levels of management. Don't isolate people.

- Develop qualitative and quantitative standards for your venture that are understood companywide.

- Since "you never know where a good idea will come from," devise a planning process that encourages creativity at all levels.

- Combine fiscal responsibility and integrity with creativity and vision.

- Balance the requests and goals of the departments in light of these companywide qualitative and quantitative standards.

- Review and give realistic appraisals and feedback.

- Resolve conflicts and trade-offs.

- Learn that good management is the final arbiter of profits, growth, image; the buck stops somewhere.

- Plan. Planning is a generic function of management; it is an organic part of the day-to-day operation.

- Using good planning tools, free the firm's management and staff from needless improvisation and error.

■ ASSUMPTIONS

In an orderly strategic planning process, a planning packet is given to each manager so that the finished products will follow the same formats and, therefore, be easy to review and consolidate. Uniformity of the packet in no way inhibits the creativity and individuality of each planner-manager.

The first page of that packet, typically, contains the *economic assumptions* that management had made regarding the coming planning period. These are the guidelines that each planner-manager should follow when preparing the plan, and they concern such basics as salary increases, expected rent increases (or decreases), expected inflation rates, industry trends on pricing, cost of goods, and so on.

This page helps each planner-manager *speak from a common base* in the preparation of the plan. It should also allow the preparer to identify *individual assumptions* that may vary from national trends (such as regional rent differences, changing regional telephone rates, salary competition, etc.).

■ PROJECT

The "Project" portion of the plan can range in scope from defining an entire company to defining a single department. It can be a simple statement, a paragraph of five lines, or an essay of five to ten pages. It answers two questions:

Mission—what the venture is.

Function—what the venture does.

■ OVERVIEW

The "Overview" portion of the plan places your venture in perspective. It concerns itself with the *environment* (the world in which your venture operates) and the *future* (your hard-nosed, no-nonsense analysis of what lies out there as threat or opportunity).

■ ENVIRONMENT

The "Environment" portion of the "Overview" addresses itself to the old vaudeville gag line, "Everybody has to be somewhere." Where are you? More important, are you in the right place? You'll only know when you research and analyze the aspects of the environment listed as follows:

- *Economic.* What is the state of the economy now, and what is it expected to be in the coming year? How will this impact on your venture? You should arrive at certain economic assumptions on the corporate level so that everyone is making the same assumption.

- *Cultural-social.* What is going on in terms of changing life-styles that could impact on your plan?

- *Political.* These winds shift more often than the Gulf Stream, but knowledge of changing laws and regulations, the power to influence them and the growth or diminution of political groups can have a profound effect on the thrust of a business plan.

- *Demographic.* This word, which has taken its place in the American language over the past two decades, predominantly involves statistical data that describe who we are.

- *Technological.* Analysis of and preparation for the technology of the present as well as the future with respect to your venture is a crucial part of your business planning.

- *Artistic development.* What are your plans to nurture the creative mind?

- *Internal.* This is the section in which you look candidly at your current internal environment.

■ FUTURE

The "Future" section of the plan is not the place to dream (that comes later, in your long-range plans). This is the place to address specific problems and opportunities you see down the years for your segment of the business.

- *Major opportunities.* Are new laws or government regulations coming soon that will open up possibilities for increased business?

- *Major threats.* Go through the same sort of exercise that you did for opportunities, only this time, identify problems that could limit future growth.

■ AN EXPLANATION OF STRATEGIC PLANNING BY ANALOGY

Assume that you are a parent with two small children. You and your spouse decide to visit the children's grandparents in a distant city. Strategic planning starts with your decision to visit. Part of the strategic planning involves the method of transportation: car, plane, train, or bus. It also involves the comfort and safety of the children, as well as the budget, the dates, and communications with the grandparents. From that point on, the operational plan is involved. It takes into account that there can be changes in weather, delays for construction, accidents, hunger, thirst, the calls of nature, and a whole range of small but important details.

Refine it even further. Assume you decide to go by car. You get a road map which indicates the various roads you will expect to take from point A to point B. That is your strategic plan. But you know that a car driver rarely can follow a road map exactly on a long trip. There are detours, accidents, and weather changes, so the sensible driver is quite prepared with an operating plan to handle the realities.

CHAPTER 8

Operational Planning

■ OBJECTIVES

Objectives are generally one-sentence, specific statements of what the company, division, or department wishes to accomplish. Some examples are:

- Increase gross revenues 15 percent.

- Increase profits 10 percent.

- Enhance image with state _____ agency.

- Increase audience reach by 3 percent.

- Expand financial reports to include _____ division.

- Implement salary administration system.

- Develop and implement national advertising campaign for product.

Remember: be specific, be succinct, and don't confuse what you want to do with how you want to do it.

■ DETAILS

The "Details" section of the plan is your chance to say how. This is the place where all the homework you did in the "Overview" section of your strategic plan begins to pay off.

In each case they must be logical and practical. In each case they may also impact on your operating budget, your capital requests, your personnel (and space/equipment) requests, and your marketing budget. Therefore, you should be able to prove that they are worth the cost or that they will provide an adequate return on investment (ROI). That justification should rightly be included in your financial backup statements.

The "Operating Plan" answers the question, "What do I do if things go wrong?" This information should be presented in two parts: (1) "Narrative" and (2) "Financial Impact." The "Narrative" section allows you to elaborate on the actions you will take in case some of the events occur. The "Financial Impact" section allows you to measure the impact (on income, costs, profits) in an orderly way.

In our experience this becomes an exercise almost akin to selecting from a Chinese menu: "one from column A, two from column B." Management has gone through its trade-off process, and you as a manager have the go-ahead for some of your new strategies and a negative decision on others. You can put in those accepted items from your "New Projects" pages, remove items that have been rejected (again using the "New Projects" pages) and have a clear picture of your approved plan for the coming year.

We also include one other "Alternate Plan" page, which we suggest that you submit to management at the beginning. Some managements have the opinion that all first plans have "fat" in them; they assume (rightly or wrongly) that you have embellished your requests in order to "give management something to cut." That may not be accurate, but if you know your company, you know how to play the game. This is not to say that we encourage the game; on the contrary, the best plan writing in our opinion is based on honest, realistic requests and goals. But on the assumption that every company arrives at hard times sometime, and that all managers have to "tighten their belts" for the good of the company on occasion, we suggest using the "Alternate Plans" form. Management can chop up your budget request like a woodcutter (with an ax), or it can allow you to trim your budget like a surgeon (carefully and selectively), so the patient will live. We believe the latter method is better, simply because it allows managers to manage. If you use that form, you will have identified both *what* you can cut and what the *impact* of those cuts will be (the obvious conclusion being that management must be willing to accept the impact if it requires the cuts).

Remember, the whole purpose of companywide back-to-basics business planning is not to develop a method of hiding something from top management; it is a way of sharing all ideas and information so that everyone may work together for the overall benefit of the enterprise and its employees.

■ ACTION PLANS

Action plans are not necessarily included in the plan package that is presented to management, but they are the *core* of your activity as a manager who is managing a department, a division, or a venture.

The simplest way to approach an action plan is to go back to the "Details" section of your "operating plan." Every detail becomes an action that must be accomplished. Every detail should therefore be written down and responsibility, due date, and budget assigned to it. Obviously, this is not an exercise performed by the manager in the privacy of his or her office, away from the staff who will implement the action plan. Since all your department heads have participated in the planning process, all the goals and strategies are a part of their plans anyway. Together, you the manager should write up action plans for each strategy, sign off on the budgets, assign responsibility, agree on the completion dates, and put the projects in motion.

These action plans can serve as status reports, which your subordinates will file with you on a regular basis (it can be once a week, every two weeks, once a month, once a year, but it must be agreed to). We have found that a status report every two weeks (assuming you have staff meetings or direct reports from your subordinates on alternate weeks) is adequate reporting to keep you informed of progress and problems and to allow your staff the necessary breathing room to accomplish its goals. Some people believe this is too often, but in the volatile world of American business, a lot can happen weekly and biweekly. While the last thing you want to do is hover over your staff, not knowing what's going on can lead to disaster.

The timing of the action plan status reports is yours to choose, but a decision to *forgo* monitoring the progress of the plan is simply foolhardy. The most satisfying word on a status report is *completed* over in the right-hand column. As you establish your plan and implement it, be sure that you monitor it and see it to completion.

■ FINANCIAL HISTORY

A thumbnail "Financial History" sketch of the progress and opportunity of your venture can be very useful. There are many variations on the theme, but even a one-page summary provides you and management with an overview that can identify meaningful trends. If you operate a department rather than a profit center, the form can be modified to include *categories* of costs, both controllable and noncontrollable. While a great deal of financial information is required in the planning process, the written narrative of the plan may be accompanied only by those details that illuminate, clarify, and project future trends.

■ RESOURCE REQUIREMENTS

Resource requirements are sometimes called capital requests. They vary with the requirements of your own particular venture. The capital requirements come from the corporate coffers—trade-offs are fundamental. Sometimes, in addition to the capital required, corporations will charge the division or unit the current interest rate the corporation itself is paying for loans (although these same corporations are often reluctant to credit the division or unit for tax credits or for interest earned on daily cash flow from profits). However, identifying your capital resource requirements is a fundamental management responsibility (even if it involves nothing more than a $1,100 personal computer). Don't overlook it in your plan; if you don't ask for something, you may not get it.

■ LONG-RANGE PLANS

Now to the future. How do you see it? What is the position of your department, your venture, your company in it? The "Narrative" portion of the "Long-Range Plans" section allows you to present your projections covering the next 3 to 5 to 10 years, depending on the nature of your company. (If you make cars, 10 years is a short period of time. If you make television programs, 3 years is a lot.) The "Detail" portion of the section on long-range planning invites sensible budgeting but aggressive ideas in your area of operation. While the long-range plan is not binding (remember, planning is an *organic* process), it allows company management to share your long-range vision of the firm's destiny. Again, the research you did in the "Overview" section of the plan will come into play here. This does not mean that you must repeat the ideas of the media and gurus, but it does mean that your projections should be based on what is as well as what you think might be.

We suggest a brief, annotated narrative, followed by some reasonable guesses as to projected revenues, costs, headcount, new projects, and profits. Although not binding, when consolidated with other plans, this allows top management to view its future through the eyes of its principal employees. If you believe that planning and progress of a venture are based on the people who make it run, then use the "Long-Range Plans" section to capture your most creative thoughts. You never know where a good idea will come from: you can get a lot of "off-the-wall" ideas in long-range plans, but just remember, going to the moon was an "off-the-wall" idea once upon a time. For executive management, the long-range plans of each department and division have to be the most interesting planning elements of all, because they give the ultimate indication as to whether or not your venture is going in a creative, profitable, and productive direction and whether or not you have the right people working with you to take you there.

▪ HEAD COUNT

Many companies and ventures expect a "head count" page as part of the plan. Such a section serves little purpose if it is not related to dollars, income, and profit. And it can be extremely useful if coupled with other numbers such as square-footage analysis of space utilized (multiply the head count number by 225 square feet to see whether you over- or underutilize office space for your personnel); if compared to your equal opportunities report of women and minorities in the top four categories (executives, professionals, technical, sales) to see whether you are a leader or a laggard in equal opportunity; or if used to analyze your medical, pension, or holiday/vacation benefits on a cost-per-employee basis to see whether you surpass or lag behind the national average. Taken alone, a head count is relatively useless. But employed by analysts in your company in conjunction with other key data, it can help define your position in the past, present, and future in a variety of very important business categories.

▪ BUSINESS

As a continuing part of the "Overview," you will now look at your business as it relates to other companies in the same field.

- *Critical success factors.* What is critical to your success next year?
- *Competitive position.*
- *Trends/industry developments.* This is where your constant, year-round reading of trade journals pays off.
- *Strengths.* Honestly and candidly, what are the strong points of your division or company?

- *Weaknesses.* Shortcomings, too, should be addressed honestly and candidly.

▪ CHECKLIST FOR THE PLANNING PROCESS

"Speak the same language."

The *process* of writing a business plan is more important to you and your staff than the written plan itself. Going through the cooperative, creative, analytical, structured process of looking at your venture and its future can make you a real "expert." Defining the elements of such a plan and agreeing at the outset on the data to be included help to ensure that all involved are "speaking the same language"—the language of back-to-basics planning.

The following are reminders of how you get everyone involved in a common planning exercise and in working toward common goals.

- Having the plan in written form ensures that it will be taken seriously, while the process of writing the plan makes the plan meaningful.

- Be sure you know the general environment in which you operate—in terms of economic, cultural-social, political, demographic, technological, artistic-development, and internal factors.

- Be sure you know the business environment in which you compete: your critical success factors, your competitive position, industry trends and developments, and your strengths and weaknesses.

- Have a clear understanding of your future opportunities and threats.

- Be specific about the objectives for your venture and target between 5 and 15 achievable goals.

- Relate the strategies to the objectives, realizing that there can be several strategies for achieving one objective.

- Plan ahead for what can go wrong: identify the critical factors and devise alternate plans to cope with them.

- Use the "Departmental Operations: Narrative" section of the plan to illuminate your operation/department/division for management.

- Use the "New Projects" section to exhibit your ability to see into the future, to visualize, to relate to the company's long-term growth.

- Use the "Alternate Plans" section accurately and in great detail so that management will be more apt to let you manage your operation rather than make decisions for you.

- In conjunction with your staff, develop action plans for all the strategies and set up a regular monitoring and review timetable.

- Be sure that your resource requirements (capital requests) include everything you may need in the coming period. If you don't ask for something, you may not get it.

- In long-range planning, present sensible budgets, but be sure they are coupled with aggressive ideas.

- Your "Head Count" page is a good tool for measuring your enterprise against the competition—in terms of space utilization, benefits, equal employment opportunity concerns, and so on.

MARKETING

CHAPTER 9

The Basics of Marketing

For the back-to-basics planner, marketing is not some strange, mysterious art. It's been done from the beginning of time. One can just picture an aggressive Cro-Magnon fellow painting appetizing cuts of antelope and succulent roots on the rocks outside his cave if he wanted to trade them with passing travelers for warm winter furs or a new set of bone needles.

Broadsides and banners were used to proclaim performances of entertainers or hawk wares back before the average person could read. And we all delight in the mortar and pestle of the pharmacist, the boot outside the cobbler's shop, and the red and white barber pole (lest we forget that the barber once doubled as the local surgeon).

That's marketing: *anything done to enhance a product or service.*

◼ THE PRODUCT

If a product or service isn't fundamentally good or needed, the world's greatest marketing effort is doomed to fail. While the case can be made that hula hoops and pet rocks were not "needed" products, they still made their creators rich. That brings up the point that marketing can create a need for something when such a need did not previously exist. But be reminded: those fads were not long-lived. The need was not real.

As a back-to-basics planner, your ultimate goal in planning is to build for long-term growth. The first priority is therefore a *good product* or *service.*

■ THE CONSUMER

What do you know about the consumer—current or intended—for your product? In the marketing plan, everything you know about the consumer determines where you should plan to position your product.

Remember, *every* business has competition. In this era of shrinking personal budgets and tightening disposable incomes, consumers are getting smarter, more selective, and harder to persuade (or change from current buying habits). Moreover, consumers are being bombarded by too many impressions (Advertising Council estimates are about 1,500 per day) of goods and services to make a judgment on instinct and impulse alone. You, the back-to-basics planner, must use your tools to devise a plan that will help consumers make those decisions.

Therefore (aside from the value of the product itself), marketing becomes the single *most important* thing you will do to guarantee long life to your venture.

■ THE MARKETING PLAN

There are some who will say that the marketing plan is your business plan. If you fail in planning, in developing and producing your goods or services, or in attracting customers to them, there is no business. To the extent that your operation's sales/revenue projections are derived from the success or failure of your marketing plans, that is correct. And to the extent that your volume and productivity of that product are the driving engine of your "variable costs," your expenses and, ultimately, the bottom line of profits or losses are mightily influenced by your marketing plan.

But we must make the distinction. Marketing is the basic element of a business plan. It is not of itself a business plan. Marketing is a way to move your products and services from your warehouse, your office, or your shop into the lives of the consumer. The back-to-basics marketing plan is a *way* to get there—spelled out in detail, with specifics of *what* you will move, *how* you will move it, and the target consumer to whom it will be sold.

A number of methods are available to the back-to-basics marketing planner to make the intended consumer aware of a product or service. The following are but a few:

- *The "tune-in" ad.* Radio and television networks use them all the time to remind listeners and viewers of upcoming programming. Why? To capture consumer interest, to make consumers tune in, to increase the audience share, to sell commercial time on those programs for more money than the competition is getting.

- *Print media advertising.* Newspapers and magazines present the product or service to get the consumer to try something new or to continue *buying* a familiar product or service.

- *The commercial.* We are now an electronic generation. We know more about commercials than any society in history. (When a slogan from a hamburger commercial pops up in a presidential campaign, we have reached the apogee of commercial saturation.) But with all the criticism, commercials *work.*

- *Direct mail.* The U.S. Postal Service has become a partner in marketing services in this country. It brings to our doors every day marketing inducements to try a new product, retry an old product, stock up on an old friend, take advantage of a discount. (Discount couponing, albeit venerable, is the fastest-growing marketing tool in America today.)

- *Publicity events.* "Live at Kennedy Center," sponsored sports awards competitions, as well as competitions and awards in other fields are all marketing events.

They bring together people who have a particular interest, and while those people are there, they become *aware* of a company, a product, a service. In order to choose the best method to create appropriate consumer awareness, the back-to-basics planner knows not only the product but also its intended market. Before an effective back-to-basics marketing plan is written, these two key variables must be examined.

■ THE BACK-TO-BASICS PLANNER'S MARKETING TACTICS

The back-to-basics planner uses the resources available to learn every feature of the product or service to be marketed. Once the "goods" are defined, the "consumers" must be defined. To accomplish this task, let's take a look at the various marketing tactics the back-to-basics planner can employ:

❏ Market and Marketing Research

Market research is research conducted to establish the extent and location of a market for a product or service. It determines whether or not your concept is viable and whether or not the dollars you plan to put into it will have suitable return. It is the gathering of factual information regarding consumer or user preferences.

To establish an important distinction in terminology, "market research" is the *action;* "marketing research" is the *result of the action.*

❏ Advertising

Advertising is simply the publishing or announcing of *news* via paid messages.

Don't let your friends look down their noses at you when you call advertising "news." The fact is, when a consumer hears about a product or service, particularly for the first time, it is news—albeit paid for. It is the opportunity, however, for you to present your message the way you want it to be said rather than have someone else say it for you. That's a very important "plus" for anybody involved in selling.

❏ Sales Approach

The sales approach varies depending on the services being sold. It can be as simple as the newspaper stand at the subway or bus stop or as complex as the movement of 20 consumer home products from a major manufacturer. It can involve one person, teams, or battalions of sales representatives.

Sales approaches include personal sales, mail order, point of sale, and many variations. While the techniques vary, the result is basic: movement of products or services to the consumer.

❏ Merchandising

Merchandising is a sales promotion activity, usually oriented more toward advertising than toward sales. Merchandising relates to couponing, the two-fer discounting in the theater, and other discounting activities, often in conjunction with some other business. (A fast-food chain might offer a discount on an entertainment complex, for instance.) The purpose of merchandising is to induce the consumer to make multiple purchases, usually in different products or services.

❏ Public Relations

Public relations is the business of inducing the public to have an understanding of and good will toward a person, service, institution, or product. Said another way, public relations involves those activities designed to develop images for products or services.

It is the ability to have a medium or the media report on your activities in a positive way—unpaid. It is important to realize, however, that there is a quid pro quo:

The medium involved must be convinced that your story is of concern to its audience—that is, the public interest must be satisfied. The story even must be worth reporting from the medium's point of view, not just yours. The persuasive (and creative) ability required for that is worth a lot in your public relations budget.

❏ Publicity

Publicity is an act designed to attract interest—free advertising, if you will. "Hype." It's a good flak beating a drum. It should be noted that good, imaginative writing is crucial for effective publicists. More often than not, when their material is used, it is because it has been presented in a press release in an interesting and well written way, and a beleaguered editor will use it for "filler" or "lead" because his or her audience will find it interesting.

■ MARKETING PHILOSOPHY

Marketing is a continuum. It is not something that you do at a particular point and then discontinue. That does not mean that a back-to-basics plan is cast in stone. But it does mean that a marketing plan, like all plans, is an organic instrument dedicated to the long-term life of the venture.

■ PRODUCT LIFE CYCLE

We've all heard the phrase *product life cycle*. A product starts, rises to a level, holds at a certain share, and then, perhaps, starts a decline.

There are (usually) many years of life in a product, albeit at varying stages of health. Part of your job marketing planning is to tailor programs for the different stages of that product's life. You will refine how you sell. Part of that depends on the *budget* that is available. Generally, you have more money at the start of the product's life and have to rely more on imagination and other types of marketing tools as the life cycle proceeds.

We must state our belief again that, in this day and age, research is the indispensable ingredient. Given the education and fragmentation of interests of the American buying public, launching a marketing campaign without research is simply like a blind person struggling through a swamp.

So we get to *budgets.* Be sure you budget enough for research—as well as for sufficient *advertising* and aggressive *publicity.* The truth is that there is a lot of competition out there, and you've got to have enough drums to beat.

Without belaboring the issue, we would recommend that merchandising be used sparingly or *not at all,* when launching a new product. That is, we don't believe in discounting or couponing at the beginning of a product's life. We know that flies in the face of a lot of current marketing practices, but in our view, the "I can get it for you wholesale" approach, as it were, diminishes the image of the product—cheapens it, perhaps—at the very beginning of its life. Later in its life, when the product needs a boost, couponing or other merchandising techniques could be helpful, but not when you're first building its image.

This does not refer, of course, to sampling (you know, those little tubes of toothpaste or hand cream that arrive in your mailbox unexpectedly). Sampling has always been a great way to launch a new product. (The method has drawbacks, of course, with services.)

■ COUPONS VERSUS SAMPLES

What is the track record of coupons versus samples? Is there a difference in cost between these two approaches? Is one more effective than the other? The answer is yes.

Larger product companies—the Colgate-Palmolives, the Procter & Gambles—obviously use every available kind of marketing technique to move their products. But when it comes to the question of coupons versus sampling, sampling is more cost-effective.

It's obviously cheaper to give away pieces of paper than it is to give away samples of the product. However, when you weigh the cost of coupons or the cost of sample product against the number of times the person uses the product during its life cycle, it becomes apparent that sampling is far and away the more effective approach to marketing a new product.

Not true, however, in marketing a mature product! Couponing and many other means are more effective in that case.

■ ELEMENTS OF THE BACK-TO-BASICS MARKETING PLAN

❑ Concept

Marketing all starts with a concept. How does a concept start? It starts with experience, with vision, with imagination, with a knowledge of trends; it all starts with an *idea.*

But maybe the idea stinks. You could be wrong. Perhaps no one needs a new flavor of toothpaste this year or a new production of *King Lear* or a pet rock that crawls. What's your next step?

You need a start-up budget.

But you're saying, "Hey, wait a minute. I thought a budget was the *last* thing you do in a plan!"

That's right. The budget is the last thing you do in developing the total strategic and operational plans for your venture. But then what do you need a start-up budget for?

❑ Market Research

Just a few thousand dollars, a simple market research program—focus groups, interviews led by moderators, mail-in questionnaires, telephone surveys—is money well spent at the beginning of your venture. Remember, *you* don't do it; you let someone else do it. You lay out a concept, write up a simple statement about the public you think is your target, and hire a professional to do the work. It will be the best money you ever spent.

What does market research do? It lets you know whether or not you're a genius.

- It may confirm your *concept.* Or it may say you're a genius if you modify the concept in certain ways. Or it may tell you to abandon the idea altogether.

- It can help define the *areas of interest* in the product or service. Who? Where? In what form? With what modifications? It can even help establish *pricing parameters.* How much will people pay for what you're offering? Is it too low or too high? Can you make money within those parameters?

- It can help *locate the market.* This can make your particular demographics more specific. And those specific demographics can be related to the wealth of demographic information now available. This not only has impact on the targets of your advertising and promotional campaigns but is a great aid to the copywriters and advertising people who have to communicate the message.

- It can help *identify your competition.* (What else are people buying that will compete with your product?)

❏ Product Development

If the marketing research tells you it's a "go," now the development people join the team. (Notice that we did not say, "the development people take over." You're building a team for the long life of the venture; no one goes off and works alone. Right? Right.)

Successful product planning follows a basic outline, which has been used by all the great companies:

- *Logic.* There is consensus among all concerned that the new product or service is logical; marketing agrees that there is a need, development says that it can be created, finance says that the funds are available, and marketing and finance have agreed on pricing and have arrived at a suitable return on investment.

- *Design.* This is where those creative talents come into play. However, be sure they design what the market said was needed!

- *Prototypes.* Build as many as necessary. Remember the space program and all those rockets that fizzled on the launch pad? Oh, my, it was depressing. But what a day when John Glenn orbited the earth! The prototypes were important to everyone— not the least of whom was John Glenn.

- *Manufacturing sample.* This is where your production and operations people really shine. If they can't make the sample cost-effective and guarantee it during the life of the product, then you've reached another plateau until they can (your product is on "hold").

- *Quality control.* In the whole marketing and development process, you are concerned with establishing procedures that will give you quality control throughout the life of the product. The consumer expects to get the same product time after time after time.

❑ Financial Plan Budgeting

Financial plans and budgets are primarily in the purview of the marketing director. Depending on the venture (that is, whether you are manufacturing personal computers, managing a theater, providing counseling services), the types of expenses and what you call them will vary, but they generally fall into the categories discussed in the following paragraphs.

- *Cost of goods and services.* Your real concern in this area is *pricing.* It's probable that when Bill Blass creates a one-of-a kind dress for a valued client, he doesn't concern himself too much with the cost of production in setting the price, but a dress house on New York City's Fashion Avenue is very concerned about the total cost of each piece before the price is set. We go into more detail on this in the chapter on quantifying, but this is where development, production, finance, and marketing must be in total agreement and have no secrets. The price placed on the goods or services must provide a healthy gross profit so that there will be a net profit when other expenses are deducted. Marketing departments (i.e., advertising, promotion, public relations, merchandising) must know the leeway (and ground rules) under which they operate: Do they discount? Can they offer group reductions? Do they sample? Is there a suggested price or a firm price? Does the offering go to the top-of-the-line demographic, or is the outreach more general? Well, you see the importance for the back-to-basics marketing plan of firming up pricing.

- *Departmental budgets.* Departmental budgets become a part of the overall consolidated plan. Each department in the marketing area must have a budget for the year.

- *Media costs.* There will be figures later in the chapter illustrating the media schedule. But the media costs can be as much as 15 percent of the total costs of your operation. How much do you plan to spend on television, radio, newspapers, magazines, merchandising, promotional events, giveaways, and the like?

It should be obvious that the financial plan for marketing should not be done "by guess and by God." It is basic to the success of the venture.

- *Sales.* In many companies sales and marketing are a part of the same department, but in many others, they are separate operations. There is a marketing department at Macy's (and other large department store chains) that handles the elements we have discussed, but there is also a huge sales staff of people who deal face to face with the public daily. Ford Motor Company has a large marketing department, but you buy your cars from a salesperson on the floor of a showroom, generally owned by a private dealer-entrepreneur, not Ford Motor Company. IBM has always marketed and sold its own products directly to the customer, but even IBM is now distributing those products through non-IBM dealers.

How to plan a sales campaign, motivate and reward salespeople, and utilize buyer input for further development of product and sales are the topics for a whole series of other books. For the purposes of developing a back-to-basics marketing plan, it is important to remember that the planning of those sales and the accounting of them on a regular basis is the basic monitoring of your marketing plan.

The advent of the computer has made it possible to track every conceivable kind of sales today. Ticket sales can be tracked by ZIP Code and therefore by demographics. Product sales can be tracked by price, color size, model, volume, and so on, making it possible to set up reasonable manufacturing and distribution schedules. Services can be tracked by location, price, number, volume, and type, allowing the company to anticipate staffing needs and service problems.

The data are available to enable you to *satisfy the customer*. It's a marketer's dream.

❏ Advertising

In the nineteenth century, advertising appeared mostly in newspapers, catalogs, and broadsides. Those were also the days when signs on hotels read, "Dogs, actors, and drummers not welcome."

Well, we've come a long way. Dogs are welcome in a lot of places, and actors and sales-advertising people are acceptable in polite society.

Frankly, our society has now reached the point where the train of commerce is pulled by the engine of advertising. Although you may discount it, you as a consumer still use advertising to help you make many of your selections. Admit it! Why this dependence on advertising? Because advertising is *news* (albeit slanted) that you need to know.

There's no secret to the advertising section of your back-to-basics marketing plan; it just involves hard work. And it's basic. The following paragraphs outline some of the key decisions you will have to make regarding your advertising campaign.

- *Positioning, strategy, copy.* One of the most interesting books in recent years, by Al Ries and Jack Trout, is called *Positioning: The Battle for Your Mind.*[1] The authors contend that positioning is what you do to the mind of the prospect. They use as examples

---

[1] Al Ries and Jack Trout, *Positioning: The Battle for Your Mind* (New York, McGraw Hill Book Co., 1981).

"Avis is only No. 2 in rent-a-cars, so why go with us? *We try harder.*" "Honeywell, the other computer company." "Seven-Up: the *un*cola."

Positioning is spending the time and research money necessary to find the positions (the *holes*) in the marketplace. Once you've found the niche where your product or service can fit, fill a need, and make a profit, you develop the *strategy* to teach the public, to reach the minds of viewers, listeners, readers, convincing them (1) that the hole *exists* and (2) that *you* can fill it.

The copy you write, the images you create, the slogan you promote pound at that *idea* day after day after day.

- *Choice of media.* Your research has given you information regarding who and where your customers are. The selection of media relates directly to that information. Someone once asked a famous bank robber (following his capture, prosecution, and conviction) why he had robbed banks. His answer: "Because that's where the money is."

Obviously, you advertise *where the people are*—making sure that the people you are going after are the people you want.

Later, we will present some forms that will help you create your media plan. For now, remember that your options are:

Print, broadcast, cable

Direct mail, mail order

Freestanding inserts, flyers

Couponing, samples

- *Length of campaign.* Allocating resources on a calendar basis is fundamental to the effectiveness of your advertising. You will do a lot of strategic analysis and engage in many "skull" sessions with the advertising agency, research and development, and production to get the "most bang for the buck," by building awareness, creating need, sampling, and attempting to create ingrained buying habits.

- *Budgeting.* Cost per thousand will undoubtedly be the criterion for your allocation of resources by medium. But rely heavily on the demographic information available from each medium so that you can be very selective about your audience and your expenditures. You many want to focus your efforts like a rifle shot rather than scatter them like a shotgun blast.

■ *Staffing.* Most companies hire agencies to handle their advertising needs. A few have their own in-house staffs. Some go to full-service agencies; others buy from "boutiques." Your decision of whether to do it all, do none, or do some will be based on dollars (the agency gets 15 percent of billing plus expenses and production costs), on the character of your company (do you need ads in a real hurry, like Macy's?), on the scope of your campaigns, on the talents you can attract, and on the buying power you as a company may have compared to the buying/bargaining power of the agency. Whatever you decide, staffing considerations are a part of your job when creating the advertising part of the plan.

CHAPTER 10

Developing
a Marketing Plan

These are the classic elements to consider in developing a marketing plan. It was published by the Conference Board, and the elements are listed in order of priority.

1. Forecast of market demand
2. Market share of business
3. Competitive strengths/weaknesses
4. Competitors' market share
5. Market segmentation
6. Customers' changing needs
7. Technological trends
8. Risk factors
9. Environmental issues
10. Government regulations

11. Alternative strategies
12. Assign product to a matrix position
13. Contingency plans
14. Product life-cycle analysis
15. Postmortem on previous plan

Whether or not you analyze these elements in the order listed, you should consider *all* of them to avoid surprises.

■ FORMS FOR DEVELOPING THE MARKETING PLAN

This section presents some sample forms that will get you started on the road to a good back-to-basics marketing plan. Other aids are available, and you will design many of your own. However, the use of these fundamental forms will help you to incorporate your marketing plan into the overall business plan.

❑ Analysis Matrix

The simple matrix shown in Figure 10.1 on page 133 is a quick method of analyzing various aspects of your current and future market(s) and aiding you in developing *facts* for your marketing objectives. The matrix can be larger or smaller, as required, and it can be used to analyze many different types of data.

The "Product" column should be used to define the variety of items you offer for sale: the list of brands you produce, the array of services you perform, the number of productions you plan to offer, and so on. "Market" can be defined by region, by demographics, by type (consumer, industrial, etc.). Then a calculation is possible in each of the squares to lay out the sales projections for easy, visual understanding.

The same exercise could be developed for the cost of goods or cost of sales for each product/service and market segment.

The chart can also be used to calculate gross profits on each product/service and market segment, as well as marketing costs, and so on.

There is no magic to this simple chart. It is primarily a visual tool for segmenting elements to identify problems and opportunities in your marketing plan.

The other charts that follow will provide you with information necessary in putting together your marketing plan. Figure 10.2 will help you define responsibilities of each department. Figure 10.3 provides the matrix for calculating the ratio of cost of marketing to sales. The Rate-of-Return Worksheet in Figure 10.4 allows you to project into the future for each product or service you are developing. Figure 10.5 helps you to assess the risk in marketing each product. Figure 10.6 helps you to monitor your promotional projects throughout the year. Figure 10.7, the Media Flowchart, shows you where and when you are spending your advertising dollars. Figure 10.8 summarizes the data from Figure 10.7 by quarter.

■ FIGURE 10.1

Analysis Matrix: Total Annual Sales by Market and by Product

	PRODUCT				
	P	*P*	*P*	*P*	*Annual Total by Market*
M					
M					
M					
M					
Annual Total by Product					

MARKET

▪ FIGURE 10.2

**Analysis Matrix: Problems and Opportunities
(Defining Responsibility)**

			DEPARTMENTS		
		Marketing	*Research and Development*	*Production*	*Other Departments*
FACTORS	*Sociological*				
	Technological				
	Economic				
	Environmental				
	Political				

▪ FIGURE 10.3

Marketing Budget Compared to Sales

	1st Quarter		*2nd Quarter*		*3rd Quarter*		*4th Quarter*		*Total*	
	$	*%*	*$*	*%*	*$*	*%*	*$*	*%*	*$*	*%*
Projected Sales ($)										
Marketing Budget ($)										
Marketing Cost/Sales	*$*									

▪ Note: The full marketing budget (media costs, promotions, staff, production) should be used, and the quarterly percentage of total put in each quarterly square. This will give you the true picture of your marketing costs to sales ratio in the last line.

■ FIGURE 10.4

Rate-of-Return Worksheet

Year	Cash Flow (× $1,000)	Market Segmentation	Market Expansion	Discount Rate (%)	Present Value
0					
1					
2					
3					
4					
5					
6					
7					
8					
9					
10					
11					
12					
13					
14					
15					

■ Note: This worksheet is valuable for each product and service you are developing, allowing you to ask the "what if" questions necessary to an effective marketing plan. Should we expand? Should we segment (break out other products or spinoffs)? How will our discounts affect us? And so on.

■ FIGURE 10.5

Risk Analysis

Element	Low (0–17%)	Medium (18–49%)	High (50–100%)
Industry			
Maturity			
Competitive position			
Strategy			
Assumptions			
Past performance of unit			
Expected level of future performance			
Overall risk			

- Note: Each "risk" should be listed in percentages as well as identified by name.

■ FIGURE 10.6

Promotional Calendar 19____

Month Project	Start Time	End Time	Type	In Cooperation with	Responsibility	Budget

- Note: This chart helps you sell the flow of your promotions and monitor their scope and timeliness.

Media Flowchart by Month

Medium						MONTH								
	Jan.	Feb.	March	April	May	June	July	Aug.	Sept.	Oct.	Nov.	Dec.	$	%
Newspapers														
Magazines														
Television														
Radio														
Cable														
Brochures														
Outdoor														
Promotions														
Production														
Advertising spending ($)														
Advertising spending (%)														100.0%

■ Note: In practice, you would break this chart down into much finer detail. That is, the chart should be divided by weeks; each week should be dated; television should be divided by network, spot, and local, as should radio; magazines should be grouped into national and regional categories; newspapers should be grouped into national or local categories; promotions should be identified. Also, this chart should be done twice—once with arrows that readily indicate the mass of coverage at a given time and again with figures indicating the dollar cost of coverage at a given time.

▪ FIGURE 10.8

Media/Promotional Expenditures by Quarter

Medium	1st Quarter ($)	2nd Quarter ($)	3rd Quarter ($)	4th Quarter ($)	Total ($)	Percentage of Total
Newspapers						
Magazines						
Television						
Radio						
Cable						
Brochures						
Outdoor						
Promotions						
Production						
Total						
Percentage by quarter						

▪ Note: This chart is a management summary of the finite detail on Figure 10.7 to be used for analysis and reporting.

▪ CHECKLIST FOR THE MARKETING PLAN

"I ain't lost."

There is a story about a man who was traveling in a rural area and needed directions. He found a young boy seated on a log and asked him the road to the nearest telephone. The boy said, "I don't know." "Well, does this road lead to a town?" "I don't know," the boy again replied. The traveler, impatiently: "Does this road lead to a bigger road?" The response: "I don't know." Finally, the man snorted,

"You're not very smart, are you?" "Well," replied the boy amiably, "I ain't lost."

Perhaps everyone preparing a back-to-basics marketing plan should have "I ain't lost" tattooed on their eyelids. That's what a marketing plan avoids—getting lost on the way to market.

The preceding tips have been summaries, at best, of the process involved and the tools required to stay on the road and make the sale. It is a complex process, but not mysterious. You will use many more tools than we have provided to achieve a working marketing plan. But these are the fundamental tools to help you form the outline of what you intend to do.

In summary, we'd like to remind you of some of the things we've touched on:

- Selling a product or service is what marketing is all about.

- The first priority is a good product or service—value received for value given.

- What you know about your consumer is the most important piece of information in a good marketing plan.

- Marketing is the way you move your products and services to your consumers. It involves *what* you will move, *how* you will move it, and *whom* you will target.

- Marketing defines your message.

- Building *awareness* is your first step. Perception is reality.

- In building that awareness, *control* of the message is why you employ advertising, publicity, public relations. Don't depend on anyone else.

- Marketing researchers are the "first among equals." They give you the *facts* from which you work.

- Market research is the action; marketing research is the result of the action.

- Advertising is paid news. Believe it or not, consumers want to know what's out there on the market.

- Merchandising is usually designed to induce the consumer to make multiple purchases.

- Public relations is the controlled way to develop images for products, services, or institutions.

- Publicity is activity designed to attract public interest.

- Marketing is a continuum. Like all plans, the back-to-basics marketing plan is an organic instrument concerned with the long-term life of the venture.

- Remember the acronym BAP. To launch a marketing plan and keep up with the product's life cycle, you must combine *b*udgets, *a*dvertising, and *p*ublicity in an orderly way.

- Sampling is very cost-effective in launching a new product.

- The first step is a start-up budget to do initial market research (remember, the indispensable ingredient).

- Research helps you clarify your concept, design the areas of interest, establish pricing parameters, locate the market, and identify your competition.

- Product planning follows the process of logic, design, prototypes, manufacturing sample, quality control.

- The marketing budget must take into account cost of goods/services, pricing, departmental budgets, media costs.

- In planning advertising you are concerned with positioning, strategy, copy, choice of media, length of campaign, budgeting, cost per thousand, and staffing.

SECTION 5

SELLING

CHAPTER 11

Selling as a Career

Selling is an old and honorable profession. For many centuries it has contributed to the spread of culture, the improvement of living standards, and the redistribution of wealth, and it has encouraged invention and the spread of technology. In ancient times, in every civilization that developed to the point where its production of goods and services exceeded its own needs, there arose markets for luxuries and for better or fancier variations on the necessities of life. Creative salespeople—including traders, merchants, and craftspeople—just as they do today—would identify these wants and needs and strive to fill them. The profits to be made were often astounding, although the risks were often just as great. The fabled spice trade involved the transportation of goods—including not only spices, but silks, rare woods, strange animals, gems, art objects, and other exotica—halfway around the world. With the rise of industrial civilization, salespeople helped expand the markets for mass-produced goods as well as newly invented items. Traveling peddlers were (and still are, in many parts of the world) a common sight. These gave way to the representatives of manufacturers who still make their rounds of retailers and, in the guise of the much maligned and ridiculed traveling salespeople, the homes of consumers.

With the advent of mass communications—national magazines, network radio, and television—in the United States (to be followed by a lesser extent in the other industrialized nations of the world), selling was enhanced by the more sophisticated use of advertising. In more recent times, the extra dimension provided by advances in market research, consumer psychology, demographic studies, and so on moved the profession into the position of "selling the sizzle instead of the steak"; in other words, the product has often been overshadowed and the salesperson sells the status or sex appeal or other benefit or advantage that is associated with the product.

In many ways, selling is the cornerstone of any competitive enterprise—or market—economy. The constantly shifting balance of supply and demand is, as Adam Smith saw it, controlled by the "invisible hand" of the marketplace—the endless stream of buying-selling transactions. In the United States, the unprecedented standard of living we enjoy is the result of our creativity, freedom of opportunity, and the efficiency of our economic system—productivity plus distribution—kept moving by salespeople and prodded by the demand created by them.

■ ADVANTAGES OF A SALES CAREER

In addition to being an important profession, selling as a career offers many advantages to the individual. First, there is a certain amount of freedom and independence for salespeople, who budget their own time for visiting prospects and servicing their customers, which is found in few other careers. Further, because selling is a broadly applicable skill, salespeople have the freedom to work in virtually any field or any geographical location. They have the advantage, too, of switching from one product or service to another, or from a product to services, or from probing (going out and looking for sales) to reactive selling (selling to the individual who comes to the seller).

There is extensive involvement with people—both peers and prospects—which many find desirable. In fact, in a well-led and well-balanced sales operation, a unique kind of camaraderie develops, leading to enduring friendships and pleasurable satisfying relationships.

In selling, there is a built-in regimen of discipline—the necessary partner of the freedom enjoyed by salespeople—regarding dependability, responsibility, and integrity, as well as grooming, attire, behavior, and the rules of etiquette. As we will see, success in selling depends in large measure on acquiring this personal discipline. Not that it is an onerous set of rules—far from it; many not only find the order and discipline appealing, but also enjoy the benefits that these bring to their personal lives.

■ WHAT MAKES A GOOD SALESPERSON?

Who should consider a career in selling? How can you determine if it might be right for you? In the following chapters, we will be exploring the specific traits and skills of the successful salesperson, but here we can consider some of the fundamental characteristics of those who are best suited to this field of endeavor. They have a good basic education, enjoy working with people, keep an open mind, and are easily motivated.

Selling seldom requires a higher education, except for areas in which technical knowledge of a product or service is required. Mastery of the basics—reading, writing, and arithmetic—is essential, although additional general or specialized education can be helpful. Since long years of schooling beyond high school are not necessary, sales is open to virtually anyone and a career can begin as soon as high school is completed.

The next requirement is a preference for working with people and for meeting new people. After all, one part of the selling equation is a buyer, and all potential buyers are people. To succeed, the salesperson must enjoy meeting a constant stream of new people. In a year, there can easily be contacts with anywhere from a few hundred to several thousand strangers.

Because of the infinite variety of people and situations with which the salesperson must deal, having an open mind is very important. In the course of selling, all types of people are met, and being flexible, tolerant, and understanding can stand you in good stead. The narrow-minded, rigid, judgmental person will alienate others.

Finally, there is the factor of motivation. In spite of the many advantages of a sales career and the many rewards, it should not be forgotten that selling is hard work. Courage, perseverance, dependability, responsibility, and great quantities of energy are required. Anyone who is not highly motivated to succeed is unlikely to achieve the rich rewards and satisfactions of a sales career.

■ CHOOSING THE RIGHT CAREER IN SELLING

For both the individual deciding on a career (whether it is one's first career or a later one) and the person already in the sales field, it is important to examine the contemplated or actual career in relation to one's interests, goals, and satisfactions. This is more difficult for the individual considering sales, because there is no way of knowing for sure if the routine and demands of the career will be satisfying or frustrating. Ideally, every person's job should be interesting, challenging, and rewarding, both psychologically and monetarily.

The wrong choice of a career or of a wrong job within a career field—the proverbial "square peg in the round hole" syndrome—can be disastrous. Among the symptoms of such a situation can be depression, migraine and other stress-related headaches, circulatory problems such as high blood pressure, anxiety neurosis, spasticity, digestive problems, insomnia, excessive weight gain or loss, excessive smoking or drinking, and impotence.

A bad choice can be prevented by examining carefully the available options. First, look at your interest, your style of life, and your expectations regarding day-to-day work life. With the help of such a self-evaluation, you can begin the process of deciding whether sales is the right field for you. After all, there are many other kinds of careers. If you are making your first career decision, learn as much as possible about selling as a career. Talk to salespeople, ask questions, take a part-time selling job to try it out. This book and others will provide you with a lot of information about selling. See how your own requirements match those of the field of sales in general.

If sales seems to be right for you, take note that that is still not the end of the process. There are many kinds within the field, and a better understanding of their differences will enable you to make a better choice of career path. This is especially important for the person who is working in sales and enjoys selling but who is nevertheless dissatisfied. In many cases, the individual is simply in the wrong kind of selling.

▪ PROBING AND REACTIVE SELLING

The major types of selling are *probing* and *reactive*. Simply stated, in the former, the salesperson goes out looking for buyers, whereas in the latter, the salesperson waits for the buyers to come into a store or showroom.

In *probing sales*, prospective buyers must be identified and located, and some strategy must be developed for approaching them. How this is done depends upon the product or service being sold and who the most likely buyers are. In the most difficult kind of probing sales—the cold canvas—the salesperson works with a telephone directory or in a geographical area and either calls or knocks on the door of each customer. This is a common approach used with any product or service that has broad general appeal—magazine subscriptions, household supplies and gadgets, home improvements–related products (roofing, siding, storm windows, insulation), and appliances such as vacuum cleaners. The challenge for the salesperson is to initiate contact with a total stranger, who may or may not be interested in the product, and to make a short presentation. As might be expected, the number of failures is huge compared to the number of successes.

For other kinds of products, such as office equipment, computers, swimming pool supplies, and so on, there are more reliable ways of identifying customers. For example, the Yellow Pages might provide names of small companies that would be likely to use a certain type of office equipment. A business directory could yield information about companies large enough to benefit from a small computer. Lists of recent purchasers of swimming pools, obtained from manufacturers or form installation companies, can be used by the salesperson selling pool chemicals or service contracts.

At yet another level, the salesperson has the advantage of a list of prospects created by the company from responses to advertising campaigns. This is common with encyclopedias, for example, and with high-priced business equipment and services. Every sales call is thus with a genuine prospect, someone who has expressed an interest in the product or service. For the most part, the company does the probing and the salesperson provides the follow-up. But good salespeople will also endeavor to develop their own prospect lists by asking for referrals in the course of their presentations.

Finally, salespeople in the probing sales field are also often responsible for providing liaison between their customers and the company's relations staff. This not only involves advice, consultation, and services, but also provides the potential for replacement and updating sales of hardware or the sale of upgraded or expanded services.

In a very large company, such as International Business Machines, various types of probing sales will be found. In selling and leasing its lines of computers, typewriters, copiers, supplies, software, and so on, IBM has territorial assignments for sales calls to small companies and offices; routes for calls on retailers; a sales staff using prospect lists; and a special division for meeting the needs of banks, brokerage houses, the largest corporations, and government agencies. Obviously, in such a company enormous amounts of time and energy are invested in the process of identifying markets and specific prospects; gathering and processing that information; training salespeople and constantly bringing them up to date on advances in technology as represented in new products and services; creating and producing brochures and other "leave-behind" material; assigning salespeople to territories; and arranging for free demonstrations and trial-use models, follow-up calls, closing calls, delivery, training and orientation of customer personnel, and periodic callbacks to check on customer satisfaction.

In *reactive sales,* prospects call or come into a store or showroom with the idea already in their minds of buying something. It is the responsibility of the salesperson to help the customer to make a purchase by answering questions, offering suggestions, and even demonstrating the product when that is appropriate. Because reactive selling is more passive than probing sales, most salespeople find it less frustrating and less challenging. Of course, the rewards are fewer, as are the opportunities for advancement. On the other hand, more people are better suited to reactive selling than to probing and find it very satisfying. I do not want to give the impression that retail selling presents no challenges. The need to be informed about all the products or services being offered and to remain courteous, friendly, attentive, and helpful—even in the face of the most belligerent, uncouth customer—is not always easy.

■ SELLING TANGIBLES AND INTANGIBLES

Almost all selling involves intangibles. That is, what is sold along with the product is a variety of benefits, uses, and satisfactions. In most instances, there is a tangible product involved, but in others there is none whatever. When an automobile is sold, the customer is interested in its physical properties (styling, materials, and workmanship, design, engineering, and special features), but such factors as fuel efficiency, comfort, status, estimated rate of depreciation (or appreciation), convenience, and other intangibles are more important. On the other hand, life insurance is completely intangible and is sold on the basis of the security it provides for the buyer's family and the peace of mind and sense of pride it gives the buyer.

Most individuals prefer selling where the tangible element is important. A person who is oriented to objects and their physical characteristics will be most comfortable selling products; there is a certain security in having a product to show and demonstrate. Others, who are more oriented to concepts, ideas, and abstractions, are perfectly at ease—and may even enjoy the challenge of—selling where the physical product is of only minimal concern or does not exist at all.

For convenience, we might call the former product-oriented selling and the latter service oriented, but the distinction is really one of degree rather than concerning the specific object of the selling process. Most products rate high and most services rate low on the scale of tangible elements. As noted earlier, it is usually the intangibles that are the focus of both types of selling. People who are (or think they might be) less satisfied or dissatisfied in a field of selling dominated by intangibles should consider selling products instead.

■ SELLING AND PERSONALITY TYPE

One of the basic differences between people is the way their functioning is oriented, whether their personality is extroverted or introverted. Extroverts are outwardly oriented and typically see themselves in relationship to other people and to their surroundings. Introverts, on the other hand, are inwardly oriented, relating their daily life to their inner sense of self, to their own mental state. No person is completely one or the other, but one orientation is usually dominant.

In most types of selling, the extroverts have a clear advantage over the introverts and will tend to be happier, more fulfilled, and more successful. The probing sales field in particular, since it requires a going-out-to-meet-the-world-head-on attitude, is the natural province of the extrovert. This is not to say that introverts cannot do very well in high-technology products and services, bookstores, educational materials, and similar areas. They are, however, generally happier in the less competitive, less highly charged areas of selling, either probing or reactive.

Both introverts and extroverts can, through hard work, learn to function in new ways to succeed in situations for which they are not naturally suited.

■ PERSONAL INTERESTS AND FIELDS OF SELLING

After a searching self-appraisal to determine the best aspect of selling to enter, one of the sure ways to be happy and fulfilled in a chosen sales career is to try to match your personal interests with a particular job. For example, if you are interested in sports, there are sales jobs with sporting goods manufacturers, retail stores, sports magazines, and even sports organizations and sports broadcasting. If you like to travel, there are sales jobs in the travel industry itself (airlines, travel bureaus) and in other types of companies in which salespeople do a great deal of traveling (publishers' representatives, agents for import-export businesses, department store buyers). The added motivation provided by such a marriage of career and interests, the added information and skills, and the insights garnered over the years of pursuing a hobby or avocation also give such an individual a competitive edge in seeking a job and in achieving excellence in it.

Whether you are about to enter the sales field for the first time or are already in it, remember that working in a job that is compatible with your goals, personality, and life-style and in a field related to your interests will make you happier, fulfill you more, and enable you to succeed. Choosing the right job or changing to it is vitally important to your overall, long-term well-being. In such a situation you are able to bring your assets, your background, your skills, and your knowledge and interests to your work. There is no reason for your work to be divorced from your life. The ideal we should all strive to achieve is the integration, the making whole, of all parts of our existence.

▪ SALES AND THE CORPORATION

For those individuals who have never worked in a large corporation, it is very important to understand how and where selling fits in. The main divisions of a large manufacturing company are research and development, engineering, purchasing, manufacturing, distribution, finance, administration, and marketing. The marketing division consists of the following departments: sales, advertising, promotion, publicity-public relations. In smaller companies, of course, some divisions or departments may be combined.

In simpler days, the coordination of the parts of a corporation was the responsibility of the chairman of the board, the president, the treasurer, a few vice presidents, and a small administrative staff. As corporations have grown, the problem of coordination and control has grown as well, as has the number of administrators and managers. For efficiency and accountability, the so-called "rule of five" has been widely adopted: executives should have no more than five other executives reporting directly to them. The ultimate in sophistication has been witnessed recently in corporations in which there is no longer just the chairman of the board and the president, but what is known as "the office of the chairman of the board" or "the office of the president," an executive committee composed of the chairman, the president, and two or three executive vice presidents.

Traditionally, the sales manager has been an important member of the management team. After World War II, with the cascade of new products being brought to the marketplace, sales managers became even more important and highly visible executives. At the same time, however, developments in marketing communications—including research, test marketing, market testing, copy testing, advertising, promotion, merchandising, and public relations—began to shift the job of the sales manager to a less visible position in the hierarchy. What was needed was individuals who could not only oversee sales, but also coordinate it with the activities of all the other departments whose tasks were complementary to and supportive of the sales efforts. Many sales managers broadened their skills and expertise and evolved into marketing managers. Others did not and ended up working under marketing managers. Just as it was once for sales managers, now it is marketing managers who move on into top management as vice president, executive vice president, or even president.

As a side note, it is worth mentioning that this development in corporate life contains a lesson for those whose goals include moving up into the high-paying, high-prestige positions of top management. Advancement comes not only as a reward for excelling in a job, but also for demonstrating the potential for assuming greater responsibility. In most cases, such added responsibility will require greater knowledge and a wider perspective. What that means is that you should learn continuously through both observation and study. The more you know about your own job, about the jobs at the next higher level, and about the company and its field, the more likely it will be for you to be considered for promotions.

The entry-level salesperson reports to a sales supervisor, a regional sales manager, or some such similarly titled person who in turn reports to the sales manager, who reports to the marketing manager, and so on. The sales force forms the base of one of the pyramids that constitute the hierarchy of a corporation. Its activities are one part of a company's efforts directed at succeeding in the marketplace. Success in the marketplace depends on the coordinated efforts of a great many people working in several divisions; specifically these are, in addition to sales, research, merchandising, advertising, promotion, publicity, and public relations.

Research, within the context of marketing, involves testing, analysis, and evaluation of the various elements affecting the success of a product or service in the marketplace. For example, there is test marketing. Before committing itself to the tens of millions of dollars necessary to bring a new product to market, corporations prefer to spend up to half a million dollars to find out if the product has enough appeal to the public to warrant full distribution. A limited number of the items are manufactured, packaged, and promoted in one or more small, carefully selected areas. The results are minutely scrutinized and are an important factor in the final decision of management. Another example of research is market testing, wherein advertising, merchandising, and sales techniques for both old and new products are tried out. One of the several highly focused types of research is copy testing. A variety of advertising and sales promotion themes are tested to see which produces the most favorable response. Often this research is carried out by the company's advertising agency or by a specialized research company. It usually involves the use of a number of panels of consumers—housewives or teenagers or other target population—who are presented with the material and then interviewed regarding their responses. The details of an advertising-marketing campaign are thus refined before being implemented.

Merchandising is a general term referring to the coordination of the various elements of the marketing strategy—everything from the design of the package, the copy and design of advertising and promotion materials, and patterns of distribution to defining the target universe of consumers. For example, when you see an "As Advertised" sign in a store, the retail point-of-sale promotion is being coordinated with the advertising campaign, each effort reinforcing the other. The *Good Housekeeping* seal, for instance, appears both in the advertising of such a product and on the package or label. It was recently shortened to the G.H. seal.

Advertising is perhaps the most obvious part of a company's marketing efforts. The carefully selected images, colors, words, phrases, and—in the electronic media—sounds of an advertisement can have a number of goals. The first, and the most basic, is to inform the public of the product, its characteristics and uses, its efficacy, and its availability. On another level, advertising can promise or imply that certain benefits—health, beauty, status, sex appeal, and the like—will accrue to the buyer. These and other goals are, of course, all pursued in the service of one ultimate goal—to get the individual to buy. Wise salespeople, whether wholesale or retail, will be sure to be aware of the marketing plan for a product, particularly the advertising, and seek to use it to enhance their sales presentations.

Promotion involves a variety of techniques that are used to enhance sales. At the wholesale level, there are convention booths, receptions and parties, brochures, advertising tear sheets, follow-up letters, and so on, all designed to remind buyers of the company and its products and to create in them a receptive frame of mind. On the retail level, promotion can include coupons, rebate plans, contests, proof-of-purchase redemption plans, and so on.

Publicity is closely akin to advertising, but with one important difference—it is free. Press releases, press parties, demonstrations, and so on are all aimed at getting the company or its products mentioned in the news columns or broadcasts of the media. Many companies participate in various projects for the sake of the publicity it will generate. For example, many furniture and home furnishing stores will lend or donate items to theaters for use in their productions in exchange for the credit they receive in the program. Other firms will be involved in community affairs such as grant programs to community projects, public television, sponsorship of youth programs, and so on.

Public relations, in many respects, picks up where publicity leaves off. It is the means a company uses to make sure the public knows about its good works, good intentions, honor, honesty, sense of responsibility, and the like. In many cases, publicity and public relations are combined into one operation; in others, public relations will be divided into several specialized operations, such as community affairs (for the areas near company offices, factories, etc.), trade relations (dealers, wholesalers, distributors, suppliers, etc.), government relations (local, state, and federal lobbying activities), employee relations (internal), foreign affairs (for companies with overseas operations), and consumer affairs (to deal with problems, complaints, and the like). Because of their increasingly important place in many large companies, government affairs and consumer affairs have been taken out of the public relations department and raised to the managerial level of responsibility, often under a special vice president.

Being knowledgeable about the activities, goals, and responsibilities of the marketing efforts of a company can help the novice salesperson better understand the place of sales in the corporation. Also, being aware of the coordinated nature of the various facets of marketing can help make the salesperson more effective.

■ WHAT TO EXPECT

Typically, upon joining a sales force, the salesperson will be given a course of training and indoctrination. This might include written materials for study, lectures, tours, slides, filmstrips, motion pictures, or videotape. During this period, he or she should learn not only the specific techniques, procedures, and policies of the sales division, but also about the company as a whole and its marketing efforts in particular. Also during the learning and acclimatization phase in some well-run companies, new people are often assigned as assistants or apprentices to more experienced salespeople. A great deal can be learned in such a relationship, with the bonus that the senior salesperson, in orienting and teaching the newcomer, gets a refresher course in some of the fundamentals of selling.

Further, lasting friendships can result from the interaction of a senior and junior salesperson. In my very first summer job, I was a junior salesman for the Royal Typewriter Company. Not yet 20 years old, I was completely without experience except for some retail selling in a grocery store. At Royal, the junior salespeople underwent a brief training period and then became door-to-door or office-to-office canvassers. Our assignment was to convince secretaries or office managers to accept a Royal typewriter for a free two-week trial. We received a modest weekly salary plus $28.87 for any machine that was sold as a result of the free demonstration. You can imagine the spirit of cooperation and excitement generated between the senior salesman and me. When I would return at the end of the day and announce that I had placed five or more demonstrations, that would be my victory. We established a relationship that has lasted more than four decades.

Such friendships, especially with other salespeople, are very important in maintaining morale, in problem solving (both professional and personal), and in making the work more enjoyable. Becoming a part of the group is one of the newcomer's first priorities, and it is not difficult. Simply remember that the foundation of good relationships is good manners—a respect for the feelings and dignity of other people. In starting out as a new member of a sales force, concentrate on being considerate and on making a good first impression. With these, you will be in a position to begin participating in the experience and interactions out of which friendships develop.

I have mentioned that at Royal I received a small salary plus commissions. The pay arrangement for salespeople, which can range from straight salary to straight commission, is a very important consideration. There are few jobs in sales involving only a salary; commissions and bonuses, because they reward the successful salesperson, are generally considered necessary. The most common formula is a relatively small salary plus commissions. In commission-only positions, there is often a system for receiving advances against future commissions (called a "draw"). It should be noted that while the commission schedule for commission-only salespeople is higher than that for salaried salespeople—making it potentially more lucrative—the risks and stresses are also greater. The idea that a person would pursue selling with no guarantee of income and allow the income that can be earned to be tied completely to the volume of sales does not sound very appealing. Nevertheless, that arrangement is not universally scorned. There are many strong-minded salespeople who willingly accept such a challenge and get great satisfaction from working under pressure and from succeeding at it. However, the stresses—mental, emotional, and physical—can be tremendous, and the person not suited to it would be foolish to consider it. Even for those who are equal to it, it is wise to beware of businesses in which "payola," kickbacks, and other improper practices are commonly utilized to induce sales. It is nearly impossible to compete honestly and on an even footing with those who do business this way, no matter how hard you work or how good you are at selling.

■ WHAT TO LOOK FOR

When looking for a specific job in selling, remember that the hiring process is a two-way street. While the company is assessing you and your background, qualities, and potential, you should be looking the company over just as carefully. As with people, companies range from the dishonest and disreputable to the ethical and humane. During the interview process and, if hired, during the probationary period, try to discover the principles and practices of the day-to-day work of the company, not what they say they do, but what they actually do. For example, watch out for what were once called "any-rate" companies; their price schedules, instead of being sacred, are a fiction, and tough buyers can literally get any price they want. A good company is honest with all its customers, suppliers, and retailers, and most of all, with itself and its employees.

Look carefully at the people for whom you will work. Are they the type of women and men with whom you feel comfortable? Do they project qualities you can respect? Do they seem to feel secure about themselves and their work?

Finally, look closely at the colleagues with whom you will work. Are they positive or negative and cynical about their work and the company? Are there many problem drinkers? How is their morale? Do people get along with one another or is there a lot of jealousy and bickering? Are there among them some with whom you could work and possibly become friends?

CHAPTER 12

Management Philosophy and Sales Policy

The rules of action and behavior and the guidelines for decision making throughout a company are of concern to all employees—executives, administrators, managers, and workers. They are of particular interest to newly hired employees who must find out how things are done and what is expected of them. Ideally, these rules and guidelines are formalized into a series of written policy statements, one for the company as a whole and one for each of the departments or divisions. Since the sales department represents the company to its customers, the sales policy is especially important.

Before discussing the specific elements of such a policy statement, however, it should be noted that policies are not immutable. Just as an individual must adapt his or her personal habits, routines, and goals to changing conditions, so must a company periodically review and reevaluate its policies, changing and updating them as necessary.

A good example of how policy guides a company and how changes of policy help it to adapt to new conditions is seen in the

159

case of the Coca-Cola Company. For several decades, Coca-Cola's slogan was "The best cola drink for a nickel," and its policy was to sell its product primarily through soda fountains. If the company had rigidly held to that policy, it would have gone broke. As conditions altered, Coca-Cola's policy shifted so that more emphasis was given to retail sales of its bottled product. Later it shifted its policies again and expanded from a cola-only business to a refreshment business, marketing noncola beverages and also acquiring the Minute Maid orange juice concern.

Most of the details of the company's overall policies and practices are contained in a general set of policy statements governing all employees. The specific policies and practices governing the sales force are included in a separate document. In general it should cover the following areas:

ELEMENTS OF A WRITTEN SALES POLICY

1. *Objectives*

   Quality, pricing, market position

   Weekly and monthly goals

   Special-target accounts

   Performance compared with competition

   Ethical considerations

2. *Organization*

   Table of organization and reporting structure

   Territory and account responsibilities

   Prospect and client contact reports

   Record keeping and reports

   Guarantees and service

3. *Sales Support*

   Lines of communication

   Advertising

   Sales promotion

Presentations

Management involvement

4. *Recruitment and Training*

Recruiting guidelines

Minimum qualifications

Training period

Basic presentation

Samples

Demonstrations

5. *Personnel*

Job descriptions

Advancement opportunities

Entertainment guidelines

Company-supplied transportation

Information gathering and reporting

Performance evaluation

6. *Compensation*

Salary

Bonus and incentive programs

Commissions

Benefits

Expense accounts

Vacation and sick leave

▪ TERRITORY AND PROSPECT LIST ASSIGNMENTS

To salespeople, one of the most important aspects of a company's sales policy is the way in which territories or prospect lists are assigned. After all, the financial success of each salesperson is affected by the assignments he or she receives and by the policy followed toward changing them. In general, if the assignment policy is perceived as fair and equitable, there will be harmony and mutual goodwill in the sales force. If, on the other hand, it is perceived to be unfair, there will be disharmony, dissatisfaction, and poor morale.

In a new or rapidly expanding sales organization, an assignment policy can be established and followed with relative ease. Accounts and territories are evaluated and graded on the basis of sales potential. Fair and equitable assignments can then be made and, with the help and cooperation of the sales force itself, adjustments and reassignments can be made as needed.

In older, well-established sales organizations, however, it is perhaps inevitable that regrettable patterns will develop. The most common is allowing an individual to have a more or less permanent territory or prospect universe. There are some salespeople who, being aware of the dangers, will combat them successfully. Others will not. They will develop friendly relationships with their customers (a good thing), but will allow that to dull the cutting edge of their competitive drive (a bad thing). What this means is that their customers might begin to feel that they are taken for granted and thus become prime targets for salespeople from competing companies. With an easy-to-service set of customers, the salespeople will often not bother to seek out the younger purchasers in the company and begin to develop good working relationships with them, on the grounds that they have the top person as a loyal friend. But when that individual is promoted, reassigned, fired, or retired, the friend and possibly the account are lost.

There are two ways of dealing with this problem: by constant evaluation and monitoring of performance and by a plan of regular changes of assignments. In the former, problems in assignments are revealed as they develop and steps are taken to improve the situation. In the latter, shifting assignments prevents problems by constantly challenging each member of the sales force.

■ MONITORING PERFORMANCE

To forestall problems of all sorts, a sales organization needs a system for monitoring and evaluating the performance of its sales force. To do this effectively, management must establish minimum standards and tell the salespeople exactly what is expected of them. Measures of success will include number of sales, total dollar volume, number of reorders, number of prospects called on, and, though they are more difficult to measure, such intangibles as attitude, morale, and professionalism.

There are several ways for management to monitor the performance of its sales force. Keeping accurate records based on the daily, weekly, and monthly reports of these salespeople provides numerical bases for many areas of evaluation. Frequent meetings between the sales manager and each salesperson reveal much about what the salesperson is doing and what challenges are being faced.

One of the most effective means is for the sales manager to accompany the salesperson occasionally on a number of sales calls. This is just one of the ways for the two individuals to get to know each other better. It allows the manager to see the salesperson in action and will reveal certain signs of problems, such as sloppiness, inefficiency, or other bad habits. If, for example, a salesperson does not know the location of the purchasing department of an important customer, there is likely some problem requiring the attention of the sales manager. The alert manager will also observe how receptionists and secretaries react to the salesperson, as well as how the salesperson interacts with the purchasing agent or office manager. Such visits also give the manager firsthand information on the potential for new orders from customers, and information that can be used to evaluate the salesperson's sales estimates and forecasts. A further benefit also accrues to the salesperson whose morale can be helped by this attention from the manager as well as providing an out-of-office opportunity for the salesperson to ask questions, seek advice, and make suggestions.

How all the data available on salespeople are handled and how evaluations and recommendations are made must be carefully organized. Since the purpose of monitoring and evaluation is both to identify problems (and help to resolve them) and to recognize outstanding achievement (and to reward it and learn from it), there is a lot to be said for not leaving the process completely in the hands of sales managers. No matter how objective the managers try to be, biases stemming from daily contact with the sales force—friendships, resentments, jealousy, indifference, and so forth—can be a problem. By involving individuals from the layer of management just above the sales managers (their supervisors), many of these problems can be eliminated. The result is more accurate and fairer evaluations. The company benefits by being better able to encourage success and to forestall failure. The salesperson benefits by getting accurate feedback, rewards, and any help that may be necessary. Finally, the process allows supervisors to evaluate their sales managers.

▪ CHANGING ASSIGNMENTS

There are times, based on the results of the evaluation process or in response to significant alterations in the market, when territorial assignments need to be shifted. Reassignments and the addition of new salespeople give management the flexibility to resolve or prevent problems. In addition, such changes can be a refreshing and rejuvenating influence on the sales force.

At other times, a sweeping, all-encompassing change of assignments—something that is seldom undertaken—can produce excellent results. To accomplish this successfully and prevent mass disorientation requires thorough consultation with the salespeople as well as advance warning of buyers and prospects. Although the benefits of new challenges, renewal of morale, and better service to customers can accrue to the sales force, such a large undertaking must be carefully planned and executed. The following plan is offered as a step-by-step way in which this can be done, one that should be used as a guideline rather than as a blueprint. The particular circumstances of a company will dictate certain changes.

OUTLINE PLAN FOR TOTAL SALES FORCE
REASSIGNMENT

STEP 1

The company announces a special sales meeting about 3 months in advance. It should have a dramatic theme, a dynamic name, and appropriate buildup.

S<u>TEP</u> 2

The company's advertising agency, working confidentially, plans and creates presentation materials for the meeting.

S<u>TEP</u> 3

At the meeting, the president of the company or the chief marketing officer should provide the opening remarks.

S<u>TEP</u> 4

The sales director announces the plan for changing all account and territorial assignments and the reason for it, pointing out that to succeed, the teamwork of every salesperson will be required, but that success will benefit the company, the sales department, and every salesperson. A part of the plan, to be explained at this point, should be that no salesperson will suffer financially for the first 18 months of the changeover. After that, because of the positive effects of the revitalization program, everyone will earn more than before.

S<u>TEP</u> 5

The sales manager explains the details of the transition. Each salesperson will accompany his or her replacement to the first call on each customer to introduce the new person and explain the change. For larger accounts, the two salespeople will be accompanied by the sales manager or the sales director. On each visit, old sales promotion materials in the customer's file should be replaced with new literature; this dramatizes *the fresh start* theme of the program.

S<u>TEP</u> 6

After the presentation, a question-and-answer period is held to give the members of the sales force an opportunity to ask management about the short- and long-term effects of the reassignment program.

Obviously, such a complete overhauling would not be suitable for all companies, but if there is real concern about boredom, stagnation, or generally bad morale, such a shake-up should be considered.

▪ SALES PEER GROUPS

Naturally, preventing boredom, stagnation, loss of motivation, and loss of discipline in the sales division is preferable for the company to its being forced to correct such a situation. While much can be done by management on a day-to-day basis to sustain morale, more grass-roots policing of morale is usually more effective—especially in light of the fact that direct control over salespeople by sales managers has waned considerably. A certain amount of individual self-discipline will exist in any sales force, but it is possible to take steps to ensure that it is both more widespread and more effective. The simplest way is to introduce a formal system or organized peer groups.

For organized peer groups to work, however, there must be a great deal of careful planning. First, there must be a very thorough evaluation of each individual in the sales force—age, assignments, territories, years with the company, salary, commissions, bonuses, and the most recent performance rating. On the basis of this information, groupings of four salespeople are made. (There is nothing magic about putting four people in each group except that it seems a manageable number. Three seems to be too few, but I suppose five would work well for some sales forces.) Every effort should be made to match individuals who live near to one another or whose territories are fairly close together. This can help members develop a sense of camaraderie through having an opportunity to meet socially.

Under the peer group system, each salesperson continues to receive the same salary and the same commissions based on performance. Besides the usual individual quotas, there should be group quotas that, when met or surpassed, will earn special bonuses for the members. This brings us to one of the added benefits of this system: there will be less competition among the members of the group (replaced by mutual support and encouragement), but more among the groups. This kind of competition is less personal and therefore more healthful. The company also benefits much more from that kind of competition. Yet another benefit is the lesson in discipline for each group when the members decide democratically on how to divide group bonuses. Only when there is a split vote should management intervene to arbitrate.

Finally, the peer group system provides the company with a means of identifying candidates for advancement to management positions. More often than not, one individual among the four will gradually gain more influence because of personality, performance, and other marks of leadership. Since this person would have no official authority, such a rise to prominence would alert management to watch, or even encourage, the development of that person.

If the system of peer groups works satisfactorily over a period of time, management may consider expanding the system. This can be done by combining 4 groups into another unit of 16 individuals, with the members electing one of their number to be coordinator. Each 4-by-4 group would be assigned a sales quota and a new level of bonuses set up for surpassing it. Once again, the company benefits from more incentive and more competition; another "laboratory" situation is set up in which the managerial potential of the group coordinator is tested.

▪ DISCIPLINE AND LEADERSHIP

As we have seen, one of the reasons that a peer group system is often needed is the waning control of managers over their staffs. When such control was still powerful, managers could prevent many problems, especially those that develop simply as a result of slowly worsening habits among the salespeople.

For example, a great many poorly disciplined people can easily fall into the habit of not leaving the office until about 9:30 in the morning. They will stop for coffee with other salespeople and not make their first call until 10 o'clock. Taking up to 2 hours for lunch, they do not see their first afternoon prospect until 2 o'clock. They meet colleagues again around 4 for more coffee or a drink, drift back to the office around 5, do their day's paperwork, and leave for home by 5:30. Simple insistence on more efficient management of time—as in a rule "on your way to a prospect's office by 9:15"—can mean hundreds of more calls each week by an average-sized sales force.

Or take punctuality. Most managers in the past were real sticklers for having their people in on time. One manager I remember had the following policy: being late once brought a reprimand, the second offense triggered a no-nonsense warning, and the third means dismissal unless there was an extraordinary reason.

Nowadays, even though management must depend to a large extent on the self-discipline of their salespeople and on such systems as peer groups, there are nevertheless things that they can do. Some are as simple as setting a good example—being on time, managing their time effectively, and so on. Strong leadership can help morale as well as discipline; it can be demonstrated through talking individually to salespeople who are not doing their best; being concerned about problems, professional or personal, that are hurting a salesperson's performance; having regular group meetings in which everyone is free to bring up and comment on problems; and taking similar steps.

Another way in which management can promote discipline is through simple mechanisms such as special bonus plans; contests; top-achiever-of-the-week, -month, and -year awards; and so on. Even simple plans or performance guidelines can help keep the sales staff on its toes. For example, to prevent the neglect of important accounts, management can issue a call-scheduling plan something like the following, set up in descending order of client importance:

A Clients (most important)

    Monthly visit by salesperson

    Quarterly visit by salesperson and sales manager

B Clients

    Bimonthly visit by salesperson

    Semiannual visit by salesperson and sales manager

C Clients

Semiannual visit by salesperson

Annual visit by salesperson and sales manager

D Clients

Annual visit by salesperson

C and D clients should receive a monthly telephone call from salesperson.

It should be noted that the frequencies given in the example are purely arbitrary. Each group of a company's customers must be carefully evaluated and the most appropriate plan of visits formulated. In a very large company, each month's list of companies to be visited could be generated by computer and sent automatically to each salesperson. In addition, prospect lists could be handled under a similar plan with all prospects graded by potential volume, odds against dislodging the competition, and so on.

■ RETAIL SELLING AND DISCIPLINE

Large inner-city retailers, such as department stores and chain stores, are beginning to lose business to small specialty stores, the modern-day descendants of the old mom-and-pop stores. A leading cause of this is the attitude of the salespeople in large stores. Too often they are brusque, uncaring, unfriendly, and unhelpful to customers. In smaller stores, often owned and operated by one or two people, friendly, courteous service is still the rule. Customers, after one or two unpleasant experiences in a large store, will even pass up lower prices to make their shopping experience more enjoyable.

The decline in personal service in larger stores has several causes. First is the erosion of effective management control over the behavior of employees. To a large extent, this erosion stems from an abdication of responsibility on the part of management in the face of the unionization of the workers. The attitude is that because of union demands, contract provisions, and the possibility of job actions, management feels that it cannot effectively maintain its own standards of performance and behavior. While unionization provides very necessary protection of the rights and interests of workers, it is never the intent of enlightened union officials that contract work rules will harm or otherwise undermine the employer's business. Discipline of unionized workers can be more difficult, especially if it is not handled tactfully, but it can be done.

Another leading cause is the deterioration of the quality of life in the inner cities—dirty streets, crowded mass transit, street crime. Such conditions affect employees and customers alike and lead to avoidance of personal interaction, suspiciousness, poor manners, and a drive to hurry through even the simplest tasks. A change, however, on the store's side can easily evince an improved response from customers.

Effective leadership—through setting a good example, instituting a system of rewards and recognition, maintaining high standards for training, retraining, advancement, and so forth—can still be exercised. This is especially true since the goals do not involve work load, working conditions, or basic wage rates, but are concerned with workers' attitudes toward and treatment of customers. Some of the specific goals are:

Friendly "presence" of each employer.

Cooperative, helpful responses to questions.

Informed answers, especially by first-floor employees, to requests for directions to other departments and to rest rooms.

Patience and forbearance in dealing with complaints.

When customers are offered an improved in-store experience, they are more likely to spend more time in the store (increasing the likelihood of impulse purchases) and to return in the future. Good manners and a friendly atmosphere are demonstrably good for business.

▪ SALES ESTIMATES AND FORECASTS

The entire sales force, including sales managers, has a major responsibility in forecasting future sales. The company depends on its salespeople, who are its eyes and ears in the marketplace, to provide the data upon which are based the planning and scheduling of production, distribution, and financing. Otherwise, the company would be "flying blind." As noted, sales estimates are better when there is a regular schedule for salespeople on those calls. Regular contact gives the salesperson a better "feel" for the customer's needs. When the initial estimates and forecasts are received, the sales manager can, based on direct contacts with both salespeople and customers, evaluate their accuracy and make any needed corrections or revisions.

Periodic reviews of estimated and actual sales figures can help reveal any pattern of overestimating or underestimating. Steps can then be taken to identify factors, including a salesperson's over optimism or pessimism, that consistently lead to estimates more than 5 percent too high or too low. While management does realize that such unpredictable factors as a major strike, industrial accidents, natural disasters, international political events, unexpected changes in the price of oil, and so on will cause deviations from estimates, the accuracy of sales staff forecasts is considered to be indicative of how well the sales managers and salespeople know their accounts and territories.

▪ THE USES OF COMPUTERS IN SALES

Two important applications of electronic data processing in the sales field are data tabulation of products sold in the retail area and the streamlining of daily sales call reports by sales representatives. In the former, each item of merchandise has an attached data card preprinted with the model number, style, color, price, and other product identification information. When a sale is made, the salesperson removes the card and adds certain details of the transaction to it—his or her own code for credit toward commissions or bonuses, data on the purchases (sex, approximate age, etc.), and so on. By processing other cards on a daily or weekly basis, the store has virtually instantaneous updating of inventory and reorder records and of payroll bonus payments due. Data can also then be forwarded to the manufacturer for tabulation of consumer buying patterns.

Many salespeople are, by temperament, very poor record keepers, and most find using the old-fashioned methods a time-consuming and altogether onerous task. Through the use of machine-readable data cards, filled in by the salesperson after each call (or twice a day or at the end of the day), this task can be far easier to do and can be accomplished more accurately and efficiently as well. The data thus generated could give management frequent updates on the current status of clients, the activity and effectiveness of salespeople, level of new orders and reorders, and much more.

CHAPTER 13

Basic Technical Skills of the Salesperson

Beyond the personal traits and skills of the salesperson are the basic technical or nuts-and-bolts skills that need to be mastered. These include using the telephone effectively; writing letters that aren't ignored; employing and exploiting symbols and other selling aids; organizing; preparing for, and delivering presentations; and managing your time and energy efficiently.

■ COMMUNICATION

Using one's language skills well—both in speaking and in writing—is of the highest priority in selling. There is no other way than through the use of language to get appointments, to present the necessary information to prospects, and to persuade them to buy. Later in this chapter we will consider presentations in some detail, but for the moment we will discuss the use of two of the fundamental means of communication: the telephone and the letter.

■ USING THE TELEPHONE

During the last 25 years, there has been a trend in American sales technique away from "cold calls" (dropping in to see a prospect without an appointment) and toward telephoning in advance for an appointment. For this reason, being able to use the telephone effectively is becoming more and more important for the salesperson. Here is a step-by-step plan for developing positive telephone procedures:

STEP 1: PLANNING

1. Decide what time of day and what days of the week are the best for making your calls.

2. Considering what you decided in item (1) and your own evaluation of your ability to maintain concentration, decide whether you will make your quota of calls at one sitting or at several shorter sessions.

3. Set up a system for keeping records of your calls, including name, date, and comments regarding appointment made, reason for no appointment, and when you plan to call again.

4. Make a list of prospects you plan to call.

5. Decide what you will say to the secretary or receptionist who will not connect you to the prospect or is otherwise uncooperative.

6. Carefully consider opening words or phrases you will use when connected with the prospect.

STEP 2: PREPARATION

1. Set up a situation in which you can make calls without being interrupted or distracted.

2. Make sure you are comfortable—proper temperature, good chair, and convenient place to write, and so on.

3. Have paper, pencils, telephone list, diary or appointment book, and so on arranged for easy use.

STEP 3: TESTING

1. Select a dozen or so prospects to call.

2. Call each one and, after each one, make notes on how well your opening worked, how well you reacted to a negative attitude from the receptionist, secretary, or prospect, and so on.

STEP 4: REVIEW

1. Analyze your notes on the first group of calls.

2. Change anything that did not work or that you think could be improved.

3. Make another dozen or so calls to test your modifications.

4. Repeat this process until you consistently get the results you want.

5. If you consistently fail to get the results you want, consult a more experienced colleague or your sales manager for advice and suggestions.

STEP 5: FOLLOW-THROUGH

1. When you have developed an effective approach, set up a daily or weekly routine for making calls.

2. Don't be afraid to try variations on your approach. Changes will prevent this task from becoming tedious and will help you get better at it.

One suggestion I would make about handling not being connected immediately with the prospect is to use the opportunity to your own advantage. Begin by simply asking, "Can you help me?" Most people will react positively to a request for help. Here are a few examples of the questions you can ask:

"Is Mr. Brown the right person for me to see?"

"Would it be better to write to Ms. White for an appointment?"

"Is the purchasing of widgets done by your office?"

"Is there a better time for me to call Mr. White?"

"Could you set up an appointment for me to see Ms. Brown?"

"I'll be in the vicinity of your office later today. May I stop in?"

A final observation I would like to make is that you should remember that a friendly attitude, courtesy, and the personal touch can flow over a telephone line. For example, if a receptionist, clerk, secretary, or assistant has been particularly friendly or helpful, ask for his or her name, write it down next to the name of the prospect or customer, and use the person's name in subsequent calls or visits. Since most salespeople do not bother to do this (some, in fact, treat such subordinates as nonpersons), your doing it will set you apart from them and in a positive way.

Although we've concentrated here on using the telephone simply to make appointments, there is a chance that its use could expand considerably in the future. With continuing increases in fuel costs, worsening traffic, and the move of businesses out of the central urban areas, it may turn out that selling will be carried out entirely via the telephone—perhaps with the addition of pictures. In any event, mastering the use of the telephone should be pursued seriously.

■ LETTER WRITING

Writing a letter to introduce yourself and ask for an appointment seems like a relatively easy task. And it would be if it weren't for the competition that your letter faces at most office "In" boxes. Malcolm Forbes, the late owner of *Forbes Magazine,* had estimated that about 10,000 letters crossed his desk every year. While lower-echelon managers probably receive somewhat less mail than that, your letter must nevertheless compete with other correspondence, memoranda, catalogs, magazines, and advertising circulars. Too many letters are stupid, dull, confusing, or annoying; some are clear, to the point, businesslike, and produce results; a rare few are bright, evocative, and memorable. With practice, anyone can write good letters. Until proficiency is achieved, however, extra care and attention devoted to the task will produce very good results. The following suggestions will help you get started; keep them in mind while composing the letter and, afterward, check the final letter against these points.

1. Decide what you hope to accomplish with the letter—introduce yourself and your company, highlight a product or service, ask for an appointment, and so on.

2. Find out the person's name, its correct spelling, and the person's title. The salutation should always include the person's last name (Ms. Brown, Mr. White); *never* use Dear Sir, Dear Madame, Dear Manager, and so on.

3. Always state your reason (the major one if you have more than one purpose) in the first paragraph.

4. Keep the letter brief if you have a limited goal—no more than one page. More complex letters can be longer but no longer than necessary.

5. Stick to specifics, especially when writing about your company and its products or services.

6. Try to point out the advantages that will accrue to the recipient of the letter—not to the writer.

7. The text of your letter should be positive in tone and sound like the work of a pleasant person.

8. Use natural-sounding, everyday words and phrases. Avoid stiff, stilted, overly formal writing, as well as the overuse of adjectives, especially superlatives. A good letter should sound as if you are talking to the prospect from across the desk.

9. Do not attempt to be cute or funny. While a relaxed easygoing tone is permissible, do not be too casual or offhand.

10. In many ways, your letter is the first stage of your effort to make a good first impression on the prospect. Therefore, make sure it is neatly typed, without errors, on good quality paper. The text should be properly centered on the page—slightly above center. Short paragraphs and the judicious use of capital letters and underlining to emphasize important words and phrases can also improve the appearance of a letter.

11. Your final paragraph is critically important. Whatever request you made in the first paragraph should be repeated here very straightforwardly.

12. Do not expect or ask your prospect to do very much in active response to your letter. In fact, announce that you will take the next step and specifically what it is you will do. For example, if you want an appointment, write "May I have an appointment next Thursday, the 16th? I will call your office on Tuesday the 14th to see if that is convenient."

13. Close the letter with a simple "Sincerely" or "Sincerely yours."

14. Finally, your signature reflects some things about you even to the untrained eye. For that reason, avoid overly fancy, flowery, gimmicky embellishments.

■ THE USE OF SELLING AIDS

In persuading a prospect to buy, there are any number of barriers to be overcome. For that reason, any extra help that the salesperson can enlist makes the task that much easier. Fortunately, the importance of selling aids is widely recognized, and thus there is no shortage of them. Many have specialized uses, but most can be used for many different purposes.

The two kinds of selling aids are *physical items* that can be shown or demonstrated and special *verbal formulas* that can be used to make various sales points. For example, to establish as quickly as possible a focal point of mutual interest with a new prospect, a salesperson can use a copy of an easily recognizable magazine or newspaper carrying an advertisement for the product or service being sold. Turning to the ad and saying, "Did you see our advertisement in this issue of *Time?*" breaks the ice and prevents early eye contact, which can make the prospect uncomfortable. If the prospect replies to the question in the affirmative, the salesperson simply comments on the ad and then glides slowly into the next stage of presentation. If the answer is in the negative, the salesperson can point out the highlights of the advertisement. In either case, an easygoing conversation is begun and then a return to eye contact can soon be made easily and naturally. If no such prop is available, photographs and other graphic material can be used to the same end.

A similar technique involves the use of hand props, either supplied by the company or improvised by the salesperson. These can be scale models, samples, or similar items that can be used to demonstrate a concept or principle. The best ones are fast, simple, convincing, and in some way memorable. Some involve a clever or humorous element. One of the very best I ever saw was a plain pocket handkerchief used to demonstrate the principle of an insulating material. It was whipped out with a flourish and then neatly folded into smaller and smaller squares to show how the layers of insulation were even and completely consistent. The salesperson should learn to use such hand props so that there are no mistakes or malfunctions. Inventing your own, where appropriate, can make selling stimulating and fun.

■ ENDORSEMENTS

The use of celebrity, expert, and institutional endorsements of products and services is most commonly encountered in advertisements. Entertainment and sports figures are also often used for their crowd-drawing ability at conventions and trade shows. The most famous institutional endorsement is the seal of approval awarded by *Good Housekeeping*, guaranteeing performance as claimed and the return of the purchase price in case of dissatisfaction. This kind of endorsement can be used as a part of a sales presentation, either directly or indirectly as part of the ice-breaking strategy. That is, the endorsement and its significance can be discussed, or the endorser can be a source of conversation preliminary to getting down to business.

■ LONG-RANGE AIDS

Companies of all sizes seek to establish a favorable image in the minds of potential customers, an effort that is of inestimable value to the salesperson. Such things as advertising (both in the general media and in trade publications), brochures, direct-mail letters and gimmicks (desk pieces, posters, calendars), seminars, booths and "events" at industry conventions and trade shows, publicity, retail displays, and so on are "conditioning" agents that prepare the way for the salesperson. Thus, the prospect knows something of the company and what it offers, and the company salesperson can begin selling without taking up valuable time providing background information or answering routine questions. In retail situations, such long-term selling aids are aimed specifically at instilling confidence in customers and in increasing the recognition of the company name. Such campaigns are often remembered for their slogans—"You can be sure if its Westinghouse," Ivory's "It floats," General Motors' "Mr. Goodwrench," or the doorbell–"Avon calling" combination.

In both wholesale and retail selling, the salesperson will take advantage of these aids, either using them directly as a part of a presentation or referring to them as a point of reference. In addition, clients or customers can be asked for their reactions to the campaign, mailing, activity, and so on. Any comments or significant reactions, positive or negative , should be reported back to those responsible for the program.

In the case of door-to-door selling, an effective long-range selling aid campaign is often critical. The doorbell–"Avon calling" combination—the message of friendly, helpful sales representatives and quality product line—has allowed Avon to counteract the public's suspicion of and resistance to door-to-door salespeople. Others, like Tupperware, hinged their sales effort on the use of neighborhood parties in the home of a resident, thus reducing sales resistance by turning the sales presentation into a social event. Other companies, selling everything from insulation to water softeners, siding, appliances, encyclopedias, and so on use advertising to build their credibility and then follow up with strict dress and protocol codes for their salespeople, brightly painted trucks and vans, and slickly produced sales materials to bolster that image.

By being aware of the aims of your company's long-range sales campaign, particularly the image it seeks to project, and by trying to find ways to take advantage of that effort, you will be enhancing your chances of success.

■ VISUALIZATION

Just as the visual image one presents—a neat appearance, good posture, friendly smile, interested expression—communicates many things to a prospect, visualization, that is, taking full advantage of form and color, can be used to communicate otherwise difficult-to-explain concepts so that they are easily understood and vividly remembered. Use every opportunity to incorporate photographs, drawings, graphs, charts, hand props, models, and so on into your presentations. Stick with evocative, vivid, concrete words and phrases in the verbal part of the presentation because these help the prospect visualize what you are talking about. Hand props, mentioned earlier, are also a good way to help in the visualization process.

■ PRESENTATION

We have mentioned sales presentations several times already but have not discussed them in detail. To begin, there is endless variety to the kinds of presentations that can be employed. In many companies, there is a prescribed general presentation in which the basic facts about the company and the products/services and the primary selling points are set forth. Often, salespeople are required to commit to memory the entire basic presentation, running to as many as a dozen pages. Some will object to this requirement as being too static, too classroomish, but the fact is that the basic presentation is rarely delivered in its entirety; its value lies in the fact that it contains the answers to virtually all the questions that company's salespeople are likely to encounter. With the presentation fully memorized, the answers are immediately available for recall, and they are the correct answers. There is no need to look them up, guess at them, or delay answering until a later time.

Regardless of the type of presentation—one to one, small group, or large group—there are a number of basic principles that should be remembered in planning and organizing it.

1. *Presentation should be as simple as possible, given the kind of information to be communicated and the audience to whom it will be given.* This is important because there is a tendency to try unnecessarily fancy or experimental methods. Critical evaluation and editing will help winnow out the extraneous.

2. *The essential facts, points, and examples should be presented in a logical and orderly manner.* This allows the audience to follow the presentation more easily, to relate the various elements to one another, and to be led step by step to the desired conclusion. Using an outline is helpful in constructing a presentation.

3. *The methods and materials of the presentation should not overwhelm the information to be communicated or in any way distract the audience.* While this problem can arise in one-to-one and small-group presentations, it is most apt to occur in those used for large groups. There has been a tendency, especially in recent years, to get carried away in the use of what are otherwise effective tools. There is much that can be done with films, slides, videotape, closed-circuit television, multiple screens, computer simulations, and so on, but when a presentation is overproduced the audience may begin to focus on the hardware or effects and not on the company and its products/services.

4. *The basic facts about the company and its products/services should be in the early part of the presentation.* This is important because it provides the audience with a context within which they can receive the balance of the presentation, and it quickly establishes the credibility of the presenters.

5. *Every presentation should be carefully rehearsed and evaluated before being used.* This gives the individual presenter, as well as other members of the sales force, the opportunity to eliminate awkward phrasing and poor organization and to check out the use of materials, props, and equipment.

6. *When a presentation to a large group is planned, care should be given to check out the facilities and other arrangements in advance.* Doing this can prevent problems from arising and allows for any necessary tailoring of the presentation.

Specifically, the following should be checked:

a. What is the size and composition of the audience?

b. What are the preferred starting and ending times?

c. Will there be a question period following the formal presentation?

d. What is the size and configuration of the room?

e. What equipment (projector easel, tape recorders, etc.) is needed? What is available and what must be supplied?

f. Is there a sound system? Is one needed?

g. Is the room air conditioned? Is it soundproofed?

h. How can brochures or other material be distributed to the audience or left behind for them?

7. *For every type of presentation, there should be suitable "leave-behind" materials that summarize the main points made.* The main themes and facts of the basic presentation, plus those covered in any special presentation, should be covered in a series of sheets, pamphlets, or brochures. Although there is something to be said for unusual, attention-getting sizes and formats for this material, it probably makes more sense for them to be of a standard 8½- by 11-inch size. Using custom-printed brightly colored file folders as holders, the sales force, prospects, and customers can easily file them for ready reference. Also, with such a standard format, sections can be assembled in whatever combination is needed for a particular situation. Besides giving ease in handling and filing, standard-sized literature is more convenient to mail.

8. *After every kind of presentation, there should be a follow-up letter or telephone call.* Oddly, it is often true that an elaborate and costly presentation will fail to produce orders immediately, but a simple call or letter within a few days may well succeed. The presentation prepares the way, so it would be foolish to overlook the critical follow-up to it to get the order.

One final observation on presentations relates to their cost, which can run from just a few dollars to many thousands. The point is that a presentation should be no more elaborate and costly than is necessary. Waste and extravagance should be eliminated. Usually the budget is calculated in relation to the total dollar amount of the orders that the presentation is likely to produce. But ultimately it is not the cost that matters, it is the effectiveness of the presentation. One that costs $100 and fails is more expensive than a successful one costing $1,000.

To illustrate some of the principles of a successful presentation, the annual Fashion Breakfast of Deering Milliken, a firm that makes fashion fabrics, can be cited. The event is held at a first-rate New York hotel and begins very early. The guests are served a delicious breakfast and then the fashion show—staged by a professional theatrical director and including a large portion of entertainment by singers, dancers, comedians, and a few big stars—is presented. As the guests depart, they receive a beautifully produced kit of information with pictures, fabric swatches, and an order form in a distinctive distributor folio recognized throughout the industry.

Since the Fashion Breakfast is the first event of the day, the guests are fresh and receptive. The show ends in time for them to return to their workplaces by 9, with no hours lost from a full day's work. The information kit reminds each guest of the show's high points. Although the shows are expensive, they enable the company to maintain their superior reputation and their share of the market.

Another original presentation concept is of great personal interest to me, because it first brought me to the attention of the top executives of the Hearst Corporation, which owns *Good Housekeeping* magazine. It came about this way: *Good Housekeeping* magazine measures about 25 percent smaller than any of its three major competitors: *The Ladies' Home Journal, Woman's Home Companion,* and *McCall's.* That was a definite negative, for by going into two or three of the others, advertisers could make just one plate for the production of the advertisement and then prepare duplicates. If *Good Housekeeping* were to be used with one or more of the others, a new, scaled-down advertisement would have to be created and a new plate made by the magazine at extra cost. Added to that was the fact that *Good Housekeeping* had a higher cost per thousand than the other magazines, all of which had larger circulations. One of the reasons for the higher cost per thousand was that *Good Housekeeping* had a higher cover price than the others.

The challenge was to make *Good Housekeeping* loom larger in influence overall than any of the competitors. I wrestled with that problem for a while and suddenly the idea surfaced. It led me to the creation of what I called the "*Good Housekeeping* area of influence." To dramatize the concept I decided upon a display revealing at first just the cover of *Good Housekeeping* magazine on a stand, under a spotlight. However, under this cover were dozens of display cards, which could be brought into sight on top, on both sides and on the bottom. By the time I got through showing the overall readership of the magazine, three times its circulation, the number of newspaper press stories about *Good Housekeeping* articles, and the sales of the *Good Housekeeping Cookbook* (second only to the Bible) and had depicted the scores of millions of *Good Housekeeping* booklets, the display towered far above my head and spread 12 feet across, down to the floor. *Good Housekeeping* management accepted the "*Good Housekeeping* area of influence" as the basic presentation for the magazine, and it was used effectively for years. One key element was that anyone could give the presentation with good effect. There was indeed very little that had to be said as the cards with their statistics were displayed. The president of the Hearst Corporation, Richard E. Berlin, was told about the presentation and about me, and a substantial raise and promotion to my first management job in sales resulted.

For stark simplicity, however, my best work was a presentation I devised for the Imagery Transfer Concept for radio. I would stand at a podium, dim the lights, then show color slides of very expensive, full-page magazine advertisements. I would read the headline copy and then describe the human trait of recovery of visual images from words that triggered the imagery transfer. The lights would go down, the last color slide would fade, and the voice of an announcer would simply state the headline of the advertisement. The audience would understand that immediately.

Imagery Transfer was an immediate success. Hundreds of thousands of new advertising dollars flowed into network radio for commercials as brief as 15 seconds.

There is nothing wrong with more elaborate presentation, however, if they are indicated by the problem. To compete with television, which had so much glamour, I enlisted the entire production staff of the NBC radio network around the world. A radio closed circuit was organized with the best-known newsmen in Paris, Bonn, Tokyo, London, and Moscow. Shortly after I started making my presentation before an audience, which had already been dazzled by a presentation on color television, I casually remarked that it was time for a report from around the world. I spoke directly to each of the NBC newspeople personally first and then asked them to tell my audience what was going on in the countries in which they were stationed. In this simple way I demonstrated the worldwide flexibility of network radio and made a pitch for advertising on "NBC News on the Hour."

▪ TIME MANAGEMENT

How efficiently salespeople use their time is critically important to how effective they are. Avoiding wasted time, reducing the time it takes to accomplish tasks, and eliminating unnecessary tasks means that more and more of your time will be productive. Good management of time can mean good office and work-area planning so that supplies, files, and equipment are at your fingertips instead of requiring an extensive search. It can mean using the time between appointments to make canvassing calls at offices in the same building or in the immediate vicinity. Or it can mean grouping appointments by geographical location to reduce unproductive travel time. The goals are to make sure there is sufficient time for all necessary tasks and to maximize one's productive time. The following pointers will help you to make more efficient use of your time.

❑ The Basics of Time Management

1. Know where your time goes. Keep a daily log for at least 2 weeks and then analyze your time. Identify trends and patterns.

2. Budget your time by priority. Rate your work projects in terms of importance and urgency; then schedule your time accordingly.

3. Practice continual planning. Constant evaluation and reevaluation of work priorities and schedules will lead to the best use of your time today.

4. Consolidate discretionary time into large chunks for uninterrupted work. Avoid overscheduling or inflexible scheduling that cannot be met.

5. Vary your work activities. Keep a healthy balance between long- and short-term projects, working in groups, working alone, and so on. This helps you maintain perspective and remain vital.

6. Delegate work to others. Avoid the pitfall of thinking of delegation as giving away your work. It is work that others could just as well do.

7. Ask yourself, "Are there things I am doing that shouldn't be done at all?"

8. Look for ways to minimize time spent on unproductive tasks, thus enabling you to spend more time on productive ones. Grouping similar activities will also often save time.

9. Gather as much information as you can before acting and thus avoid wasted time and effort. For example, take care in clarifying the objectives of your communications and seek feedback. This could prevent unnecessary rewriting or callbacks to correct information.

10. Take time to create a positive work climate. Avoid criticism and defensiveness, which can drain energy that could otherwise be utilized for creative, purposeful work.

11. Time invested in your own professional growth can pay handsome dividends. Keep up with developments in your field, including the various other divisions of your company.

12. Change fixed routines as a way of increasing your own alertness and adaptability.

CHAPTER 14

Advanced Skills in Selling

While the salesperson masters the basic skills and gains experience in the field of selling, there are a number of more advanced, more complex skills that require his or her attention. For the experienced salesperson, certain difficulties may arise from inadequate mastery of these skills. The first of these skills is to be able to distinguish between those situations in which the opportunity to sell must be pursued and those in which the opportunity is present and selling can proceed. The second of these skills is to learn the techniques that can be used to overcome nervousness and stress. Coping with the inevitable rejections encountered in selling is the third. Finally, there are a number of what might be called "tricks of the trade," techniques that the best salespeople devise to aid their selling efforts.

◼ OPPORTUNITY TO SELL VERSUS BEING READY TO SELL

These two activities could be described as knowing what is involved in getting your foot in the door and knowing what to do when you

189

get through the door. The former is basically an administrative function and includes the following:

1. Identification of prospects

2. Identification of decision makers within prospective companies

3. Knowledge of each prospect's buying cycle or pattern, if any

4. Knowledge of the competitive factors faced with each prospect

5. Evaluation of the best ways to get an appointment with the decision makers in each prospective company

6. Evaluation of the value of entertaining a decision maker, say, at lunch or dinner, to prepare the way for or as part of a sales presentation

7. Preparation of a letter or for telephoning to ask for an appointment

8. Selecting the best day of the week and time of day for the appointment, if there is a choice

Once the opportunity to sell is achieved, the salesperson must be ready to capitalize on the situation. This involves the following:

1. Mastering the presentation to be given, including any customizing that might be necessary for a particular prospect

2. Selecting the appropriate presentation materials and props and leave-behind materials

3. Based on a quick evaluation of the prospect's secretary (who will often mirror the prospect's personality) and then the prospect, selecting the best opening remark and strategy for handling the meeting

4. Carrying out the selected strategy smoothly and professionally

5. Taking steps during the presentation to put the prospect at ease (more on this later in this chapter)

6. At the close of the presentation, asking the prospect for the order—the all-important "detail" surprisingly overlooked by many

Take a look at your list of prospects and determine which ones involve achieving the opportunity to sell and which are ready for the selling to begin.

■ OPENING REMARKS

Having a variety of greetings and opening remarks gives the salesperson the flexibility of choosing just the right one, basing that choice on the initial evaluation of the prospect. There are scores of "ice breakers" that can be used quite naturally. A forced or "formula" opening, an overhearty manner, or excessive familiarity must all be avoided. It is better to say nothing beyond "hello" than to strike a false note. Good openings can be as simple and straightforward as "Thank you for letting me visit on such short notice" or "Our companies have had a long, friendly history," or they can be designed to initiate friendly conversation before getting down to business, such as comments on pictures or other items, in the prospect's office. ("That's a beautiful horse!" or "This is an extraordinary desk!" or "What a spectacular view!")

The reaction of the prospect to an opening remark can be a good clue to that person's personality or attitude. If the response is friendly and further information or comments are offered, then the meeting is likely to be friendly. If, on the other hand, the response is curt and businesslike, that is a signal to proceed immediately with the presentation. Once that is done, pause to allow the prospect time to react and, it is hoped, ask questions. Questions are important because they reveal that the prospect heard the presentation and is responding to it. If not, bring the call to an end, hand the prospect whatever leave-behind materials you have, and thank him or her for the meeting. Although such a lack of responsiveness can be disheartening, it may be that that particular prospect is always that way with salespeople. A follow-up letter might be a good idea. If the account is very important, report any less than positive reaction to the sales manager and suggest that both of you go to a follow-up meeting.

CHAPTER 15

Managing Stress

■ STRESS IN THE PROSPECT

In the area of assessing a prospect quickly upon first meeting, the experienced salesperson will look for the signs that the person is experiencing stress. Some of the telltale signs, all readily observed, are:

Compressed or tight lips

Narrowing of the eyes

Frowning

Fidgeting or nervous movements, including fluttering hands

High-pitched or reedy voice

Hacking, barking cough

Very rapid eye blinking

Excessive licking of the lips

Darting, restless shifting of the eyes; avoidance of eye contact

Deep, frequent inhaling of cigarette

Shallow breathing

When shaking hands, cold, moist hands, erratic pressure

Each of these symptoms is caused by the body's reaction to the experiencing of stress and is part of how we cope physiologically with stress.

When you notice any of these signs, make every effort to overcome it before getting into the critical part of your presentation. This can be done in a variety of ways. The salesperson's smile, relaxed manner, and friendly, easygoing attitude can do a great deal to help a prospect to relax. The conversation–starting remarks, discussed in the preceding chapter, can be used to draw the individual into a less stressful frame of mind. Above all, avoid high-pressure techniques and aggressive selling. These only increase the prospect's distress and could lead to a negative association in that person's mind between seeing you and feeling distress.

▪ STRESS IN ONESELF

The problem of stress, it must be remembered, can work both ways. If you show the signs of stress, even if the prospect does not, you will not make a very good impression or give a very effective presentation. If both you and the prospect are experiencing stress, it will be doubly difficult to accomplish anything at the meeting.

Stress can be produced by frustration, insecurity, self-consciousness, anxiety, and similar feelings. Improper management of stress over many years is not only unpleasant in one's work and counterproductive in trying to succeed in it, but it can also lead to a variety of ailments such as migraine and other stress-related headaches, spasticity, anxiety neurosis, digestive problems, ulcers, insomnia, weight problems, excessive smoking and drinking, high blood pressure and other circulatory problems, and even impotence.

Periodically check yourself for such telltale signs of stress, and, once alerted, take steps to reduce the stress you feel. A simple short-term "first-aid" response is to sit quietly somewhere, take a number of deep breaths, and concentrate on some pleasant thought or memory.

For effective, long-term prevention of unhealthy levels of stress, there are a number of helpful activities. Adding any of them to one's life can contribute significantly to the reduction of stress. Some of these are talking openly about frustrations and problems with close friends or sympathetic advisors; meditation; sports such as swimming, jogging, racket sports, and walking; dancing; calisthenics; better diet; listening to music; developing creative activities or hobbies (painting, clay modeling, sculpture, woodworking, gardening); and biofeedback self-regulation training. A number of books on stress management are listed in the bibliography.

Here is a simple regimen of activities that, in about two weeks, will get you started on improving your ability to manage stress. Note: A physical examination and consultation with your physician should precede any major change in diet or level of physical exertion.

S<u>TEP</u> 1

Before breakfast each morning, spend about 10 minutes exercising. Begin with a minute or so of stretching exercises. Adding 2 or 3 minutes of jogging in place or shadow boxing (make sure you wear proper shoes) is also a good idea. The objective is to stretch the muscles and to get the heart pumping more vigorously to increase the circulation of blood. After a few days of doing this, exercise more strenuously by increasing the number of repetitions of each exercise until you begin to perspire lightly.

S<u>TEP</u> 2

After exercising, lie down in a comfortable position and call up a mental picture of a person, place, or situation that is pleasing to you. Clear your mind of all other thoughts (this gets easier with practice) and contemplate the pleasing image for about 10 minutes. During this time, breathe deeply but slowly; try humming quietly with each exhalation.

S^{TEP} 3

Conclude the period of meditation by spending an additional minute or so thinking about the way you would like the day to proceed for you and your loved ones. Reaffirm that you will do everything you can—by your actions and by your attitude toward your work and the people you encounter—to make the day go as you envision it.

S^{TEP} 4

Repeat steps 2 and 3 toward the end of the morning or early in the afternoon if there is sufficient time and a quiet place is available. Once you have mastered these two exercises, you will be able to utilize them to relax unobtrusively almost anywhere.

S^{TEP} 5

At the close of the business day, either before or after your evening meal, take another 5 or 10 minutes to review the day, but do so in reverse, as though you were looking at a motion picture of your day being run backward. As you do this try to notice both the most pleasant and unpleasant episodes. The people or situations that irritated or angered you are what cause stress and should be avoided if possible. If they are unavoidable, try to be more philosophical about them and to take them less seriously.

S^{TEP} 6

Schedule at least two 1-hour periods a week for some strenuous exercise—swimming, tennis, dance movements, jogging, bicycling, skating, or brisk walking.

■ OTHER STRESS MANAGEMENT TIPS

During hectic, high-pressure times, stress is much more likely to be experienced. Badly managed stress, when combined with overwork, can lead to confusion and then disorientation. One method for correction is to take a sheet of paper, draw a line down the middle, and write the word "Critical" at the top of the left half and the word "Important" at the top of the right side. In the column headed "Critical," list those things that absolutely must be accomplished during the next day, things which if left undone would count heavily against you. In the column headed "Important," list—in descending order of importance—those things that would be desirable to accomplish. The immediate benefit is a certain amount of relief stemming from the fact that you have isolated and identified the most critical problems and will begin the next day by working on them. On the job, concentrate your efforts on those critical problems. When they have been dealt with, you can begin attacking those tasks listed on the other half of the paper. Doing this every day helps you keep control of the situation, focuses your energies, and reduces your anxiety about how well you will perform.

Try not to "fly off the handle" unnecessarily. Such a "hot" reaction to everything that goes wrong, irritates you, or offends you involves a tremendous output of energy and is highly stressful. In most cases, the simplest thing to do is to just let them go by or bounce off you. Consider the possibility that you contributed to the situation that irritated you. If so, a change in attitude or behavior could prevent its recurrence.

Have your blood pressure checked regularly. High blood pressure is fairly common, affecting one out of four individuals; since there are virtually no easily discernible symptoms, it is often unsuspected, and if it is left untreated it can be life-threatening in the long term. Once diagnosed, a simple, easy-to-follow, and effective program of exercise, diet, and relaxation is prescribed.

If you feel frustrated and unfulfilled because of limits and prohibitions on your freedom, look at the limits closely. Very often, we learn certain standards while growing up that are not necessarily suited to present-day realities. The guilt, anxiety, and resulting stress can be prevented by a thoroughgoing reappraisal of our codes of behavior, restructuring of our life-style and outlook, and setting more humane, more reasonable, less harsh standards for ourselves.

Another stress-producing time is when things have gone really badly. Sometimes it was preventable, just as often it wasn't. Regardless of the reason or even the specific problem, the secret of coping with the problem and of reducing the stress it causes is to be active and to avoid brooding about it. Almost any activity is preferable to sitting and doing nothing. Do devote as much time and energy as you can to resolve the situation, but once you have done that, go ahead and engage in some physical, mental, or emotional activity. Walk, jog, swim, soak in a tub, take a sauna, see a funny or wildly adventurous movie, flirt, make love, get together with friends, and so on.

Finally, it cannot be denied that there are unusual frustrations in selling—surly, uncooperative receptionists, unsafe streets and neighborhoods, poor public transportation, hostile prospects, and so on—especially in those positions where the salespeople must go out and "beat the bushes" for each sale. For those who are successful at it and in dealing with the stresses, not only is there a feeling of accomplishment, but that feeling will spread into other areas of life. The skills grow stronger with continued success and help make the person a better, warmer spouse, friend, lover, parent, and citizen.

On the other hand, if you give being in sales your best shot and you cannot deal with the pressures and the stresses, think about another position in the company or a different line of work altogether. There should be no reluctance to consider this option. After all, no job and no rewards are worth submitting yourself to daily misery. The best way to cope with a stressful situation is to avoid it; if it is the job itself, do something else.

■ COPING WITH NERVOUSNESS IN GROUP PRESENTATIONS

Many salespeople who have no trouble dealing with situations involving one other person or even a small group are far less comfortable when called upon to speak before a large group. While a trace of nervousness is to be expected before and at the beginning of a group presentation—and audiences often react sympathetically to such stage fright—its continued manifestation will be distracting and will detract from the presentation. Ideally, the salesperson gains confidence as the presentation proceeds and it is projected.

The primary manifestations of nervousness are fluttering hands; grimaces; shifting from one foot to the other; fiddling with papers, clothing, glasses, and so forth; and lack of personal focus. There are a number of techniques and tricks that can be used to eliminate these. Immediately prior to the presentation, use the relaxation procedure described in the preceding section. Regarding the presentation itself, here are some helpful suggestions:

1. *Rehearse the entire presentation.* An audience of experienced peers can provide valuable suggestions.

2. *Request a glass and a pitcher of water.* Pausing occasionally for a sip is certainly acceptable, whereas smoking, chewing gum, or eating are not, except during breaks.

3. *Speak clearly and loudly enough to be heard.* If a sound system is available, use it. Rehearse with a microphone, because it takes some getting used to.

4. *Stand erect.* Good posture enhances your message by giving you more credibility. You are more pleasant to look at than if you slouch. This does not mean standing ramrod straight and immovable. If you change position every few minutes, it will prevent you from tiring too quickly and let the audience do the same. Do not, however, move about too much by pacing, stooping, or turning. Also be careful to keep your feet flat on the floor and not to rock back and forth or from side to side or to bounce on your toes. Such movements reveal insecurity and are a distraction to your listeners. Never sit if that places you on the same level as the audience.

5. *Begin your presentation by identifying yourself if you have not been introduced.* Use your own words rather than a prepared text, and make frequent use of quotations, personal experiences, and anecdotes. Include as many visual or picture words and physical descriptions as you can. Also, visual material—slides, charts, graphics on a flip chart, scale models, and the like—will help any presentation.

6. Much as you would do in a one-to-one conversation, *pick out various individuals in different parts of the audience and focus on them,* shifting your attention from one to the other every 5 or 10 seconds. Speak directly to each person, make eye contact with them, smile at them when it is appropriate, and so on. If you do this correctly, those sitting near the individuals upon whom you focus will feel that you are speaking directly to them and will pay more attention to you. Avoid looking constantly at your notes, props, the floor, the ceiling, or anywhere but at the audience.

7. *Except when making deliberate gestures, keep your hands and arms still.* If there is a lectern, you can use it to anchor your hands. Simply hold on to it. The idea is to concentrate your energy in your face and voice, thus providing the audience with a point of focus. When you are more experienced, you may want to try working without a lectern. Credibility and a sense of openness can thus be communicated.

8. *When making gestures, use your whole body.* Using just the hands and arms can make the gestures look jerky and unnatural. Gestures of enthusiasm, reaching out to the audience, and using your hands to emphasize or reinforce visual images are good. Use gestures of threat or rejection only sparingly and then only for dramatic effect. Unconscious gestures and movements, such as crossing arms across the chest or putting them behind you, touching the face or hair, and covering your mouth, should be avoided. These are negative signals of nervousness, defensiveness, and withdrawal.

9. *Don't worry about making a mistake*—even the most experienced speakers make them.

10. *Learn to monitor the body language of the audience so that you can direct yourself to those who indicate the most interest.* If signs of restlessness and boredom begin to become generalized throughout the audience, take steps to regain their attention—change your pacing, go immediately to a more interesting part of the presentation. If you are giving a long presentation, take frequent breaks or interrupt yourself to ask for questions.

▪ HANDLING REJECTION

One unavoidable occupational hazard of selling is rejection. Even the greatest salespeople in the world do not make a sale every time. When you are just beginning, however, your rejections will probably far outnumber your successes, and that can be a problem. If a generalized sense of rejection and failure develops, you may begin to doubt the value of the products or services you are selling or, worse yet, your own abilities as a salesperson.

In most of those cases in which you fail to make a sale, the reason will be clear—a purchase from a competitor may just have been made, you hit the wrong point in the prospect's buying cycle, there was a mismatch between what you were selling and what the prospect wanted, and so on. One common reason is that the prospect is just having an off day and is thus distracted, in a bad mood, or simply unwilling to be cooperative. Such rejection can be put down to bad luck. Furthermore, there is always the chance of making the sale at a later time.

Some lost sales can be seen, when viewed objectively, to have been the result of an error or miscalculation on your part—misreading the prospect, botching the presentation, or some such. In these cases, the damage may sometimes be undone in a subsequent call or by another salesperson. In any event, you should use the opportunity to analyze your errors, work on correcting them, and prevent them from recurring.

There are often instances of lost sales—and these are the most difficult to identify and to deal with—in which you are certain that you did a good job in presenting the values of your product or service, in answering questions, and in countering objections. You may know that the prospect was ready to buy, that what you had to offer was right, and that you had a price advantage, or at least no disadvantage. A rejection in such a situation is, of course, difficult to understand. Speaking to your peers about the matter can be very helpful. You can get good suggestions, answers, sympathy, and support. In fact, the group may decide that consulting the sales manager for evaluation and action may be warranted. If it is decided that the buyer has been unfair or unduly influenced by personal factors or unethical practices, the sales manager may decide to face up to the buyer. An unsatisfactory outcome from that meeting may lead to consultation with the buyer's superiors. The point is that sharing the problem with peers and management will help ease the feelings of rejection. In companies in which the policy is to call in the sales manager for assistance at an early stage, the failure to make a sale is shared. If the help of others produces a sale, the pleasure and satisfaction of succeeding are multiplied.

■ TRICKS OF THE TRADE

As individuals work in the field of selling, they learn to do little things that can give them a slight competitive edge or make coping with certain problems easier. I remember, for example, when I was a junior salesperson for the Royal Typewriter Company and my job was to call at every office in my territory to offer a free typewriter demonstration to the secretary or office manager. I was moderately successful in meeting my daily quota of demonstrations. Whenever the secretary was reluctant to allow the demonstration, I would leave my business card and a small brochure extolling the virtues of the machine. The senior salesperson with whom I was working was impressed with my industry and persistence. To help and encourage me, he took me to a perfume wholesaler one morning and out of his own pocket bought me two dozen small vials of perfume. He told me to attach one of my cards to each vial and to give one to each of the secretaries I visited. Within a short time, the number of demonstrations I arranged had nearly doubled.

A common problem that salespeople encounter is having to field unexpected questions or arguments. Too often the immediate response is either defensiveness or hemming and hawing, neither of which makes a very good impression. The problem is that because the question or argument is unexpected, you need time to formulate an answer. To do this, immediately break your response down into three parts: past, present, and future. Since the past is known and the present is obvious, speaking briefly about them gives you time to consider the real question, which is about the future.

Here is an example. You work in an automobile showroom and are talking with a married couple. The woman is obviously favoring your brand, but the man is silently resisting. Just as you think you are nearing a sale, he blurts out, "Yeah, but what about that lemon you had to recall last year?"

You begin with an acknowledgment of the prospect's concern and then proceed with the past-present-future response. "That was a very serious matter, sir, and no one took it more seriously than my company [concern acknowledged]. Every one of the problems was corrected [past]. We learned a great deal from that experience, and four new inspections have been added to make sure it never happens again [present]. The best proof of this is the new warranty on our cars, which specifically covers that part [future], making it the best warranty in the industry."

This technique can also be used whenever you are asked unexpectedly to speak in a meeting or even at a social gathering. Say, for example, you are at a farewell dinner for a retiring colleague and you are suddenly asked to "say a few words." Using the past-present-future formula, you rise and say, "I have known Bill Jones for 20 years and have some very fond memories of those days [past]. One story you might enjoy was the time Bill did XYZ . . .. Now Bill tells us that he is going to Arizona [present]. I am sure, knowing how much he hates our weather, that he will prosper and be sinfully happy there [future]."

There are endless variations on the past-present-future type of response. Although it will not, of course, work in every situation, having it available is a valuable time-buying device. Just think of the similar technique used by Richard Nixon, who typically responded to every question by saying, "I'm glad you asked that question. Now I want to make this perfectly clear . . .,"which he seldom did.

■ A NEW VIEW OF CLIENTS

I have always believed that once a prospect becomes a client, an unfortunate shift too often takes place in the salesperson's mind. It is a natural one, I suppose, but it should nevertheless be avoided. As has been shown in preceding chapters, research and preparation regarding a prospect's needs, personality, and so on are very important in getting a sale. Once the sale is made, however, too many salespeople give significantly less attention to clients and continue to concentrate on their new prospects. Now certainly, pursuing new prospects is important, but giving attention to clients is equally important. After all, any buying customers who are lost have to be replaced. If you call on clients only periodically to take their orders, some will resent it, and all of them will be vulnerable to any extra attention they are given by your competitors' salespeople.

The trick is to continue to get to know your clients even better than you did when they were prospects. An interest in them and the concern you show for them will help to cement your relationship with them and ensure their loyalty to you and to your company. Focus your concern both on them as people and on their success in their job. Here are a number of suggestions for how to go about this:

1. Put yourself in the client's position if you can.

2. Realize the pressures faced by the client.

3. Show respect for the client's time.

4. Learn about the client's company and the competition it faces.

5. Find out both the client's personal and professional objectives.

6. Do everything possible to make the client look good to the people in the company—employees, colleagues, and superiors.

7. Keep clients informed of new developments—in advance, if possible.

8. Entertain clients well but suitably.

9. Help any client who is obviously under stress to relax.

10. Keep the client's file on your products and services up to date.

11. Keep in touch by telephone and letter between visits.

12. Bring members of your company's management to see your client occasionally.

13. Ask the client for advice.

14. Invite clients to attend trade shows, exhibits, and conventions and to visit your company.

15. Invite clients to your sales meeting when it is appropriate.

CHAPTER 16

Basic Personal Traits and Skills of the Salesperson

In Chapter 11 we touched briefly on the subject of "what makes a good salesperson." The qualities and qualifications noted there—sound basic education, people orientation, flexibility, open-mindedness, and motivation—are important, but very general. In this chapter, we will examine in greater detail the specific traits and skills required by anyone who wants to succeed in the sales field.

■ SPEAKING

The first of these basics—and probably the most important—is speaking. I have often been asked if I had some secret weapon or a special talent to explain my successes. My response then and now is that the key for me has been my ability to speak well and persuasively whether it was one-on-one, to a small group, or to a large audience. Among my contemporaries, there were individuals who were as intelligent or more intelligent than I, who had as much motivation and experience as I had, and who could have gotten the promotions that came my way. I believe that my major advantage was my ability to speak. Some of the credit for this must go to my early upbringing; mine was a typical Irish family, with a tradition of talking, joking, and constant arguing. In school, I enhanced my ability to make "chin music" by participating in such activities as debating, voice training, and acting.

Why is speaking well so important? Because, simply, the basis of selling is communication, and speaking is the salesperson's primary means of communication. In fact, it is such a critical factor that the poor speaker works under a crushing handicap. The mastery of that handicap will often compensate for weaknesses in other areas. In addition, superior speaking ability can literally double or triple a salesperson's income and affect every aspect of his or her career, including the kind of account and territory assignments that are offered. The subject of speaking can be broken down into two separate parts: the voice and speech.

▪ THE VOICE

Whether a voice is appealing or not depends upon its quality—its pitch, modulation, and texture. The right combination produces a mellow, pleasing voice; the wrong one produces a harsh, discordant, or otherwise unpleasant voice. Because the quality of the voice is largely determined by the configuration of the larynx, or voice box, and adjoining parts of the mouth and throat, little can be done to change it significantly. On the other hand, proper care can prevent or eliminate certain unpleasant qualities. A raspy, harsh voice can be the result of heavy smoking or drinking, misuse of the voice (such as with excessive shouting or screaming), or some other condition that is correctable through a change of habits or through medical intervention.

Temporary changes in voice quality can be produced by changes in breathing patterns, and by the individual's mental, emotional, or physical state. Stress, fatigue, illness, anxiety, or depression can raise or lower the pitch of the voice; produce a reedy, tense, quavering or discordant quality; or otherwise distort the voice. In fact, careful attention to changes in voice quality can provide an early warning of such dysfunctions. Correction or alleviation of the condition will restore the voice to normal.

▪ SPEECH

The other aspect of speaking is speech itself—the words we use, how we say them, and how we use them. Here we are in an area where significant improvements, if needed, can be made through what is sometimes called the "cultivation" of the voice. Most of our habits of speech are learned during childhood and, therefore, can be un-learned—albeit sometimes with tremendous effort and application. But since how we speak is more important in getting ahead than the clothes we wear, the car we drive, or the size of our bank account, the investment of time and energy is more than worthwhile.

For example, a strong regional or sectional accent can be a distraction to prospects encountered outside that region or section. Nonstandard "dialects" in particular limit the salesperson to territories where there are similar speakers. A vocal coach can be a great help in eliminating such a handicap; improving pronunciation; and replacing nonstandard words, phrases, and constructions.

A good vocabulary is a minimum requirement for the salesperson, since it makes it possible to speak more effectively and to understand other people. Good salespeople are ever on the lookout for ways to improve their vocabulary. There are courses and self-help books for this purpose that can be quite helpful, but the most effective way is through paying constant attention to the words encountered in listening to others and in reading. Whenever a new word or an unfamiliar meaning or sense for an already familiar word is met, check it out as soon as possible in a dictionary. With a clear understanding of its meaning, pronunciation, and proper use, try to use it in speaking or writing if an opportunity arises. In this way, through using it, the word becomes yours and will thereafter be a part of your lexicon.

Vocabulary is, of course, only the raw material of communication, the building blocks of sentences. Far more important than a bagful of "twenty-dollar" words is the ability to speak and write in a clear, concise, easily understood way. The implication of jumbled, incomplete sentences that do not follow one another logically is that the speaker-writer has a jumbled, confused, illogical mind. In other words, poor communication not only fails to communicate, but implicates the communicator as well. Here, again, courses and seminars in speech, public speaking, and writing can provide the training and guidance for improving these all-important skills.

■ LISTENING AND RESPONDING

Of nearly as much importance as the ability to communicate effectively is being able to listen effectively and to respond to the communications of others. A common fault of salespeople is their habit of delivering their "spiel" or "pitch" straight through without stopping. Naturally there are advantages to being able to complete a presentation, which is often very carefully designed, without interruption. On the other hand, in selling, there are at least two people involved, and if the prospect gets the feeling that a lecture is being delivered and that comments or responses are unwelcome or unheard, it should not be surprising that the prospect may resent being treated in this way. The secret to listening effectively is always to be aware of the fact that the other person is a human being who is entitled to respect and consideration. What others have to say is important to them for its own sake, but even more to the point, it represents the other half of a dialogue and can provide the salesperson with valuable insights into a prospect's feelings, needs, desires, doubts, questions, and so on. Effective listening permits the salesperson to respond appropriately and thus move ever closer to the transformation of the prospect into a customer.

Try to be aware of how you treat other people—both professionally and in your dealings with family, friends, colleagues, and others. Do you let others finish their sentences, whether they are making a statement or asking a question? Do you interrupt simply to correct a minor misstatement instead of waiting? Do you often cut people off by saying, "Yes, I know," or "Oh, I know all about that"? When another is speaking, are you listening or are you preoccupied with what you want to say next? Obviously, you have to be thinking ahead to the points you still need to make, but it is just as easy—with practice—to respond first to what the other person has said and then go on to your own comments or statements.

■ PERCEPTION, OBSERVATION, AND RESPONSE

An expansion and extension of listening and responding is the more general ability to perceive and observe the entire environment and thus be able to respond more fully to it. Perception is the notice we pay to sensory stimuli of all sorts—sights, sounds, odors, temperature, and so on. Observation is the somewhat more conscious process of seeking out significant details of the environment, sorting through them, connecting one with another, relating them to our perceptions, and attempting to arrive at conclusions about what they mean, what they tell us, or where we should look for more information. Apparently, some individuals do this sort of thing instinctively, while others learn through practice to focus their attention and concentrate on taking in their environment until doing so becomes second nature to them.

To show how important these skills are, we will analyze a typical situation. A salesperson goes to the office of a prospect. Among the significant clues to understanding this until-now-unknown individual before the first words are spoken are:

The decor and furnishings of the outer office.

The demeanor and professionalism of the secretary.

The neatness or messiness of the office, particularly the secretary's desk and adjacent areas.

The manner in which the secretary handles calls, greets guests, and interacts with the person for whom he or she works.

The decor and furnishings of the inner office.

The demeanor of the prospect.

The way in which the prospect interacts with the secretary.

The personal items found in the office—family pictures, awards, trophies, desk paraphernalia, and so on.

The way the prospect is dressed.

The indications of good or bad grooming and of the habits of personal hygiene.

The physical fitness and posture of the prospect.

The state of the prospect's desk and the room in general—neat, messy, cluttered, chaotic, and so on.

Each of these clues reveals something about the prospect, and taken together, they present a rather full, though preliminary, picture of that person. As we will see later, these observations can provide the salesperson with opportunities for "ice-breaking" comments or questions. Most important, however, the quick hypothetical composite of the prospect can warn the salesperson of potential problem areas. For example, if the person seems to be extremely disorganized, there may be a problem with holding the prospect's attention or of continuity on follow-up visits or calls. An overbearing individual might try to cut you off without a fair or complete hearing. It might be difficult to get information regarding needs or preferences from a very meek, shy, or nervous person. In each case, an early awareness gives the salesperson an opportunity to take countermeasures.

■ BODY LANGUAGE

One area of observation that has been studied extensively is called body language. Simply stated, people communicate their moods or attitudes without realizing it through the way they hold their heads, shoulders, torsos, arms, and legs. In other words, the attitude of the body is a sort of language that tells the careful observer about the attitude of the person.

In addition to aiding the individual in observing others—prospects, colleagues, and superiors—an awareness of body language can be used to monitor your own moods and attitudes, many of which may be unconscious. For example, if you observe your hand gestures closely, you may find that you are symbolically pushing people away. Seeing this, you may realize that although you consciously strive to draw others toward you, some insecurity, fear, anxiety, or other unconscious process is leading you to subvert your best efforts. This, in turn, allows you to analyze your feelings about yourself and other people and seek to overcome your unconscious resistance. Other clues will reveal other things, but achieving greater awareness of both conscious and unconscious actions promotes understanding and more effective focusing of our energies on achieving your goals.

▪ STRAIGHT THINKING

Thinking logically and clearly is important to the salesperson in two primary ways: planning and problem solving.

Planning involves such day-to-day details as how you organize your desk and office space; how you set up your appointment book, expense diary, and personal telephone directory; how you establish the routing of your workday—making and returning calls, setting up appointments, handling correspondence, record keeping and reporting, professional reading, scheduling travel, and so forth. The most efficient planning and organizing of these seemingly mundane and trivial matters frees the salesperson to concentrate on selling. The elimination of confusion, wasted efforts, misplaced information, and neglected details can be immensely helpful and in some cases will provide the salesperson with a competitive edge.

Problem solving, in our context, is the specialized effort required to handle events and circumstances not foreseen by the planning and organizing already done. It is dealing with the unexpected, the exception to the rule. In come cases, after appropriate analysis and action, changes in day-to-day routines can be instituted to prevent the recurrence of a particular problem or to incorporate its proper handling within the routine. In any event, developing one's ability to identify the problem, determine its origins, discern its components, analyze alternative plans of action, and forecast the probable results, including side effects, and then to follow through or resolve the problem should be a high priority.

■ PERSONALITY

I remember hearing about a study conducted by a sales organization to determine the characteristics of its top salespeople—roughly 25 percent of the sales force (who were, by the way, responsible for 75 percent of the sales). No significant differences could be found. The high performers were not better looking, better dressed, educated, smarter, or younger. Oddly enough, the one characteristic they all had was the somewhat ill-defined one of *niceness*. Time after time, customers rated the top salespeople as nice. When a top sales manager was told about this result, he replied, "I'm not surprised. I always try to hire people I like to be with. If I like to be with them, then the chances are that the customers will feel the same."

And what is niceness? Can it be defined? It is, I believe, a complex mixture of such traits as self-respect, respect and consideration for others, courtesy and manners, pleasant personality, good humor and sense of humor, and thoughtfulness. The sum of these characteristics in someone, I think, is what is identified as niceness. But I believe there are other qualities contributing to that perception and that are probably a part of niceness. These include honesty, loyalty, character, forthrightness, dependability, honor, sense of fairness, tolerance, and empathy. It is, in the final analysis, all those traits one expects to find in a well-rounded, secure, responsible, mature individual. The chances of success in selling, as in other endeavors, including one's personal life, are certainly enhanced by everything we do to mature, to free ourselves from our insecurities, and to become better, more functional individuals.

■ MAKING GOOD FIRST IMPRESSIONS

The first impression we make on a stranger—whether in business or socially—can have a lasting effect. But when you consider that the first impression can be good, neutral, or bad, the odds are not all that unfavorable. A neutral impression can be improved upon, and even a bad one—although it requires time and effort that could be invested elsewhere—can sometimes be reversed over a period of time.

There are certain attributes and behaviors that foster a bad first impression and that should simply be eliminated. Examples of these are rumpled, soiled, spotted, or inappropriate clothing; offensive personal hygiene—dirty hair or nails, body odor, bad breath, and so forth; lateness; profane language; disrespect for people other than the prospect; rambling, disorganized presentation; argumentative or combative responses; unresponsiveness to questions or comments.

Other attributes and behaviors are a matter of degree, usually involving something that is quite acceptable or even necessary if not taken to an extreme. For example, it is obvious that a good opening for a conversation is important. If it is clever and memorable, you've made an important step toward creating a good first impression. A cheerful, friendly remark is generally quite acceptable. Mumbling unintelligibly is almost as bad as saying nothing. Obviously, saying something silly, stupid, or in poor taste is also to be avoided. Other weaknesses in approach include an overly bluff or hearty manner; rushing the presentation or dragging it out; unnecessary repetition (although some repetition of key points to dramatize their importance is an excellent strategy); mishandling of eye contact (since eye contact is important, seek a balance between avoiding it and staring, both of which make others uncomfortable); and pushing or avoiding the personal touch (the former seems like prying or confession, which puts people off and makes them defensive, whereas the latter makes you seem cold or distant).

Finally, there are things that a good salesperson can do to promote a good first impression, but that seldom detract if they are not done. Here are some examples. Develop a repertoire of good stories and jokes to be used as appropriate. Keep up on current events—especially sports, national news, and, most important, news that could affect your field—so that intelligent, informed conversation is possible. Be curious and don't be afraid to ask questions; in this way you can not only increase your store of knowledge, but also let the prospect know that you are genuinely interested in hobbies, activities, travel, family, and so on, if any of these or other topics come up in conversation.

Remember, though, that making a good first impression is as much a matter of judgment as it is technique and preparation. What you do and how you act must be tailored to the particular individual you are meeting. By being flexible, you will be able to adjust, to react appropriately, and to say or do what is right. Although it would be an advantage to know something about a prospect before calling on her or him, that is rarely possible except for the clues you can gather just before the encounter begins. Because of that, it will sometimes happen that there is very little you can do to succeed in starting off the new relationship on the right foot.

I remember just such a situation when I was a young "apprentice" salesperson. I was working part time one summer and was surprised and thrilled to be invited by the regional sales manager to accompany him on a sales call. He was the most impressive man in the organization; tall, handsome, well dressed, hearty, with a booming voice and unusually broad vocabulary. His handshake was firm, and his hand was always warm and dry. He exuded confidence and competence.

We entered the prospect's office and I immediately noted the contrast between my hero and the buyer, who was a small, shy, balding man who stuttered nervously during the early stages of the meeting. As he sat, his feet barely reaching the floor and listening wide-eyed to the beautifully flowing language of the sales manager, he appeared awe-struck. Then, subtly, his attitude began to change. I watched him and thought I could see a look of envy stealing over his face. It suddenly occurred to me that there was something wrong with this match-up. On the one side was the huge sales manager who seemed to be blessed professionally, physically, and socially. On the other was the little man who had almost none of those gifts, but who did have the power to buy or not to buy. At that point, I realized that in spite of the sales manager's skill, we would not get an order from this man. I could almost read his thoughts: "This guy has everything. Why should I give him my business, too?"

This is an example of first-impression overkill. There were other salespeople and other managers who would have done much better in confronting that particular buyer, individuals who would have had something in common with him. And having something in common with a prospect is a critical basic element in creating a good first—and lasting—impression.

■ FORMULA FOR SUCCESS

The personal traits and skills that we have been discussing, while valuable, are not sufficient in themselves. There are still other elements involving the salesperson's orientation to his or her work that are crucial to success. These traits are the keystones, and, when present, make it possible for the individual to acquire, correct, or refine any of the other skills or traits discussed in this book.

■ PRIDE AND MOTIVATION

The first of these is personal pride. It means that the way one acts, looks, and is perceived by others makes a difference. Pride leads the individual to strive to behave in a way consistent with a personal set of values, to meet certain standards of excellence. With this sense of self-value, or self-respect, the individual has a personal stake in learning to speak well, be attentive to others, be observant and perceptive, think clearly, avoid pettiness, act responsibly, and be clean, well-groomed, and well-dressed.

Closely related to personal pride is what is commonly called motivation, the desire to do well, to succeed, to do whatever is required to reach one's goals. It is what makes people put in extra effort, study and take courses, constantly look for ways to be more effective and efficient, and, in general, take seriously both what they do and how well they do it. It can be said that a person who has a sense of personal pride and is highly motivated will be equal to any challenge and be able to overcome any difficulty—or at least give it the best possible effort.

■ ATTITUDE

One of the characteristics commonly found in successful salespeople is good attitude. This is not just a matter of being positive or optimistic, although that is surely an element of a good attitude. Even more important is acceptance of the realities of a situation with equanimity. What this means is a disinclination to carp, complain, or whine about unfair conditions or other problems. To react negatively is destructive to one's morale and to team spirit and is a waste of time and energy. For example, no product is perfect in every way for every prospect. Despite the huge amounts of money devoted to research and development, to design, and to testing, there is always room for improvement. The salespersons, who become aware of a product's deficiencies or a competing product's advantages, do not serve their own interests or that of the company by complaining about them. To succeed, never forget that your job is to sell what your company offers, whether it is services or the products in current inventory. This is not to say that deficiencies are not of concern to you. Constructive criticism and suggestions are welcomed by progressive management; griping and complaining are not.

■ FOCUS

The question of attitude is related to the quality called focus, or perspective. This is the ability to channel one's time, energy, and attention on those things that matter most and to avoid distractions, side issues, and trivial matters. I ran across an excellent example of the importance of focus in a story about a former New York Giants football player, Dick Lynch, one of the very best linebackers ever. A linebacker's primary goal is to defend against runs and passes in the zone he patrols. Lynch was so good that opposing quarterbacks rarely attempted passes to receivers in his zone, which meant that he effectively reduced the opponent's field of action and hampered their offensive strategy. But for a linebacker, the ultimate in fun and excitement is surely to make an interception. Also, the press and the public notice linebackers who have high rates of interceptions. Thus, Lynch decided one season to work on getting more interceptions—and he did—but his opponents were also completing more of their passes to his zone. In several conferences with the coaches, it was concluded that the change in focus was the problem. Where previously he had had only one objective in mind on pass plays (preventing completions), he now had two (preventing and intercepting passes). The change had made him a split second less decisive in his actions and that was all the opposing quarterbacks and receivers needed. Dick decided to return to his original focus, and in the very next game his effectiveness returned.

The focus of a salesperson should be on selling and on doing all those things that promote making each sale. Competing with others, making friends with colleagues or clients, building up one's feelings of self-worth, and even getting ahead in the business world flow from concentrating on one's primary goal. Focus on selling and the others will probably follow and, in fact, are more likely to follow.

■ PREPARATION

One last characteristic of successful salespeople is the priority they put on preparedness, on being ready for virtually any eventuality. This includes total mastery of the facts, figures, and procedures related to the products or services they are selling and their company's policies, prices, and discount schedules. It means carrying a sufficient supply of leave-behind literature, business cards, order forms, samples, and so forth. It also means making each call prepared to do their best by being physically and mentally alert (getting enough sleep, being moderate about lunchtime cocktails, and so on). Proper preparation can even include being ready with an umbrella for foul weather, even when there is only a slight chance for it.

CHAPTER 17

The Basic Rules of Selling

Here are the basics of selling, a review of the main points of our discussion presented in the form of a series of brief rules, suggestions, and guidelines for behavior.

1. Work to develop a clear awareness of what you really want out of life. Then decide if sales is a path to those goals for you.

2. If sales appears to be the right path for you, decide whether you would rather sell products or services.

3. Think carefully about territorial sales work, particularly about whether it would adversely affect your spouse and children. There is more money, but your frequent absences may not justify it.

4. Decide whether you are best suited for the probing kind of selling (in which you seek out prospects) or the reactive kind (in which the customers come to you).

5. Research the top companies in the field in which you have the greatest interest. If you are conservative by nature, you may be better off working for the bigger, more established organizations. If you are more adventurous or daring, take aim at the companies that are third or fourth in their fields.

6. Avoid cutthroat or unethical businesses.

7. Ask questions about the amount and degree of sales training each of the companies in which you are interested provides to its new salespeople. If you have a choice, go with the company providing the most training.

8. If you are very ambitious for advancement into management, you can enroll in some evening classes in marketing, public speaking, advertising, and other subjects allied to sales. There are easy ways to let your superiors know this. Getting to the office a bit earlier and leaving a bit later than the rules demand does not go unnoticed. It should not be overdone, however, as associates may resent it. Keep your records better, make your call reports frequent and complete, be available and helpful to your associates and friendly to the new arrivals, and avoid making obvious judgmental errors. You will undoubtedly receive consideration for greater responsibilities and, ultimately, promotions into sales management if that is what you want and you do not have any major deficiencies.

9. Make friends with the older, more experienced salespeople and seek their advice when possible. Listen and be respectful.

10. When you have become established in sales or sales management, give some thought to good business citizenship. Businesses do many, many great things for communities through public service programs. There are also ways in which individual business people can be of service. Such good citizenship is good business; it not only improves one's image in the community, but it also often puts sellers and buyers together in programs for the common good.

11. If there are sales drives and contests, do your very best to make major contributions and to win. That is the best kind of visibility for a salesperson interested in advancement.

12. Do not socialize with competitors during business hours.

13. Remember that your job is to sell the products and services your company offers currently. Do not waste time worrying or complaining about the products and services of the future. However, if you lose accounts to a competitor because of specific features of its products or services, advise your sales manager. Better still, take your sales manager to visit clients whose business has been lost.

14. Subscribe to the best trade magazines in your field and read as much as you can about other people's methods and successes. If you do not have a very retentive memory, make notes and refer to them when possible.

15. If you work for a public company, buy a few shares of stock. You have some surprising rights as a stockholder regarding information about the company's overall operations, as well as some legal rights.

16. If you have some accounts and prospects that are also public companies, either buy a share or two of their stock or get copies of their annual reports by contacting a brokerage house or by writing directly to the corporate secretary. You may be surprised by what you can learn about a business from such documents.

17. Make full use of whatever system of administration is provided by your employer for record keeping, call reports, and follow-up schedules.

18. Try to develop a reputation for accuracy and for being slightly conservative in your sales forecasts. You will never embarrass your immediate superior by doing a bit better than you anticipated.

19. Learn to read the signs of stress in yourself and others. Check for signs of stress in yourself before calling on prospects. Learn to read the signs of stress in your prospects and develop some ways to help relieve their stress.

20. Consider that each of your sales begins before you walk into the reception room of the prospect. It starts when you look into

a mirror to check on your appearance and for any outward signs of stress.

21. Project friendliness and respect for the receptionists and secretaries of your prospects. You never know what their relationship is to their superiors.

22. If entertaining customers and prospects is part of your sales style, you should quickly survey your territory for the best places to entertain. This does not mean the most expensive or fanciest. You must consider the emotional as well as the physical well-being of your guests. Some individuals feel out of place in expensive or ostentatious restaurants. You should be able to judge that fairly quickly from the persons themselves and their office surroundings.

23. If your company has a basic presentation, commit it to memory.

24. Prepare and rehearse before people who have the experience and competence to give you constructive criticism.

25. If you think you can make a good suggestion(s) about improving the company's presentation, put it (or them) to the test *outside* the organization with some friends, relatives, or acquaintances who have experience and competence in presentation techniques. Do not risk looking amateurish within your own organization with untested suggestions. If you are told your ideas are good, take them to your immediate superior, and let that person share in the credit for the development of the idea.

26. If there are group presentations involved in your selling, make sure that you are among the best 10 percent of the sales force in your presentation technique.

27. When you join a new company and are assigned a territory or if you are given a new territory, start with as much of an overview as possible—literally. In almost every part of a major population center there are tall buildings from the top of which you can look down on *your* territory. You might even do a bit of sketching to show where the biggest concentration of large buildings is. You can thus examine the whole territory in terms

of coverage so that you do not waste time in getting from prospect to prospect. You can also make a decision about whether to cover the territory in concentric circles, radiating out from one central point, or to divide the territory into quadrants and cover them in order. But do make such a decision rather than plunging into a territory without a set plan. You can always change it later. By taking this kind of overview of your whole territory, you will develop a proprietary feeling. That territory in a way is your own small business. Out of it you will provide for your family and the education of your children. That kind of feeling will add to your presence when you start making your sales calls. It can also give you some good points of conversation when you make first calls.

28. Build your case for salary increases and more responsibility steadily. Some good indicators of superior performance are increases in sales each year; your performance compared to that of competitors; and a positive attitude toward the company and its products and services, and toward your associates.

29. Give some thought to the timing of requests for salary increases or additional responsibility. When your company is not doing well overall, it is not a very good time, and in fact, there may be policy restrictions on salary increases. If your immediate superior shows signs of stress from personal or business problems, wait until that situation changes, as it almost certainly will.

30. Once employed, budget a fixed part of your income for clothes and personal grooming. Keep fit; avoid gaining weight.

31. Despite the difficulty, try to save some of what you earn to give you short-term independence and long-term security. Ideally, you should have enough reserves to leave a bad sales career situation before it affects you negatively. But remember, it is always easier to find a new job when you have one than when you are unemployed. One of the advantages of being a salesperson is that you can look around for a new job with relative ease.

32. Develop your own personal policy of standards and goals; keep upgrading them as you get older and, it is hoped, wiser.

33. Make a commitment to being dependable. Do not make promises unless you are sure you can deliver. If you make a commitment and later realize that you cannot deliver at all or not on time, tell the person and give the reasons.

34. Be prepared to whatever degree that is possible, but do not let yourself be thrown off balance by the unexpected. Do not let your impulses run wild. Take a few seconds before reacting to anything that appears to be hostile or offensive.

35. Be a really good listener. These suggestions will help if you make them part of your listening policy:

   a. Keep your emotions in control as you listen.

   b. Keep your mind clear and respond to what the speaker is actually saying to you.

   c. Avoid distraction and eye movements away from the speaker.

   d. If the speaker uses numbers to make points, try to remember them in the same sequence.

   e. If the circumstance indicates that you should make notes, ask if the speaker has any objections.

   f. Remember that the reason you are listening is to learn something that will help you make a sale this time or on a subsequent call.

   g. When the speaker is finished, you are well within your rights to repeat in your own words what the speaker said. Misunderstandings can be avoided that way.

36. Sit up front in meetings and conferences. If the speaker did a particularly effective job, go up after the speech and congratulate him or her.

37. Praise others when their appearance, actions, or words merit sincere kudos.

38. Grudges are for spoiled children. If you find that you cannot reconcile differences with others, avoid them.

39. Avoid jealousy for the corrosive sickness it really is. Generosity is the antidote to jealousy.

40. Do not automatically reject criticism; there may be something to be learned from it.

41. When you are paid a compliment, don't "ham it up"; just say, "thank you."

42. Get in the habit of using positive, affirmative language.

43. Make a point of walking more erectly and at a good pace. As you get older, do stretches and bends and other exercises to keep the muscles in the backs of the legs stretched and strong. The first sign of an aging person is a stiff-legged walk.

44. If you have been forced to sit still for some time in a meeting or conference, get your circulation going normally by doing some discrete warm-up exercises.

45. Do not let disadvantages (ethnic, economic, or other) blind you to the bright prospects of a career in selling. Whatever your background, be on guard against feelings of resentment or mistrust of colleagues, clients, and prospects. Such feelings almost inevitably will reveal themselves as an edge of anger in the voice, less than businesslike behavior, a look in the eye, and so on. Just as inevitably, the other person will react negatively to these projected feelings. Seek to come to terms with these feelings in yourself; try looking upon your career and your contacts with individuals from differing backgrounds as an opportunity to learn more about them and yourself and to achieve your goals.

46. If you are a woman in what has been a man's world, be tolerant of the initial reaction of some of the salesmen who may act like idiots for a time. Study the developing situation and speak up for your rights if you think they are being threatened. Women do very well in selling. There are also an increasing number of women buyers, so friendly, supportive relationships can often develop.

47. Give thanks every day that you live in a country that, despite its flaws, has the best system of government in the world for a large, very populous country. There may be times when you think our country is committing suicide, but remember that the

competitive enterprise system is still a modern miracle, despite some abuses resulting primarily from greed. As long as the great majority strive to improve it by working within the system, there is hope.

SECTION 6
PUBLIC RELATIONS

CHAPTER 18

What Is Public Relations?

Public relations did not start in 1946, as some people claim. It goes back as far as human communication.

The Romans had their Plutarch; Alexander the Great, his Aristotle. The beliefs of Jesus of Nazareth would have remained confined to the small country of his birth had not St. Paul determined to spread his message.

In England, The Plantagenets, The Tudors, The Stuarts—all had their official "historians" who presented facts to suit the interests of the ruling family. Without a doubt, the greatest public relations man of his time was William Shakespeare. His completely distorted picture of Richard III, for instance, was created to please Elizabeth I, his monarch and sponsor, whose grandfather, Henry VII, had usurped Richard's throne. Today, only professional historians realize that Richard was not a cripple or a villain, that there is no evidence that he had his nephews or anyone else murdered, and that, had he lived, he would probably have been one of the greatest of

England's kings. The rest of us believe the picture that the skilled publicist Shakespeare created.

England was not unique. Richelieu in France, all the popes and Holy Roman Emperors, and the other rulers of the Middle Ages had their court historians and publicists. Many a throne was lost not to the sword, but to the broadside, gossip, and rumor.

Public relations in the United States started with George Washington. Whenever he wrote a letter he made sure that copies were sent to the local papers. Abraham Lincoln did the same. The people who helped Washington, Lincoln, and the presidents in between to get their words into print were not called press secretaries or officers, they were called administrative assistants. But, basically, they were doing a public relations job.

The first publication devoted to public relations that we have discovered was called *Persuasion,* and it was published in England in 1919.

The actual beginnings of modern public relations in this country might well be traced to World War I and a book by Walter Lippmann entitled *Public Opinion,*[1] which lays down the basics of what we now know as the public relations profession.

George Creel was the first actual full-time propagandist for the U.S. government. He was in charge of public information during World War I. When it was over, he, Edward Bernays, and other pioneers who had cut their teeth in government service set up their own agencies. They had limited media with which to work and called themselves "counselors," advising their clients on how to get their names into the papers and how to change their public images. The classic examples, of course, are the publicity stunts Ivy Lee pulled off on behalf of old John D. Rockefeller to make him more "lovable." Lee's classic, of course, was to have John D. distribute dimes to crowds whenever he appeared. This not only implied generosity in those depression days, it also guaranteed him a cheering mob wherever he went.

---

[1] Walter Lippmann, *Public Opinion* (New York: Free Pr., a division of Macmillan Publishing Co., 1965).

During the first decades of the twentieth century, the railroads and utilities ran wild, casually stomping on the rights of the American people. They hired publicists to make their outlaw tactics palatable. Those of us in the profession today would like to forget that many of these early practitioners bought publicity in newspapers by buying newspapermen. We'd like to forget it, but it is a fact. When Samuel Insull, a power company executive, fled to Europe to avoid prosecution, it was revealed that he had more than 50 newspapermen in his home state of Illinois on his payroll.

It is almost unnecessary to point out that this could not happen today. The safeguards built into every newspaper and radio or television network make it impossible for a single reporter, or indeed any group of reporters, to plant false information deliberately. Editors, managing editors, publishers, and copy editors are all involved in the final news product. But the line between news and entertainment has been too often crossed in television. The recent NBC/General Motors controversy was shocking. Trucks were rigged with devices to make sure there were gasoline explosions and fires for the television viewing audiences. The head of NBC News Department was fired because it happened "on his watch."

In addition, the public relations profession has so monitored itself through the Public Relations Society of America, publicity clubs in various cities, and other organizations that a dishonest practitioner would be quickly exposed.

The pattern of today's public relations began to evolve during World War II with the appointment of Stephen Early as press secretary to President Roosevelt. The creation of the Office of War Information headed by Elmer Davis was another step. Into it were drawn some of the finest writers in the country. The war spawned many of the deans of the public relations profession. They left the service with a relatively new and marketable skill, opened agencies, and went to work for corporations.

There is little relationship between the naive practice of the 1930s and the complicated, sophisticated public relations business of the 1990s. On the scene now are public relations agencies that offer total services; counselors who sit on the boards of directors and do nothing but advise; corporations with staffs of hundreds of public relations people; and advertising agencies with public relations departments or subsidiaries. There are experts in financial public relations, product publicity, media placement, fashion and technical writing, and perhaps a hundred other specialties.

But all this skilled and competent work force has a single objective—the same objective George Washington had when he sent copies of his letters to the local newspapers. Public relations then was as it is now: *the total communications effort of a person, a company, an agency, a group, a government, or any organization to its various publics.*

There are as many definitions of public relations as there are people who follow the craft. Almost everyone has a version, and most of them are incomplete. Perhaps, then, it might be profitable to start by outlining what public relations is not.

Public relations is not advertising. Although this is one of the most prevalent misconceptions about the field, it often uses advertising as a tool; in fact, a public relations campaign is almost always coordinated with an advertising program. But it is not "paid-for" space and time that you buy in newspapers, magazines, on radio or television.

Public relations is not publicity. It is not getting your name in the paper or on radio or television. Publicity is generally an important and essential element of public relations, but it is always just one part of the whole. It is true, however, that getting unpaid editorial space or time in the media is a primary objective of most public relations programs.

Public relations is not sales promotion, point-of-sale displays, contests, speeches, personal appearances, membership in organizations or, for that matter, any single isolated thing. A public relations program involves all these and more, but it is larger than the sum of its parts. These are some of the tools that public relations uses, but they do not define the general term. What, then, is public relations?

When a customer deals with any member of your organization and is satisfied, that is good public relations. When your appearance and knowledge make a favorable impression on anyone in your community or in your industry or in the media, that is good public relations. When you contribute your time and effort to a worthy cause, that is good public relations. In short, any contact you have with another human being is part of public relations—your personal total communication effort.

The purpose of this book is to suggest ways that a communications program can be made more effective, ways in which you can better use tools and opportunities now at your disposal and develop new ones, and ways in which your individual activities can reinforce the entire program of your company or organization.

▪ MANY PUBLICS

Any person or organization planning a public relations program must analyze the various "publics" upon which it depends and that it must influence.

For the purposes of this book, we will presume that you are a line public relations executive for a division of a publicly held company that has a corporate public relations department with which you can cooperate. The principles and techniques we discuss should have validity for you no matter what your specific situation.

Who are the publics of such a publicly held company that manufactures products for industrial and/or consumer use? To what groups must we direct our communications? There are many:

❏ The Ultimate Consumers

How do they break down demographically in terms of age, income level, geographic locations, and so forth? You must identify your public before you can design a program to reach it. Appealing to the teenage market with a product for senior citizens would be pointless. It might be possible to sell refrigerators to Eskimos, but there are easier ways to make a living.

❏ The Shareholders

If you expect your company's securities to enjoy a good market, you must certainly keep the holders of those securities informed and confident. How many stockholders are there? Where do they live? How many shares of stock do they own? All these factors will influence the ways in which they might best be approached.

❑ The Investment Community

This includes security analysts, brokers, bankers, investment bankers, and so on. These people must be familiar with the company and its management so they can support it in the marketplace and recommend it as a sound corporation.

❑ The Primary Consumer

These are the wholesalers, retailers, jobbers, builders, and others who are the primary customers for the company's products and who make the initial purchase. The ultimate consumer will never see these products unless the "middlemen" are confident of their profitability and reliability.

❑ The Communities

The communities are those in which the company has factories, offices, or other installations. A reputation as a good corporate citizen is vital to the well-being of any firm. Opposition from misinformed special interest groups, local officials, or other concerned citizens can be a major problem. Open, effective communication is crucial for developing a mutual understanding of the needs and goals of both the company and the communities in which it operates.

❑ The Company Suppliers

They are important to the company's existence. Building mutual trust and a feeling of interdependence with your company's suppliers is essential for a smooth, profitable business life.

❑ The Media and Other Opinion Molders

The various media must be prime targets of any complete public relations effort, for they are the conduit through which the company's story will flow to all its other publics. They require—and deserve—intensive cultivation and attention.

❑ Government Agencies

Government bodies on all levels—federal, state, and local—must be sympathetic to the company's goals and activities because, whether we like it or not, they can have a profound influence on the firm's success.

❑ The General Public

This large, nebulous, indefinable mass includes all the foregoing. It involves the complete environment in which the company exists. Ultimately, the general public holds in its hands the power to determine the success or failure of the company. It is the master.

These are some of the publics to which our fictitious company must tailor its public relations program.

The next logical question: Why bother? Why must any company communicate with these publics? Why can't it just go about its business and ignore them? It can, of course. Thousands of bankrupt companies attest to this possibility.

■ WHY IS THERE A NEED FOR PUBLIC RELATIONS AND WHAT DOES IT ACCOMPLISH?

An essential step in creating a public relations program, then, is the clarification of objectives. In other words, what does a company hope to accomplish through this effort?

1. *To improve sales.* This is a prerequisite for a healthy company.

2. *To increase earnings.* Companies are in business to make money. (There are other reasons, but this one is primary and basic to corporate existence.)

3. *To broaden the base of ownership of the company's securities and to assure the proper valuation in the marketplace.* The shareholder and the financial community as a whole will support excellent performance if they are told about it clearly and professionally.

There are many barometers used to measure the effectiveness of public relations and publicity. The price of a public company's securities on either of the major stock exchanges ranks very high on this list. Corporate managements have risen and fallen with stock prices or price-earnings ratios.

One pointed example is in the field of commercial broadcasting in the P/E ratio game. RCA's stock price theoretically relates to a composite of the earnings of many divisions of this gigantic corporation. However, when NBC, which is owned by RCA, slipped from first place in the television network ratings into second, RCA stock price was inordinately affected. When NBC slipped further, into third place, the RCA stock dipped again in actual value and its P/E ratio dropped as well.

So stockholder and financial community relations must command the attention of the public relations and publicity practitioner.

4. *To convey the company's message to the community.* This is particularly important since the community can have an impact in the critical areas of environment, employment, taxes, and so forth.

5. *To secure for the company a respected position in its parent industry.* People enjoy doing business with a "winner." Since this program is built on performance, the public relations story must convey the company's expertise, past successes, future potential, and general strength and reliability.

6. *To establish, maintain, and constantly reinforce the company's relationship with all segments of the media.* Defining publics, determining objectives, and deciding how best to tell the story are all basic to the program. However, they accomplish nothing by themselves. They must be translated into action. The predetermined messages must be conveyed to the selected audiences to achieve the desired objectives. The media are of primary importance in accomplishing this task.

CHAPTER 19

The Elements of a Public Relations Program: The Media

The successful use of the media is key to any public relations effort. In this chapter we will discuss the elements of a public relations program, focusing on the media, both print and electronic, and on the all-important press conference.

■ ADVERTISING

Advertising offers several advantages. It tells the company's story directly and in precisely the way that is desired. The advertiser, within certain limitations imposed by law and good taste, has complete control of content. And, since space is purchased, the message always appears at the desired time and in the chosen media.

Advertising does, however, have two major limitations: it is expensive, which tends to inhibit its use, and no matter how well it is put together, it bears the stigma of self-interest. The most naive of readers, viewers, or listeners is aware that an ad is telling the story from the point of view of the advertiser. It is impossible to claim objectivity.

This is not meant to denigrate the effectiveness of advertising. Its success stories are too numerous. But it is important to recognize the limitations of our tools so that they can be used for the greatest effect.

■ PUBLICITY AND MEDIA RELATIONS

Publicity is any print space or air time that the company obtains in the editorial segment of the media without payment. Publicity is valuable, of course, only if it reflects favorably on the company and is consistent with its self-image. The old adage "I don't care what they say about me as long as they spell my name right" still might be valid for circus performers and politicians, but it is long out of date for business organizations.

Knowing your local media people will not guarantee you a story if your material doesn't warrant one. If they are good reporters—and many are—nothing will do that. But establishing a consistent relationship with local media, based on reliability and truthfulness, will assure that your ideas get a fair hearing. Many reporters and editors, once they come to rely on you and trust you, may suggest that a story might interest them if you could develop another approach. When this happens, you know you have established excellent media relations.

These suggestions are important, but there are two hard and fast interrelated principles that must never be violated when you are dealing with the media. They are:

Always tell the truth.

Never say anything to a media person, anywhere, at any time, on any subject that is "off the record."

The first principle appears to be simple, but sometimes, it is not. If you are not authorized to impart certain information, admit it. If, for example, you are asked a question concerning corporate policy or finances, do not give the classic "no comment" answer that newspeople hate. Inform them that it does not fall into your area and that you will have someone from corporate public relations call them. If you are asked an esoteric question in your own field that you cannot answer, again, admit it. However, assure the reporter that you will be happy to get the requested information and, of course, do so.

As for the second principle, this applies no matter how close a friend or good a contact the media representative is. Telling a reporter something "off the record" puts him or her in an uncomfortable position of conflict between loyalty to you and the concept of the public's "right to know." If you don't want to see it in print or hear it on the air, don't say it.

▪ A NOSE FOR NEWS

We cannot proceed to the more detailed discussion of the media without considering the need for developing the ability to recognize news, the basis of much of the public relations effort.

Newsworthy events occur in any organization. The big stories are obvious: a major change affecting many people, a new discovery, an expansion plan, the construction of a plant—activities such as these deserve public attention. But these are not the only newsworthy items. Many a news story has been published because an alert executive recognized its worth when no one else in the organization was aware of its interest or timeliness.

You must constantly look for news. You must develop a sense of what news is and which media will use it. You must be aware that an item might be old to you and to your organization but new to the readers of some publication.

Consider the following: More than 1 million corporate news stories produced by 16 billion-dollar companies were analyzed by computer and broken down by categories as follows:

34.5%	Product publicity
28.9%	"Growth" stories (increased earnings and sales, merger and acquisitions, expansion, and so forth)

7.8%	General marketing activity
7.6%	Corporate social concern
2.8%	Negative news (sales and earnings off, strikes, employment down, and so forth)

This leaves a little less than 19 percent for miscellaneous stories. Your company will get its fair share of the first four categories if you function properly. The additional space, almost 19 percent, is up for grabs. It must be obtained with your imagination and your ability to communicate. Your ability to find the news will get your company a piece of that space.

Remember, if you think something is a story, then it may well be. If you think you have a great idea, you just may have one. Be a mental miser. Throw away nothing that is in any way creative.

■ A GENERAL SURVEY OF THE MEDIA

Dealing with the media is a complex subject. The first, and most important, step is to identify the media that will be targeted by your program. If you do not already have them, prepare lists of:

1. The electronic media

2. The daily press

3. The wire services

4. The business news wires

5. Trade papers

6. Magazines

7. Weeklies, shoppers, club papers

8. Feature services

❏ The Electronic Media

The late Marshall McLuhan became rich by writing books that proclaimed that nobody reads anymore. While this is an extreme claim, it is true that television and radio have certainly become a vital element of any communications program. Incorporating them into the program can be a complicated process. The first step, however, is locating them in your area.

Begin with the local affiliates of the four major networks. While you may seldom have news or features of interest to a national network, these channels and stations function, much of the time, as local outlets. Add to this list the independent television (including cable) and radio stations. Their "call letters" can be found in your area's telephone directories. Use the phone, once again, to find out the names of the assignment editors, news editors, and producers of local interview and talk shows. There will be additional broadcasters you will want to contact with specific stories, but your basic electronic media list will include these people.

Realistically, the proliferation of radio stations and the differences in organization of various television channels might make these lists more difficult to assemble. There are, however, excellent reference directories available.

❏ The Daily Press

List all the dailies in your "affect community." This may include papers in neighboring cities and states and, conceivably, as far afield as New York, Chicago, and Los Angeles, if your activities affect those areas. Having the addresses of newspapers is not enough. You should list the names of business editors, reporters covering your industry, new products people, and others who might be interested in news from your company. Directing your material to the right person has a lot to do with whether or not it will be used. This may seem a monumental task, but, really, it is not. Usually, one phone call to each paper will accomplish your purpose. Remember, newspapers need your material and generally will cooperate to see that it reaches the correct person. Before you make your call, write out your questions. When you call the paper, identify yourself and your company and indicate the kind of information you require. When you are asking questions about the source, be brief and concise. After you get your information, if the person on the other end seems interested, discuss your needs with him or her but be aware of the limits on the time of a working newspaper person. Try to avoid calling when the reporters are on a deadline. For morning newspapers, the deadline is usually late afternoon of the previous day for the early editions and early evening for the final editions. With afternoon papers, the deadline is generally early evening for the final editions. With afternoon papers, the deadline is generally early evening of the previous day for the first editions and later in the night of the previous day or early in the morning of the same day for finals. These deadlines apply to the kind of material you will usually supply. Late-breaking, immediately important hard news will be accepted whenever it comes in. These are general rules. You will have to obtain the specific deadlines of the papers you contact.

There will be two general categories of material you will be distributing to your daily press list: such information as appointments, openings, moves, new products, plant expansions, and so forth is not exclusive. That is, you are not promising any publication that it will have the story to the exclusion of all others. These releases should be distributed to your entire media list. However, when sending material to more than one person on the same publication, note on the release the names of others who have received it to avoid confusion.

You should attempt to establish a distribution schedule which ensures that all publications receive the release simultaneously, taking into account deadlines and time for delivery.

Generally speaking, it is preferable to distribute news releases on Monday, Tuesday, or Wednesday, since this gives the editor the option, if he receives it on a heavy news day, of holding the material without running into the weekend.

❑ The Wire Services

These are the two giant wires that supply news to thousands of newspapers, electronic media, and publications throughout the world. Start by finding out if there are AP (Associated Press) and UPI (United Press International) bureaus in your city. If not, the bureau in the nearest larger city will usually be responsible for covering your unit's activities. Call and get the name of the person to contact should the need arise. You will discover that except for the major bureaus (New York, Washington, D.C., Chicago, and so forth), there is less departmentalization on the wire services than in the daily press. Your AP list, for example, might consist of just one person to whom all material should be sent.

❑ The Business News Wires

The Dow-Jones and Reuters financial news wires are interested primarily in business news. Their wires go to investment houses, brokerages, banks, and other members of the financial community as well as to media. Generally, contact with them will be restricted to corporate public relations, if your company has such a department, but there might be times when you wish to contact them, with the approval of your corporate office. Once again, use the telephone to determine the bureau nearest you and the person or persons most interested in your material.

❑ Trade Papers and Magazines

In preparing your list of trade publications, it is important to remember that what your customer or potential customer reads is more important to you than what you yourself may prefer to read. This list should include the publications of your own industry, of course, but it should also contain the papers and magazines of your customers' business. For instance, if you sell to the auto repair industry, its publication should be on the list. Just about every industry—from hardware, do-it-yourself, interior decorating, home repair and remodeling, office supply and design, to any one of the dozens of other industries—has one or more trade publications. Analyze any customer and potential customer lists available to you and from them create your trade publications master list. Structure the list for use in whole or in part, as the news warrants.

❑ Magazines

General interest national magazines are usually either staff written or will accept contributions only from well-known free-lance writers or from literary agents. For the most part they will not consider unsolicited material but will, occasionally, follow up on ideas suggested to them. When you think that you might have such a story, attempt to develop specific approaches suitable for a particular publication. Regional and special interest books will sometimes accept contributed material. To the greatest extent possible, familiarize yourself with those in your "affect community" area and with those interested in your field of activity.

The news gathering structure of news magazines such as *Time, Newsweek, U.S. News & World Report,* and others is very much like that of a major daily newspaper. These weeklies have offices in principal cities around the nation. Find out where their closest offices are. While all their material is staff written, they do appreciate tips, leads, or story ideas and frequently seek help from organizations involved in the field with which their story is concerned. In addition to the address of the magazine, list the editor or reporters who cover your business.

❑ Weeklies, Shoppers, Club Papers

Wherever you live and do business there are weekly newspapers and "shoppers." The latter are mainly advertising vehicles for local merchants. These papers, of course, have much smaller readerships than dailies, but they often have loyal readerships with money to spend. These papers are usually hungry for material. Since you are interested in results, not prestige, they deserve your attention.

Use the Yellow Pages in your area to draw up a list of these publications and find out the names of the editors. In most cases, he or she will be the reporter as well, and therefore, the correct contact for any kind of story.

Many organizations in your community will also produce their own publications, and many of them use general interest material. Large corporations with external publications, church groups, fraternal organizations, men's and women's clubs, and many other organizations may offer possibilities for placing stories. Get as many of these as you can from the Yellow Pages and other sources.

❑ Feature Services

On a smaller scale than the AP and UPI, there are a number of services that distribute feature material to publications throughout the country. They may be useful to you since they are not interested in hard news but are receptive to "how-to" human interest, industry trend, and changing life-style stories. Since these services are national, lists of them are available in publicity directories.

▪ PLACEMENT SERVICES

Over the years, different service organizations have grown up to aid in the placement of material in the media. These include the following:

❏ Public Relations News Wires

They teletype your material to newspapers, radio and television stations, trade magazines, and press associations, using their own leased wires.

❏ Mat Services (or Feature Syndicates or News and Picture Services)

They will put your stories and pictures on mats for reproduction onto letterpress or "slicks" for offset use and distribute them to an agreed-upon number of publications.

❏ Public Relations Mailing Houses

They will send your material to general or specialized lists in categories that you select.

All these services, and some that we have not listed, have one thing in common—they charge a fee. We would suggest, generally, that you avoid using them simply because we believe you can do the job better yourself for less money. There might, however, be specific situations where time or other factors indicate that using one of these aids might be advantageous. Such services are usually listed in the

Yellow Pages and will be happy to send you price lists and other information.

Taken together, all these elements make up your media public.

Now it is important to discuss methods and techniques for using the various media sectors that we have identified and that you have listed.

■ FEATURES

For our purposes, we designate all stories that are not hard news as features. This also includes editorial interviews, with which we will deal in a separate discussion.

Every publication offers innumerable opportunities for feature placement. You should read and understand the specific needs and areas of interest, not only of each publication but also of any of its departments that may relate to your program.

If, for example, your company manufactures building products, then the real estate editor, the financial and business departments, the editors and reporters responsible for construction, science, the environment, how-to stories, and general features might all be markets for stories you have to sell—each from a different point of view.

You may not be a skilled writer. You probably do not have professional newspaper experience, but you will not need it, since most papers are mainly staff written. Instead, you are going to suggest the idea, offer to provide the background material, and aid the reporter in putting the story together.

Experience has demonstrated that the best way to do this is through a "pitch letter" to the appropriate editor. This letter should outline the story you are suggesting and list the background material you have available, the names of people you can provide for interviews, and all other pertinent material.

Give the editor a reasonable length of time to consider your suggestion—two or three days—and then call to discuss it. If he tells you he is considering the story, ask when you might call again. *Do not become a pest.* Do not invent reasons to call.

A feature suggestion is exclusive. This means that you are promising the editor you will suggest the story to no one else until you hear from him. After a reasonable length of time—perhaps a week—it is perfectly logical for you to call and request a final decision. If he rejects the idea, you are, of course, free to send your story idea elsewhere. If he stalls, you must determine if it seems profitable to wait any longer. If it doesn't, inform him politely that you intend to seek another placement opportunity.

Once a story has been used, it can be reworked and placed again by approaching the basic material from a different angle.

For example, suppose a business editor has used your story on the importance of the do-it-yourself market to the construction industry. (We are still presuming you are in that business.) You have arranged an interview with one of your financial executives to ensure mention of your company's name in the story.

After the story appears, you might rearrange the material, delete some figures, and change the focus of the piece to emphasize trends in the do-it-yourself movement—what people used to do at home and what they are doing now, how inflation has sent Americans back to their workbenches, and so on. You now have a new story to "pitch" to the do-it-yourself or general features editor of another newspaper, this time offering a different knowledgeable company executive to be interviewed. A good idea is hard to find. Get all the mileage you can out of it.

Whether you are dealing with hard news or features, it is wise to remember that the most important reality of a newsperson's life is the deadline. Promised material must arrive on time, even if you have to hire a messenger or deliver it personally. Answer a reporter's calls promptly—he or she might be working on a story. When you send out a news release or suggest a feature to a newspaper person, try to be available at all times. If you are out of the office and there is no one else who can answer important questions, emphasize to your employees and/or coworkers that this is top priority and that you are to be contacted if at all humanly possible. It is by exerting this kind of extra effort that close media relations are built.

One of the most successful financial relations people in highly competitive New York City has given his home telephone number to every newspaper person with whom he has contact, in the event they might need him after he has left the office. His dinner is frequently interrupted and he's been awakened late at night once or twice, but he enjoys better relations with the press than any other public relations practitioner in the entire city.

A small but welcome gesture is to show your appreciation when a story or press release is used. A phone call or short note is sufficient. Do not thank the reporter. He does not feel that he has used the material as a favor to you. Simply compliment him on the accuracy and interest of the story.

▪ THE EDITORIAL INTERVIEW

Within your total program you may be setting up interviews with many media—magazines, wire services, financial wires, radio, and television. But since you will be arranging interviews most frequently with the daily press, that is what we will discuss here.

A reporter might request an interview with you or one of your fellow executives or you yourself might suggest it. Guidelines should be established at the time the interview is arranged. There should be agreement on which areas the person being interviewed is equipped and willing to discuss. There are the so-called ground rules. The reporter will occasionally "go fishing," asking questions outside the established boundaries. You are entitled to remind him, politely, of the agreement and, if possible, to suggest other sources for the information he requires.

Let us presume that you, as the public relations person for your company, are the one being interviewed. Keep the following guidelines in mind (or, if the interviewee is another executive, simply make sure that he or she follows these procedures):

1. Do your homework. Be familiar with the publication for which the reporter works. Read some of his by-line stories, if they are available. Bring along all possible backup material to substantiate any statements you make.

2. Be friendly and natural even if you have never met the reporter before. You are peers talking for your mutual benefit.

3. Keep the subject of the interview in mind and get to it as quickly as possible. Make your points concisely. If the reporter wants greater detail, he will ask for it.

4. Make sure the approach is always "low key." Do not emphasize your company unless the interview is primarily concerned with it. If you have agreed to talk about the industry, for instance, do so. You are not buying ad space. Company credits will develop naturally.

5. Do not be surprised by what seems to be a naive question. The reporter may be putting himself in the position of the uninformed reader, requesting a basic, simple answer.

6. Be ready to back up any statement with facts.

7. Be aware of the reporter's specific areas of interest.

8. If you don't know an answer, admit it. Offer to get the information if that is possible. If it is not, tell the reporter so. Above all, don't bluff. You are not expected to be the world's greatest expert.

9. If you promise to provide information, deliver it as quickly as possible. (Deadline!)

10. When you have nothing more to say, stop talking. You have no obligation to keep the conversation going. If the reporter wants any further information, he'll ask for it.

11. Never ask the reporter if he is going to use the story. The decision is not his. He must submit it to an editor who will make the final judgment based on the news load that day, similar stories he may have published recently, the material's immediacy, and innumerable other factors. Simply thank the reporter and assure him of your continued cooperation, should it be required.

12. *Never ask to see a story before it is printed.* On many publications, if the reporter were to agree he would lose his job. Should a newspaper person ever ask you to check a story for accuracy, do just that. Make no comment on the editorial approach. The press is extremely jealous of its independence.

13. And, finally, to repeat one of our basic principles, never say anything to a media person "off the record."

These basic precepts apply whenever you are interviewed, no matter which of the media the questioner represents.

▪ PHOTOGRAPHY

The factors that govern photos for the daily press are essentially true for all print media. You should have some knowledge of when and how to use them. A good photograph will often "sell" a marginal story. Many local papers have an overload of written material but a real need for artwork to break up the layout and add interest. But photos cost money and should be used judiciously. It is preferable, of course, to get a commitment from a specific editor in advance. It is possible that he will not have a staff photographer available to cover an event but will indicate, nevertheless, that he could use a photo, if it is good and is supplied to him. Getting the photo, then, will be up to you.

Once having decided to take pictures, you should carefully consider which photographer to hire. Many people working for local papers do free-lance work on the side. Retaining such a person has distinct advantages. He or she comes to the assignment with knowledge of the kinds of photos a newspaper uses. If the photographer offers advice on setting up the picture, you should welcome it. If your local paper has a staff photographer who does free-lance work, the photo editor will usually be happy to furnish you with this information. The Associated Press and United Press International have commercial photo departments in many cities. These people, too, are experienced news photographers. Their fees will usually be a little higher than local fees because the service itself must make a profit.

If this kind of help is unavailable, find out if any of the commercial photographers in town have news experience. Hire one who lives nearby, since you don't want to pay extensive travel expenses, and supervise him carefully.

Remember that you are not creating a work of art; you are taking a news photo. There are several simple rules to keep in mind:

1. Be aware that the best pictures portray action.

2. Be sure they are in sharp focus or they will not reproduce well.

3. Always take at least two shots of each setup, but three or four are preferable. Once you have hired a photographer, the additional cost will be negligible.

4. If you are going to service more than one publication, come up with a different shot for each one, even if you simply alter the pose, the background, and some of the people involved.

5. Whenever possible, take photos close up.

6. Remember that anything or anybody in the shot should be visible and in focus.

7. If you use objects, try to select light-colored ones. Dark ones will often lose detail or disappear into the background.

8. Avoid deadpan shots and overposing. Try to show some emotion and a casual appearance. Once you have decided what you want, the photographer is in charge of the picture. Let him place and pose the people.

9. Try not to put more than three people in a picture; two, if possible, would be preferable. Group shots are a waste of time and money. They will not be used.

10. Take a picture you would be interested in seeing.

After the photo session is over, have the pictures developed quickly (within an hour or two if possible) as 8- by 10-inch glossy prints. Make sure they are underdeveloped rather than overdeveloped. Newspaper reproduction will darken them. Make sure that a "cut line" or caption is *pasted* to the back of the picture, which details the event, the people in the picture (from left to right), and all other pertinent data. Do this even if the picture is included with a story or release. In a busy newspaper office, the two items might easily be separated. Never write on the back of a photo.

Most important, remember that a news photo is just that—news. Get it to the paper more quickly than seems humanly possible. This might entail pushing the photographer (who will automatically tell you, "it can't be done in that amount of time") and having someone wait in his studio while the pictures are developed, with the captions, paste pot, and releases in hand, ready to assemble the package and run it over to the paper. The closer to the actual event you can get the photo to the editor, the better the chance of its being used.

Finally, never send a paper a picture that you know is bad.

Sometimes, despite all your efforts, you just do not get usable shots. If you have promised pictures to an editor, call him and tell him the truth, or reshoot if you have the time. The editor will realize that you are knowledgeable and that you would rather lose a placement than provide inadequate material.

CHAPTER 20

The Elements of a Public Relations Program: The Community

We have noted the importance, to any company, of the communities in which it operates and the public relations program that affects those communities. This chapter examines in detail various techniques for developing positive and useful community-company relationships.

■ DEFINING YOUR "AFFECT COMMUNITY"

As this point in your public relations program you need to determine the confines and components of the community, or communities, in which you do business.

The community includes all people and organizations affected by, or who can affect, your company because of its geographic location. Your community may include employees, shareholders, customers, suppliers, and others with whom you have some direct relationship. But it includes also a great many more people with whom you have no direct involvement.

If you are a giant corporation, your community includes all the people in your plant cities and, to a lesser degree, most of the people in the United States. If you are multinational, your community will be worldwide.

Your particular community is probably more limited. It cannot, however, be determined by simple physical boundaries. It is more than a neighborhood, city, region, or state. It extends just as far as the effects of your actions reach.

For example, a company that pollutes the streams and waterways may affect people who live in the neighboring state or the one beyond that. Those people become part of the company's "affect community."

Make sure you are aware of your community's specific problems, its interests, its economic situation, its political position, and its special emotional attitudes.

Community complaints are seldom directed to the company that is considered guilty. One person will, generally, complain to another, and the dissatisfaction will grow and snowball while the company is still unaware of it. To prevent this from happening, you must understand your community and its needs and concerns, and address those concerns before the relationship is jeopardized.

Start by listing organizations and individuals with whom you wish to maintain a dialogue. In preparing such lists, include:

- Opinion leaders
- Groups and individuals who possess economic power
- Significant politicians and political organizations
- Environmental groups
- Churches, synagogues, and other religious bodies
- Civic and fraternal organizations
- Cultural institutions
- Trade, labor, and business organizations

- All other groups and people who appear to have influence in molding community attitudes

This will be your work list for community action.

■ TOTAL COMMUNITY RELATIONS

There are some general guidelines for good community relations. There must be a corporate sensitivity to issues that concern the community such as noise levels, pollution control, and the appearance of an installation and its environs.

The company should make an effort to keep local and regional government agencies apprised of the company's activities and sympathetic to its objectives.

Community participation in events such as plant openings and tours can create a feeling of friendship and involvement. Most important, information regarding all positive aspects of the company's performance must be communicated continuously to the targeted public—in this case, the people who live in the area. The company is of real significance to the economic well-being of the towns, cities, localities, and states in which it operates. It employs people, pays taxes, represents buying power, and is, in many ways, a key element in maintaining the desired life-style. These contributions must be made clear to the citizens on a consistent basis in a forceful and intelligent manner.

In no facet of your program is it truer that public relations is good performance, publicly appreciated. We must, therefore, discuss two phases of this segment of the work—performance and the reporting of that performance—in order to win the desired appreciation.

These are some of the basic elements of good community relations performance:

1. A regard for the appearance of your unit. It should be clean and attractive and fit into the surrounding area in a way that is as aesthetically pleasing as possible.

2. An awareness of pollutants that your unit might be releasing into the air or water supply and a concentrated effort to eliminate such emissions.

3. A similar awareness of noise and odor problems and a vigorous attempt to control them.

4. A concentrated effort to adjust to the community's traffic patterns without disrupting them.

5. An involvement in all reasonable projects to protect and conserve the natural resources and ambiance of the area.

6. A quick, courteous, and concerned handling of all complaints from the community. No matter how unfair they may appear, regardless of your inability to act in certain circumstances, every complaint should be addressed individually and answered thoroughly and sincerely.

7. Maintenance of working conditions within your unit on a level that will assure the approval of the entire community.

8. Participation in community service activities (discussed later in this chapter).

9. An effort to purchase materials and supplies on a local level. This should be discussed with company headquarters.

All these elements will achieve only minimum results unless you have made your community aware of them. This communication can take several forms.

❑ Community Involvement

Invite your unit's neighbors to plant openings; organize tours of the various facilities for church, school, and other groups; initiate periodic "open houses" where community members and your unit's executives can exchange ideas on mutual problems (and, ideally, satisfactions); investigate the possibility of hosting parties on occasions of particular significance to the area, such as the anniversary of a city's founding.

❑ Media Activities

As we have seen, an effective placement program in the local media will be of great significance in communicating with your community. In all material emanating from your unit, the feelings, sensitivities, opinions, and concerns of your community should be considered.

❑ Direct Communication

By using the list of leaders and organizations that you have compiled, you will establish direct communication with your community. You should send to all the people on this list copies of all pertinent news releases, corporate financial messages, invitations, announcements, and specifically designed material when the need arises. Every effort should be made to establish dialogue between your unit and these organizations and individuals. You should also solicit replies to your communications. Only in this way will you be made aware of problems early enough to solve them with minimum disruption of relationships.

Another important element should be mentioned in this section. Since local, regional, and federal government agencies in your area are important members of your "affect community," you must be concerned with them as well. This is obviously a sensitive area. Except under unusual circumstances, your communications with government personnel should be confined to the regular mailing of company-approved material to the list of such people and agencies that you have already compiled. If special information is requested or particular problems surface, corporate headquarters should be consulted first. Policy decisions might be involved, and those are made by the offices of the chairman and the president.

❑ Open Houses, Dedications, and Tours

Open houses can have a variety of specific purposes: to display a new installation; to observe some special occasion, such as an anniversary or a significant production or safety achievement; to participate in some local civic celebration; or to officially dedicate new facilities or equipment. An open house may be scheduled purely for the benefits to be derived. The results—and the problems—are the same.

The facility should be given every possible preparation to make it attractive, clean, and convenient for the guests. Displays should be arranged and signs erected to designate tour routes. Special guides should be selected and instructed. Refreshments may be served and literature and/or souvenirs distributed. Invitations may be extended to the public-at-large, to special groups, or to both. Films or talks may be scheduled.

A dedication ceremony can serve as an important means of gaining community recognition and of involving local business and civic leaders in your communications program. It is an important platform for favorable publicity as well.

For any dedication ceremony, invitations should come from your company's top official (or the executive of the particular installation).

Tours of company facilities are handled in much the same manner as open houses or dedications, but less preparation is required and fewer people are involved. Tours can be scheduled on a regular basis; one or two guides are the only unit personnel required. Regular tour days may be established or requests from groups may be accepted with a few days' notice.

Your company's management might encourage tours by civic clubs, professional societies, women's or men's groups, youth or senior citizen groups, high school science or business classes, teachers, clergymen, government officials (with prior clearance from the corporate headquarters), suppliers, dealers, and others. Printed material should be distributed to tour groups, and, if it is feasible, simple refreshments may be served. If at all possible, a company executive should take a few minutes to welcome each tour group.

Children under the age of 12 should not be admitted to production facilities, and safety precautions should be taken whatever the event.

When a general invitation is to be made for open houses and dedications, it should be done through the local newspapers and radio and television stations. In addition, letters should be sent to the heads of local organizations, to school officials, to the press, and to other opinion molders.

In the case of a tour, or if only a particular, special group is being invited to a dedication or open house, the invitation should of course be extended by letter.

The checklist on the following pages will be of help in planning open houses and dedications. Certain items will be applicable to tour planning and preparation.

A CHECKLIST

Objectives

- Facilitate good community relations.
- Facilitate good employee relations.
- Illustrate company or unit policies and benefits.
- Demonstrate how products are made.
- Dramatize free enterprise in action.
- Convey company, unit, and industry message.
- Attract prospective employees.
- Create new customers.
- Support the company's securities.
- Other _____.

Who Is in Charge?

- Consult with executive in charge of installation.

- Appoint committee, if needed.
- Advise supervisors and obtain their support.
- Choose staff, hosts, guides, lecturer.
- Notify employees.
- Designate press officer.

Guest List—Whom to Invite

- Employees and families.
- Customers and prospective customers.
- Civic leaders, opinion molders.
- Shareholders, financial community members (with prior corporate approval).
- Educators.
- Suppliers.
- Clergy.
- Dealers, jobbers, distributors.
- Retired employees.

- Youth, men's, women's and senior citizen groups.
- Business and science classes.
- Professional societies.
- Officials of other companies.
- Special guests suggested by executives.

Setting the Time and Date

- Tie in with company or unit anniversary or special event.
- Check with other local events to avoid conflicts.
- Choose least busy day of week.
- Consider a school holiday so entire family might attend.
- Set alternate date in case of bad weather.
- Set plan for announcing change, if necessary.

The Budget

- Estimate attendance.
- Check cost of refreshments, catering services, supplies, decorations, special safety precautions, rented films, hired speaker.
- Check cost of printing displays, signs.
- Check cost of identification badges.
- Check cost of souvenirs, prizes.
- Figure mailing expense, postage, press releases.
- Figure cost of transportation, if required.

Facilities

- Select and mark adequate parking space; assign attendant(s).
- Locate large convenient reception area.
- Establish simple registration procedure; assign staff.
- Designate ample checkroom space, if required; assign attendant(s).
- Prepare facilities to be seen:

  All facilities must be clean and neat.

  Machinery must be clean, in good working order.

  Tour route must be absolutely safe.

  Information signs and arrows must be installed.

- Arrange for adequate space to serve refreshments.
- Install or test public address system for music and announcements.
- Put up suitable displays.

- Make sure rest rooms are convenient, clean, and clearly marked.
- Provide box for drawing if prize is to be given.
- Brief guides and have practice run.
- Give guides uniform explanation of machines and processes.
- Instruct guides to be precise and nontechnical.

Format for Tour

- Arrange for short welcome speech by official.
- Show film, if available.
- Limit size of groups for better handling.
- Route tours to save time and steps, to avoid unattractive areas, to ensure safety and smooth, rapid movement of guests.
- Demonstrate how quality is built into products.
- Illustrate how standards are maintained.
- Demonstrate safety and health precautions.
- Tour modern offices as well as plant.
- Include recreation areas, lounge, library, cafeteria facilities.

- Schedule question-and-answer period at end of tour.
- Note problems for consideration in preparation for subsequent tour or open house.

Refreshments

- Select only quick-service items.
- Contract for cafeteria or catering service to handle refreshments.
- Check on adequate paper containers and disposable utensils.
- Arrange for necessary waste containers.

Printed Material

- Invitations.
- Return postcards, if required.
- Mimeographed instruction for guides.
- Company and industry literature.
- Programs, if required.
- Identification cards or badges.
- Maps of building layout and tour route, if required.
- Registration forms or book.
- Cards for drawing, if prize is given.

Displays

- Prepare displays on scope of company's activities and operations, photos of other facilities, importance to community.
- Prepare displays explaining working of equipment.
- Prepare displays of company products.
- Prepare displays conveying company and industry messages.

Souvenirs and Prizes

- Select inexpensive souvenir bearing company logo and name, if occasion warrants.
- If company produces consumer products, consider a door prize made up of a selection of products.

Publicity

- Invite press, television, and radio in advance and follow up on invitations the day of the event.
- Distribute news releases in advance of the event.
- Place advertising as an invitation in advance of event, if needed.

- Prepare material for reporters who attend.
- Arrange for company executives to be available for interviews at reporter's request.
- Make sure that company press officer maintains contact with all reporters throughout the event.
- Arrange for your photographer to cover the event.
- Distribute follow-up news release and photos to local and area media while event is in progress.
- Use the event as a springboard to place feature stories and interviews.

Follow-Up

- Encourage comments and suggestions from visitors.
- Give recognition to employees who worked on project.
- Hold critique to analyze and improve procedures.
- Maintain file of correspondence, news releases, reports, work sheets, media coverage, for future use.
- Consider sending photographs and/or follow-up letter to key people who attended.

■ SPECIAL EVENTS

❏ An Idea List

Open Houses

- Anniversary of company's founding or acquisition
- Anniversary of the opening of a facility
- Other company anniversaries
- Industry events
- Completion of new facilities or offices
- Purchase of facilities or entrance into new community
- Significant achievements, such as production or safety records
- Announcements of new process or product
- Community events, such as salutes to industry, historical commemorations, Business Education Day, Junior Chamber of Commerce Day

Dedications, Celebrations, and Similar Ceremonies

- Dedication of new facilities
- Dedication of new equipment, office buildings
- Dedication of new parks, employee recreation areas
- Dedication of historical markers or commemorative plaques on company property
- Ground breakings, laying of cornerstones
- First batch of new product produced

Tours

- In connection with other events, such as students during Public School Week, professional societies during the week honoring their profession
- Press tours in connection with any newsworthy announcement
- An annual tour by retired employees
- Tours by college classes for recruitment or customer development program
- Regular tour days: publicize the day and time when guides will be available to conduct tours for anyone who appears

Other Events

- Banquets, luncheons, dinners on special occasions to which opinion molders are invited

- Annual reunion of retired employees

- Presentation of scholarships, safety awards

- Executive or employee retirement ceremony

■ COMMUNITY SERVICE

The surrounding communities will be more friendly and cooperative if the company becomes involved in service activities that benefit the residents.

This entails executives and employees becoming active in charitable, fraternal, and other organizations as individuals and, in certain instances, as representatives of the company. It may involve providing financial assistance and, in some cases, materials and equipment to aid these organizations in their tasks. It may be valuable for company executives to investigate the possibilities of its facilities being used for shelter, first-aid, and other purposes in the event of emergencies or disasters. If this is feasible, contingency plans should be drawn up in cooperation with the responsible civilian and government authorities.

Once again, it is nonproductive for the company to hide its light under the proverbial bushel. For its contributions to do the most good—for the community in which it functions and as a positive reflection on the company itself—its activities must be properly publicized.

Setting aside for the moment the civic responsibilities attendant on your role as a corporate employee, you will, presumably, as a private individual, want to make a contribution to your town, city, state, and country. By doing so, without consideration of personal gain, you will automatically help to accomplish one or more of the important objectives of your company's public relations program.

Become active in those organizations that interest and move you, groups whose objectives you strongly support. There are general charities such as the United Fund, Catholic Charities, and the Federation of Jewish Philanthropies; those directed to a single problem or group of problems such as Big Brothers or Big Sisters, Boy Scouts or Girl Scouts; organizations such as the Masons and Knights of Columbus; civic and businessmen's groups such as the Rotary and the Chamber of Commerce; local churches and synagogues; colleges and other educational institutions—all these and many more deserve your support.

▪ PUBLIC AFFAIRS

The extent to which any company becomes involved in the issues and problems that confront its industry and the nation is a decision to be made at top-management echelons. No matter what policy is established, carrying it out becomes an important element of the public relations program employing a broad range of tools and techniques.

CHAPTER 21

The Elements of a Public Relations Program: The Shareholders, Financial Community and Other Publics

There are a number of other publics and techniques that may not be as visible as those already discussed but that must, nonetheless, be a part of any total communications effort. This chapter will cover the development of relationships with special publics, such as shareholders and the financial community, and will explore several additional public relations techniques, including direct-mail-communications and person-to-person contacts between company and community members.

■ SHAREHOLDER RELATIONS

While the shareholders comprise an extremely important audience for the overall company public relations effort, unless you are a corporate public relations executive, you will probably be less active in this area.

In most publicly held companies, maintaining and improving relations with shareholders is the responsibility of the corporate public relations staff. The annual report, quarterly reports, special reports, and meetings are all part of this effort.

If you are a line officer, your primary responsibility will be to help establish the performance upon which this phase of the program is based. It is your job, as well, to communicate that performance accurately to corporate headquarters so that it can be utilized in the total effort.

As we mentioned earlier, activities that are routine to you may be of great interest to people unfamiliar with your operation. Pass such items along to corporate headquarters for dissemination to stockholders.

Obviously, letters, phone calls, or visits from shareholders should be treated as if they were from your bosses. In a sense, they are. Of course, you will be courteous. In addition, be cautious. Be aware of what information you should not reveal without prior approval from headquarters.

If you do not know the answer to a question or if you think the requested information is outside your area of responsibility, refer the stockholder to the proper corporate executive. When in doubt, do not commit yourself. This is not withholding information, but it is, rather, an attempt to give out correct information at the proper time.

■ FINANCIAL COMMUNITY AND INVESTOR RELATIONS

Basically what we have said about the shareholders pertains to the financial community at large and to potential investors. A corporate public relations department communicates with this public through meetings with security analysts, bankers, brokers, investment bankers, and via contacts with the financial services, regular mailings, personal discussions, and other methods.

The chief responsibility of the line officer is to communicate results to corporate headquarters.

Of course, any financial or investment consultant who contacts you may possess the power to make a significant difference to the well-being of the company. He or she should be treated with the same courtesy—and caution—as a shareholder. To repeat: when in doubt, say nothing.

▪ EMPLOYEE RELATIONS

It has become an accepted fact of business life that a company is as good as the people who work for it. Their skills, attitudes, and dedication create the corporate personality.

The principal motivation for any worker is the compensation that he or she receives. It would be naive to deny this. However, in our complex society, many elements other than a paycheck influence employee attitudes. These might include working conditions, recognition by the management, peer approval, personal involvement in decision making, and the conception that the individual has formed about his or her own relationship to the company.

Specifics of employee relations vary with each company, but every member of management, both staff and line, can contribute to this important part of the program.

▪ CUSTOMER RELATIONS

No wheels turn, no factory works, no goods are distributed, no profits are earned or dividends paid until a sale is made. The most important single individual to any company is the person who makes that sale possible—the customer. On his or her shoulders rests the entire corporate superstructure. Without the customer, there is no company.

Customer relations must permeate every phase of the public relations program as well as every phase of corporate life. From the worker in the mine or factory, through the salespeople and management staff, to the chairman and president, the customer must be the "main man."

All the techniques outlined in this book, all the activities suggested, have, as the final public, that customer.

You, as a public relations officer for your company, have the most complete knowledge of your primary customers. They serve the ultimate consumer you wish to reach. You know if you sell to dealers, retailers, wholesalers, or jobbers. You know where they are located and what their position is in the industry. In short, you know who your customers are.

However, it might be advantageous to clarify your relationship with them in your own mind and to assess in what ways that relationship can be improved. Determine, once more, which of them has the possibility of becoming a more important purchaser. Consider, again, potential new customers—those people to whom you *should* be selling. If you have not already done so, list all present customers, indicating those who should be more active, and then list, as well, firms that might become customers. (You probably already have such lists. Make sure that they are current.)

This does not presume to suggest sales approaches. But public relations can reinforce your company's sales effort to make the prospect a customer and the moderate purchaser an important one.

■ INDUSTRY AND TRADE RELATIONS

The industry in which your company functions is your immediate family. Among its members are your primary customers, your suppliers, and your competitors. These people are your peers, and their view of your company will do much to influence a broader public and will play a part in the atmosphere in which you do business.

Your company should keep the trade press informed of its activities, participate in industry associations, and sit in on their decision-making councils, establish itself as a leading spokesman for the industry's needs and objectives, and, in general, play a significant role in its prosperity.

Frequently, an individual company's public relations program will be directed to the promotion of the industry as a whole. Activities will be initiated in which the company name or its products are not even mentioned. Management should be aware that when the industry prospers, the company will benefit by capturing its fair share of the new markets opened and current ones expanded.

■ SALES PROMOTION AND POINT-OF-SALES

Sales promotion cannot be dealt with effectively in general terms. It can include contests, giveaways, awards, tie-ins, window displays, and many other special projects.

In addition, if your company has its own retail outlets or supplies others directly, point-of-sales promotion is an important part of its public relations effort. Obviously, a person who enters an establishment for any purpose is the best potential customer.

The attractiveness of the displays, the completeness of the lines, the interest created, and the attitude and knowledge of the sales personnel can convert a shopper into a buyer or a small purchaser into a large one.

This will have particular application to those departments that concentrate on the consumer.

■ PERSONAL CONTACTS

When an executive of any company enters a social situation, he or she is a representative of that company, like it or not. Presuming normal, friendly behavior, the reflection on that firm will be favorable. But the executive can accomplish more than that.

Americans are interested in what other people do for a living. In very few other countries around the world would a newly met acquaintance ask, "What do you do?" or "What business are you in?" In the United States this is accepted social behavior. A company executive should be equipped to answer—to really *tell*—the interested questioner what the company does, makes, and sells. This is an effective and inexpensive way to acquaint a broad audience with the company's story. Of course, the more friends the executive makes in varied circles, the broader that audience will be.

■ DIRECT MAIL

Direct mail is a well-accepted communications tool that must be carefully and conservatively used. Not only is it very expensive, but it also must be expertly prepared, or it will end up in innumerable wastebaskets.

Any company must consider in great detail to whom it will send direct mail. Each piece must be targeted to a specific audience and the response must be carefully monitored and analyzed.

Coordination with all levels of management, including corporate, is essential in this phase of the operation, as in all others.

■ MERCHANDISING RESULTS

The impact of a story in a newspaper or magazine, an interview on radio or television, a particularly effective ad, an impressive direct-mail piece, a speech before a group or club—all these communications accomplishments can be multiplied many times over if they are merchandised properly.

A company should reprint montages of magazines and newspaper stories that have appeared, texts of speeches and interviews, advertisements, and other pertinent material and send them to customers, shareholders, and other interested parties. It should use them for point-of-sale displays and in kits for its salespeople.

What others say about a company has a ring of authenticity that nothing it says about itself can equal.

CHAPTER 22

How to Write a News Release

Before we break down the mechanics of news release writing, it would be a good idea to outline some of the general principles governing the procedure.

■ WHAT IS A NEWS STORY?

A news story answers some basic questions. Foremost is "What happened?" or "What is going to happen?" To understand the event, however, it is also necessary to answer:

To whom did it happen?

How did it happen?

When did it happen?

Where did it happen?

Why did it happen?

Of course, this has been summed up by editors since time immemorial as the "what," "who," "how," "when," "where," and "why." Every news release you send out must answer these questions, or it should not go out at all.

For the event to be newsworthy, it must contain one or more of these elements:

timeliness	romance
human interest	meaningful predications
public interest	money
well-known people	exclusivity
conflict	sex
mystery	novelty
tragedy	humor

Your releases will usually be based on timeliness, public interest, conflict, human interest, or information or speculation about the future, but look for all these elements.

As we have emphasized, there is no guarantee that your release will be used, but if you prepare it properly you will increase its chances of becoming a story.

Your release should have a general objective but be written for a specific audience. It should be interesting and timely, and, once again, it must answer the editor's questions: what, who, how, when, where, and why.

Your news release should resemble a pyramid in construction. The first paragraph should tell the essential story very briefly, and the succeeding paragraphs should amplify and elaborate, each giving greater detail and background. It is your job to assist the editor to do his or her job. If your story is too long for the space available, he or she will cut from the bottom of the release. If the editor can't do that, your story is likely to be discarded and another story of approximate news value will be used instead. Your story must be complete even if the last few paragraphs are cut.

In addition, the reader will tend to glance at the first paragraph and not read the entire story. You want to give him or her the necessary information early on.

▪ MECHANICS OF PRESS RELEASES

A release to any news medium should be typed, double-spaced on 8½- by 11-inch white paper with side margins on both sides (you are supplying plenty of room for the editor to use his or her blue pencil). Type on only one side of the page. Try to limit all releases to one page, but if that is not possible, then be sure to number each page and, at the bottom of each page, except the last, type: "(more)." A sentence or paragraph should never be split between two pages. The old news tradition of using the symbol -30- to end a story is out of fashion. Now, either the date or three asterisks (***) is usual.

A headline should indicate the contents of the release. Although this headline will seldom, if ever, be used by the paper, it can influence acceptance of the item. For instance, COMPANY EXECUTIVE DELIVERS SPEECH is a dull headline. The same release might be entitled CHAIRMAN SUGGESTS ALTERNATIVE ENERGY SOURCES (or whatever he is discussing). The second headline obviously has more news interest.

A typical news release follows. The numbers refer to the corresponding notes that follow the release and explain its various elements. If you have little experience in this area, use the text of the release and the covering notes to give yourself some foundation.

ABC Division   1.
Company X
345 Smith Street
Pawling, New York 12345

CONTACT: James Stewart, Assistant to the Manager   2.
          Telephone: (914) 555-5666

FOR IMMEDIATE RELEASE   3.

          COMPANY X APPOINTS DIVISION
                    MANAGER   4.

PAWLING, N.Y.—Robert E. Less has been   5.
appointed manager of the ABC Division of
Company X, the nation's largest producer of

left-handed wrenches, John Johnson, Company X
president, announced today.

"The appointment of Bob Less is an example of
the company's policy of building management
strength from within," Mr. Johnson said. "We are
confident that he will continue to make an
important contribution to our success."

6.

Mr. Less, who will serve on the corporate
executive committee in his new position, was
previously assistant to the manager of the ABC
Division and has been with the company in an
executive capacity for fourteen years.

7.

(more)

8.

ABC, the company's largest division,
manufactures the wrenches that are the
company's most popular product. Mr. Less will
be executive as well as operational chief of the
division.

9.

Mr. Less was president of the Less Wrench
Company before joining Company X. He is a
graduate of MIT and holds a degree in business
administration from the Harvard Business School.
He lives with his wife, Martha, and three children
in Peekskill, New York.

10.

Mr. Less replaces Alfred Ingliss as division
manager. Mr. Ingliss has resigned in order to
concentrate on private business matters.

11.

5/15/94

12.

■ NOTES ON RELEASE

1. If you send the release out on your letterhead, be sure to note
   that it is a news release and use the letterhead only for the first
   page.

2. Even if you use a letterhead, the name and phone number of the correct contact must also be typed in. This is the person ready and able to answer questions. He or she must be available to take calls.

3. Try to label all stories FOR IMMEDIATE RELEASE. It presents fewer problems to the editor. If absolutely necessary, however, you may say: FOR RELEASE ON OR AFTER AUGUST 12, 1994, or FOR RELEASE AUGUST 25, 1994, AFTER 9 A.M.

4. This is a pedestrian but informative headline. A more interesting alternative might be, COMPANY BUILDS MANAGEMENT FROM WITHIN.

5. The city of origin should appear at the beginning of the news release. The first paragraph tells your story. If the editor chooses to use it alone, you will have accomplished your objective.

6. This is important because it states company philosophy and provides the chief executive with exposure, so you put it near the top in the hope that it will be used.

7. Simply expands the basic story.

8. Make sure that "(more)" is on every page but the last.

9. (Same as 7.)

10. This is a paragraph you do not expect the large dailies to use. You put it in for the papers in Peekskill and the alumni publications of MIT and Harvard.

11. This is a paragraph that you would like to lose. Mr. Ingliss retired with some resentment, but he agreed to the explanation used in the release. You include it in an attempt to satisfy the editor's questions before he asks them.

12. The date should appear at some place in every release.

CHAPTER 23

How to Write a Pitch Letter

The pitch letter is one of your primary tools of communication with the media. You will use it to place feature stories, set up interviews, and obtain coverage for press conferences and special events and for a number of other purposes.

Since the uses for a pitch letter are so varied, the kinds of tight rules that apply to the writing of a news release do not apply to the composition of a pitch letter. The letter permits a much greater use of your imagination and initiative.

■ THE MECHANICS

Write your pitch letter exactly as you would any business letter, using your regular stationery. If your title appears on the letterhead, do not repeat it under your signature.

Leave plenty of white space, write several short paragraphs rather than a few long ones, and, in general, make the letter easy to read.

Be sure that your name and phone number appear prominently. If there are specific hours when you can be reached, include that information in the letter.

Unless the story you are pitching is as world-shaking as a war or a natural disaster, or as complicated as Einstein's theory of relativity, keep your letter down to a page or a page and a half.

Newspeople are deluged with releases and resent unnecessary padding.

▪ THE CONTENT OF THE LETTER

Although pitch letter form is freer than that of a news release, the pitch letter must answer the same questions: what, who, how, when, where, and why. However, it does not impose the same limitations. You do not have to tell your story in the first paragraph. You can use the opening lines to grab the reader's attention, to sell the entire concept of the story.

Your letter must accomplish several objectives. It must:

1. Present the concept of the story.

2. Summarize the facts supporting the story.

3. List the material you have available: statistics, graphics, photos, and so forth.

4. Offer an interview on your story subject with an expert, if there is one available.

5. Suggest a follow-up for the letter.

Since this tool has so many applications, we will not attempt to write a "typical" letter. Instead, we will offer several letters and opening paragraphs that actually were used in specific situations. It may be that none of them will be relevant to your particular company, but they will serve to broaden your awareness of the versatility and effectiveness of the technique.

❑ Example 1

To make it timely, try to tie your letter into a newsworthy event or trend. The following example was used several years ago by a computer leasing company and achieved excellent results:

> Mr. John Smith
> The Iowa Dispatch
> 123 Main Street
> Crowley, Iowa 13579

> Dear Mr. Smith *(or first name, if you are on that basis)*:

> As you know, today XYZ announced a radical change in pricing policies. The cost of equipment has been slashed and rental prices have been increased. The obvious purpose of this move is to encourage cash sales and discourage rentals. The reason is that XYZ must improve its cash position.

> One of the immediate effects of this development is that it provides an absolute bonanza for computer leasing companies. These companies buy equipment from XYZ (which makes XYZ very happy) and lease it for 15 percent less than XYZ does (which makes the customers equally happy).

> The new XYZ pricing policy means that leasing companies will be able to pass on an additional 4 to 6 percent savings to their customers.

> Grandex Computer Leasing Company is one of the largest in the field. I am enclosing their annual report and other relevant information. Company and industry statistics on growth, trends, and future prospects are available for use in a story on this mushrooming sector of space-age industry.

> Mr. Gerald Gerald, president of Grandex, is a computer engineer and a pioneer in computer rental. He has a degree in business administration from the Harvard Business School. He will be in this city from July 10 through July 17. I would be happy

to arrange an interview at your convenience. I'm sure you will find Mr. Gerald informative and imaginative.

I will call you in a few days to discuss this story possibility.

Sincerely,

John Doe

JD/gg

Enclosures

You will notice that this letter accomplishes the objectives we outlined: it presents the concept of the story, it summarizes some of the facts supporting the story, it lists additional available material, it offers an expert to be interviewed, and it suggests a follow-up phone call.

In addition, the letter takes advantage of a recent development of which the editor should be aware. This is a great strength, and you should be alert to similar possibilities. For example, if housing starts fall off dramatically for a month or a quarter and your target publication prints that news, you might suggest a story on the way in which the repair and remodeling industry is taking up the slack. Your lead might be:

Mr. John Smith
The Iowa Dispatch
123 Main Street
Crowley, Iowa 13579

Dear Mr. Smith:

The new cry of the American homeowner seems to be, "If you can't move, improve!"

As you know, last month's new housing starts were off _____ percent from the same month last year. This is not good news for anybody, particularly for construction and building products companies. However, there is a bright side.

Consumer expenditures for remodeling and improving homes increased a whopping _____ percent over the previous year in the same month that housing starts fell off.

You would then proceed to develop the story, present additional facts, suggest available material, offer one of your officers or yourself for an interview, and tell the editor how you intend to follow up.

❑ Example 2

An important development within your unit might serve as the "hook" for a story. If you are sending your letter to a local paper, the unit activity might be enough. If you are approaching a regional, national, or trade publication, you might have to expand the specific event to illustrate a general trend.

When the ABC Division of Company X expanded its production facilities for left-handed wrenches, our imaginary executive sent out the following letter:

Dear Mr. Smith:

In July of this year the ABC Division of Company X will open a new modern facility for the production of left-handed wrenches at Storeyville, Georgia. In addition, the division will expand and modernize existing plants in Boston, New York State, and Oregon.

These expansion moves will make Company X the largest producer of left-handed wrenches in the country.

Important as these developments are to our company and to the industry, they are even more significant as an indication of an emerging national trend.

Industry is no longer ignoring left-handed people. Until now, "southpaws" had to make do with tools, equipment, and artifacts designed for the right-handed majority. American business, ever open to the lure of new markets, is changing that situation.

We have researched this trend. We have available for you a long list of products from back scratchers to sewing machines, from complicated tools to simple household materials, which are being made specifically for left-handed people.

Irving Irving, vice president for marketing of Company X, is one of the few specialists in this new area of marketing concentration. He will be in our city from June 5 through June 12. I would be happy to arrange a meeting to discuss the possibilities of this story.

For your information, I am enclosing the annual report and other background information of Company X and a bio of Mr. Irving.

I hope you agree that the "left-handed wrench" can introduce your readers to an interesting and unusual aspect of American business. I will call in a few days to discuss it with you.

Sincerely,

Obviously, you are not making left-handed wrenches. And not every development of your unit will lend itself to such an interesting story idea.

However, whenever there is significant unit activity—the opening of a new facility, the expansion of an existing plant, the introduction of a product line—you should initiate a three-phase program:

1. Send out a news release to all interested media.
2. Consider the possibilities of a pitch letter to local media, based simply on the significance of the development to your company and to the community.
3. Carefully analyze the event as to its broader significance. Does it indicate a trend? Is it unusual or interesting enough to justify a feature story? Does it relate to current economic or industry news? In short, how can you use this development to get a story in a regional, national, or trade publication?

Of course, you will not be successful in obtaining all three kinds of coverage every time. But it is always worth trying. Unlike an advertisement, a pitch letter costs you only your time and postage. And even if the reporter or editor turns you down, you will have made a new press contact or reinforced one you have already established.

❑ Example 3

Perhaps "example" is a misnomer for what follows. The heading might more properly read, "Find the Hook." Every feature story must provide a reason for being used. Sometimes the reason is obvious—John Jones is appointed secretary of commerce, IBM declares bankruptcy, General Motors acquires Ford, and so on. There is no way that a newspaper cannot use a story like that.

However, you will usually be dealing with less earthshaking stories. They will be used or not, depending upon the news judgment of the editor. That judgment can be influenced considerably in your favor if you supply an interesting angle, an unusual approach—a "hook" upon which to hand your material.

There is no way to outline specifically how such an approach can be developed. That will depend upon your imagination and the "nose for news" we discussed earlier.

It helps to have a thorough knowledge of the target publication. Through careful reading and analysis of the stories used therein you will discover ways of shaping your own material to meet the specific requirements of that publication.

In addition, give your imagination full rein as you write. Do not be afraid to be a little "far out," to stretch the bounds of relevance. Your own good taste and business background will prevent you from going too far. Remember, the worst that can happen is that the story will be rejected. And you will learn something from every rejection.

Following are the openings of actual pitch letters that were successful. The names of the companies and people involved have been changed, but not the letters themselves. They illustrate how far from the actual material the hook might be:

Dear John:

Nobody knows what would have happened to the history of the world if Nero had put down his fiddle and turned his attention to matters of more importance.

However, we know a man who put away his saxophone and made millions of dollars for himself. The man is Jim Doe and he found a pot of gold at both ends of the rainbow—with two firms making beauty preparations for the professional beautician. One of the companies is now a giant in the retail cosmetics field.

Doe started as a successful saxophone player with the name bands of the thirties. Tired of the traveling and working nights, he took a job as a salesman in the New York area with Joseph Laboratories, manufacturers and distributors of supplies and equipment for beauty salons.

The letter proceeded to outline Doe's road to success. Background on the two important companies that he now heads was enclosed, and his availability for an interview was mentioned. The story was accepted, written, and published by one of the most prestigious business publications in the country. The editor used the "saxophone player turned businessman" hook as his lead.

Examine your own background and also interview your fellow executives as if you were a reporter. You might be surprised to find a number of interesting angles that you can use to introduce a story on your unit or its activities.

We offer another example:

Dear Ms. Jones:

Manuel is a man of many worlds. He is of Mexican, Greek, and Turkish heritage, but he is the prototype of the American business executive. Moreover, his creative efforts provide a seemingly impossible synthesis of Mexico, Spain, and the United States.

His full name is Manuel Manuel, and he owns the Fiesta Shop in Mexico City and the House of Manuel in New York, He may well be the presiding genius of the surge of interest in Mexican and Spanish furniture in this country.

The letter went on to expound on Manuel's history and philosophy. Pertinent material was enclosed and an interview was offered. A story in a major metropolitan daily resulted.

This is another example of using an individual to sell a company story. For you to do this, you must overcome a natural reticence on the part of many business people. You and your colleagues should understand that in presenting yourselves for interviews and as the basis for stories, you are not seeking personal publicity or self-glorification. You are making an important contribution to your company's communications program.

> Dear Tanya:
>
> Although diamonds may be a girl's best friend, ladies seem to prefer pearls. Or, at least, are able to afford pearls, since they are America's most sold precious jewelry.
>
> The oyster's creations were treasured in China as early as 300 B.C. They are mentioned in the ancient Talmud, the sacred book of Judaism. It says that the clothes Jehovah made for Adam and Eve were "as beautiful as pearls."
>
> The Arab who enters heaven, according to the Koran, lives in a "tent of pearls." And, of course, the New Testament speaks of the "pearly gates" of the new Jerusalem.

The letter went on to relate a number of interesting facts about pearls and then told the history of cultured pearls and of the writer's company, which was the largest importer of cultured pearls in America. It included background on that company and offered the vice president, a scholar on the history of pearls, as an interviewee.

The result was a feature in a major Sunday supplement which quoted the executive at length and gave excellent coverage of the company itself.

If your unit deals with a product or products, be assured that there is probably an interesting history behind them which can be used to get an editor's attention. Investigate this history, compile a list of unusual facts, and then send out your pitch letters. If one editor turns you down, there may well be another who is waiting for just such a story.

The examples are endless, limited only by your imagination. A good hook can be something very simple—a startling statistic, for example:

American industry is being buried under a mass of paper.

Business in this country used enough paper in 1991 to stretch to the moon and back five times, with enough left over to paper the entire earth.

This was a lead for a pitch for a business form printing company. There are many such amazing facts to uncover relating to almost any product.

Here is something on an industry trend:

The United States Armed Services are considering renting their uniforms. This is consistent with the decision in the last ten years of most uniform users in private industry to rent rather than buy.

This story on a uniform rental company was placed.

In conclusion, in a pitch letter anything that makes sense and excites interest is acceptable. Remember what the letter must accomplish. It must present the story concept, include supporting facts, list available background materials, offer an interview if possible, and establish a follow-up procedure.

Be imaginative, be creative, but, above all, be persistent. Keep sending out those letters. If they are rejected by one editor, try another. If one idea seems not to work, then by all means, try another.

CHAPTER 24

Public Relations in an Emergency

It is most difficult to maintain good public and press relations when an accident or emergency occurs. In such situations there are persistent, seemingly unrelenting inquiries from the press, the community, business associates, government agencies, friends and relatives of employees, and other interested people. Fatigue and tension can cause short tempers and lapses in efficiency. Unless great care is taken, months of good public relations work can be undone in a single day.

A delicate balance must be achieved between refusing to answer questions at all and giving hasty and ill-conceived responses. On the one hand, the company can be accused of withholding vital information. On the other, partial or unclear answers can result in unfavorable stories and false rumors.

However, providing good emergency services for the media can earn friends for the company regardless of the nature and scope of the problem.

Presumably the company has an excellent safety record. Thorough precautions have been taken to eliminate accidents. The company does not anticipate any serious incidents, but it must have a plan for dealing with such contingencies, or it may well be considered incompetent and poorly managed, should an emergency arise.

The following emergency operations and communications policy is adaptable for several corporate setups, with logical modifications determined by the nature of the specific company:

> An authorized spokesperson, usually the unit's senior executive, should be designated in advance to represent management on the scene and to be responsible for the implementation of this program.

> If there is a person other than the senior executive who is in charge of the unit's public relations program, he or she should automatically assume the responsibilities of press officer. If not, a press officer for emergencies should be designated in advance by the senior executive.

> The senior executive should assure that the chief executive officer is immediately informed of the nature of the emergency and is kept constantly up to date on all developments for the duration of the problem.

> Factual information on all personnel injuries should be given to the employees' families as soon as the senior executive has confirmed the facts. If at all possible, this information should not be given to the media until after the families have been notified.

> The press officer should provide the media with information as soon as facts can be verified, and within the parameters of company policy.

> No company employee should speculate on anything that has not been positively and officially verified, such as the cause of an accident. The company should take the initiative in informing the press and local government authorities if they are not already aware of the situation.

> The press officer, and all company personnel, should emphasize to the media the company's safety record and the continuing precautions taken to avoid accidents.

The press officer should utilize all means of communication to provide factual information to offset rumors or misstatements; the company should, as quickly as possible, inform all interested publics, including employees' families, shareholders, the financial community, suppliers, customers, members of the "affect community," and, of course, all media.

■ WHAT CONSTITUTES AN EMERGENCY?

A public relations emergency is a situation or event that may be interpreted in a manner that could or would be harmful to the company, and that is subject to coverage by the news media in a way that is not in the interests of the company. Such emergencies include, but are not limited to:

- A plant accident involving serious injuries or fatalities.
- Any event that requires the assistance of such outside agencies as police, fire, or medical.
- An explosion or fire.
- Death of a company executive from causes that appear to be related to his or her official duties.
- A riot or civil disorder on or near company property.
- A so-called act of God—a natural disaster such as an earthquake or flood.

In short, any incident or situation that focuses unusual media and public attention on the company must be considered a public relations emergency.

■ EMERGENCY PROCEDURES

Immediately upon becoming aware of the emergency, the senior executive (who is the executive in charge), should alert the designated press officer. (Each of these people should appoint substitutes to back them up in case they are unavailable when an emergency occurs.)

The senior executive should confirm that the police, fire department, and so on have been properly alerted and then should inform the company chief executive officer.

The press officer should contact the corporate public relations office, if such a department exists. If the situation warrants, a member of that department should proceed immediately to the location to assist in press relations and to provide counsel when required.

■ PRESS HEADQUARTERS

Each unit should designate two locations—a primary and an alternate—to serve as central media information points in case of a serious emergency. Each location should be equipped with a number of telephones and adequate office equipment. These may, of course, be facilities that are normally used for regular business purposes.

If the emergency is centered in or near the primary press location, then the alternate area should be utilized. Employees should be informed of these plans in advance so that they will be able to direct reporters.

At least two secretaries should be assigned to the press officer to take calls from media people, whether or not a press headquarters has been established. If the press officer is unavailable to take calls, all of them should be listed, and he or she should return them as promptly as possible.

■ PRESS RELATIONS

Upon notification of the emergency, the press officer should assess available information and determine if a press headquarters is required and, if so, at which of the predesignated locations it should be established. The seriousness of the situation influences the need for such a facility, which can help keep media people out of the way of rescue personnel and facilitate the accurate, prompt delivery of information to the media by the press officer.

The press officer should maintain contact with all media personnel for the duration of the emergency; assure that they remain in approved, safe areas; and issue all pertinent information, in accordance with company policy, as quickly as possible.

The press officer should discuss the text of announcements and releases and, whenever possible, the answers to questions, with the director of corporate public relations, if there is one.

When the senior executive determines that it is completely safe, the press office should escort media people to the area in which the emergency occurred and explain the event from the company's perspective.

Safety equipment, such as hard hats, should be readily available and provisions made in advance for distribution to members of the press, as required.

The senior executive should be available for interviews as frequently as possible. In his absence, other company spokespeople should substitute.

Regardless of the amount of coverage made individually by members of the press, the press officer should be constantly gathering facts for the purpose of issuing the company's own releases.

In cases where statements relating to the emergency are made by persons outside the company, such as government officials, the media should be invited to request the company's comments to avoid a situation where incorrect information is being made public without challenge.

The same full cooperation, within the requirements of safety, that is accorded to the print media should be given to radio and television representatives.

■ COMMUNICATIONS WITH OTHER PUBLICS

Depending upon the nature and duration of the emergency, special measures may be required to communicate with employees. Spot announcements on local radio stations, newspaper ads, and telephone calls on an organized basis are devices that may be used. Radio spots might also be used to reassure employees' families, if the emergency occurs during the workday.

If the problem is a severe one, the company might want to contact key community leaders by telephone as quickly as possible so that they have the facts at hand for those who might question them. If such phone contact is necessary, the senior executive should assign specific personnel to make the calls.

All communication with shareholders and members of the financial community is the responsibility of corporate headquarters.

■ WHEN THE SMOKE CLEARS

A story never ends when the emergency is over. The follow-up can be of great importance.

Stories should be developed and placed regarding the company's efforts in aiding victims, reconstruction, and future safeguards. Actions to thank the community for its help and other activities that demonstrate the company's concern for its employees and the public should be included as well.

A letter to employees reassuring them about future operations might be valuable.

You might send positive follow-up material to your list of community leaders and organizations. The same or a similar mailing might go to your lists of customers and suppliers.

Material might be provided to corporate headquarters for distribution to shareholders and members of the financial community.

Immediately after the emergency, it is advisable for the unit's public relations executive to discuss with corporate headquarters a complete and well-coordinated follow-up program.

CHAPTER 25

The Speaker's Bureau

In planning a complete communications program, the public relations executive must determine who is available to appear on television or radio, who can be interviewed by the trade and consumer press, or who can speak to organizations whose memberships are important to the firm.

He or she must look for people who are experts in a particular field, even if it is only remotely connected with the company's business. A toy manufacturer might have a child psychologist on staff; a food company, a qualified nutritionist; an electronics firm, a specialist in that field.

The public relations executive should always be interested in arranging speaking engagements and personal appearances for company representatives, even if nothing is mentioned about the company's products or services. The fact that the representative is introduced as vice president of the company, and then speaks with expertise and knowledge, has great value. The demonstrated competence of the speaker is transferred to the company in the mind of the listener, viewer, or reader.

In addition, a public appearance by a company executive is the launching pad for attendant publicity: releases to the media; announcements to customers, shareholders, and the financial community when appropriate; and follow-up reprints of the speech or interview are all effective. If properly used, this phase of the program can be extremely productive at a relatively low cost.

Certain people in your unit might be qualified to handle such general topics as energy sources, ecology, or good corporate citizenship. Others will be more effective in specific areas of expertise.

The first step in creating your speakers' bureau is the compilation of a card file of speakers, even if you have only two or three available. This file should list each speaker separately and include name, biographical data, subject or subjects the speaker can discuss, record of speeches made, and, to the extent possible, reaction to those speeches. This file will be used in selecting speakers for specific audiences and in maintaining a running record of accomplishments.

The second step is the identification of audiences. Business clubs, chambers of commerce, fraternal organizations, and many other groups are always in need of good speakers for their programs. They usually have program directors—volunteers charged with the responsibility of providing their groups with interesting and stimulating talks. Develop a list of these organizations and their program chairmen in your area, once again by using the phone books and the telephone.

When you have completed your speakers' file and your audience list, you will have set the foundation for a valuable and versatile public relations tool.

■ TIPS ON SPEECH WRITING AND DELIVERY

You have now established a speakers' bureau and are ready to book appearances for yourself or for other executives.

Once an engagement has been scheduled and a topic chosen, either in consultation with the audience group or at their request, the speaker is ready to begin preparation.

In many cases the subject matter will be so familiar that little research will be necessary. No matter how knowledgeable the speaker may be, however, he or she should carefully marshal facts, statistics, and other materials to support the positions he or she intends to take.

After the research has been completed and the required facts and anecdotes assembled, the next step is the preparation of an outline. It is advisable to begin with a rough listing of the points to be covered, then to develop it into a detailed outline, working with the material that has been collected.

■ THE FINISHED SPEECH

When the outline is completed, two methods can be used in developing the working of the speech. It may be written word for word and read, or it may be spoken extemporaneously, following the outline without preparing a full written text. The extemporaneous method of presentation gives the speaker more flexibility and permits more spontaneity, but if policy statements are to be made, it may be desirable to prepare a written text to avoid misinterpretations.

Many good public speakers combine these two methods. They prepare a full text and go over it many times until they become very familiar with it. For the actual appearance, however, they use the outline, depending upon their knowledge of the text to give them mental and verbal ease.

A crucial element to be considered in the preparation of the speech is the nature of the audience. Age, sex, and profession of the audience, as well as other demographic factors, must influence both the content and the phraseology of the speech. Technical terms should be avoided unless the group is familiar with them.

In general, use short, uncomplicated sentences. A simple word or phrase is always preferable to long, involved explanations. A speaker should not be interested in displaying erudition. The objective is to inform, educate, and interest the audience. The speech should be just long enough to cover the topic. The material should not be padded.

One of the shortest speeches on record was delivered by Henry Ford at Light's Golden Jubilee in Atlantic City in 1929. The other businessmen and politicians on the platform spent hours extolling the benefits of electricity. When the crowd shouted for Ford, he said, referring to the manufacturing of automobiles, "We build at Dearborn eight thousand complete electric light plants every day. This being an electrical meeting, I thought I'd like to tell you that. Thank you." And he sat down.

Abraham Lincoln's famous address was by far the shortest speech given at Gettysburg on that historic day. Obviously, longer is not necessarily better.

Most of us are not comedians. The old after-dinner speaker's habit of including "jokes" in a speech is obsolete. They are usually strained, inferior jokes that half the audience has heard before. Many speakers have the wit and sense of humor to find amusing aspects in the material itself. This kind of light, informal approach is far superior to the overworked joke. The speaker should not, however, feel an obligation to be "funny." That is Bob Hope's job, and he gets paid very well for it.

To sum up, the speech should be brief, simple, and as light and informal as the material permits. It should be well researched and completely accurate. Remember—the speaker is the voice of the organization.

Whenever possible, the speech should be submitted to corporate public relations or the office of the chief executive officer in advance of presentation. If statements of company and/or industry positions on national issues are included in the remarks, then this is essential.

■ THE PRESENTATION

Before going in front of the actual audience, the speaker should practice delivering the speech. This should be done alone, aloud, and, ultimately, without script if possible. Even though the outline or the verbatim text will be used by the speaker at the time of the talk, it is essential that he become thoroughly familiar with the material beforehand.

In many cases, it is desirable to enhance a speech with the use of visual aids. These might consist of slides, filmstrips, enlarged photos, charts, drawings on a blackboard, or product samples. These aids should be used only when they serve the purpose of making the presentation more interesting and effective.

The physical appearance of the speaker is very important. All speakers will, of course, be well groomed. They should have good posture and a confident manner and be relaxed, warm, and friendly.

The speaker's first task is to establish contact with the audience. It is a good orator's trick to speak to them directly, one after another, until as much of the audience as possible feels that he or she has been personally addressed.

The speaker's voice must, of course, be loud enough to be heard throughout the room, but not so loud that the audience would begin to feel harangued. The tone of voice should be conversational, and not pompous or stagey. The speech pattern should be slow and distinct so that every word is heard and understood. The speaker should be careful to avoid a monotone and should allow easy and natural voice shifts as frequently as the material dictates, for interest and emphasis.

The less the speaker has to refer to notes the better, but if a certain statement must be read to ensure accuracy, this should be done openly and obviously without any attempt at concealment. Any visual aids used should be presented so that the entire audience has a clear view.

If questions and answers are to follow the speech, the company representative should be prepared beforehand. He should try to anticipate what might be asked and formulate answers. During this period the speaker should be courteous, positive, confident, and avoid guessing at answers he does not have. Once the presentation is completed, the speaker should be warm, friendly, and appreciative of compliments and expressions of thanks.

From the instant the speaker enters the room until the time he leaves, he must be aware that he is the face, the voice, the representative of the company.

In most instances, the speakers' bureau that you have established will be able to fill requests from organizations in your area. There may be occasions when a speaker is required to discuss a subject about which no one in your unit has expertise. Do not automatically refuse the booking. Consult first with corporate public relations or the office of the chief executive officer—such a person may be available in another unit of the company.

CHAPTER 26

The Basic Rules of Public Relations and Publicity

In this chapter you will find summarized the basic rules of public relations and publicity, distilled from the material presented in the foregoing chapters. You might find it useful to have it photocopied so that it can be kept handy for review and easy reference.

■ ALWAYS DO THE FOLLOWING THINGS

1. Develop an overview of the whole company or organization for which you work. Learn how various elements interrelate.

2. Use the corporate identity logo, trademark, colors, and motto on all possible occasions.

3. Discuss your unit's activities, its products and services, with all your publics, within the confines of corporate and division restrictions.

4. Work closely with the division staff and corporate public relations, if they exist.

5. Use freely all material contained in annual and quarterly reports, leaflets, brochures, and other printed material published by your company.

6. Be sure all information you use is accurate.

7. Recognize the synergistic connections between your unit, your division, all other units and divisions.

8. Call upon corporate public relations, if your company has it, for guidance, assistance, material, and ideas when necessary. Regard it as your external public relations agency.

9. Use this checklist as a guide for action in all phases of public relations.

10. State, but do not try to interpret, company or organization policy.

11. Always tell the truth to the media. When in doubt, say nothing.

12. Admit you don't know the answer to a question, if that is the case, and arrange to get the reporter the required information, or refer him or her to someone who can be of help.

13. Be "low key" rather than "hard sell" in your relations with the media.

14. Seek only tasteful, positive publicity.

15. Get to know the media people who are important to your program.

16. Prepare and keep current lists of all the media people with whom you deal.

17. Direct all material to the proper media person.

18. Send all material to media in time to meet deadlines.

19. Include on your media list the trade publications that interest your customers.

20. Promote your unit, its products, and services.

21. Develop a "nose for news."

22. Promote local media use of press material issued by division headquarters and corporate public relations, if your company has them.

23. Take advantage of the interest created in products by ads to place stories in local media.

24. Show no favorites in the distribution of "hard news" releases.

25. Keep your word when you give your story exclusively to a reporter.

26. Examine all departments of a publication for feature placement possibilities.

27. Be aware of opportunities in the electronic media.

28. Use the "pitch letter" as a tool.

29. When a feature is turned down, try to place it elsewhere.

30. When a feature is used, rework it with a new angle and try to place it with another publication.

31. Set up editorial interviews whenever possible.

32. Use photography when it will enhance the possibility of a story being used.

33. Be sure that a "cut line" or caption is pasted to the back of every photo you send out.

34. Attempt to place wire service stories when your material is of broad national interest.

35. Pay special attention to trade papers and magazines.

36. Service the weeklies, shoppers, and club papers in your area.

37. Take advantage of the opportunities presented by the feature services.

38. Be sensitive to issues, specific problems, and economic factors that concern your "affect community."

39. Cooperate in reasonable efforts to protect the environment and to control air, water, and noise pollution and conserve natural resources and the ambiance of the area.

40. Keep local government apprised of your unit's activities and contributions to the community.

41. Encourage community participation in events such as plant openings, tours, and open houses.

42. Communicate your unit's participation in community affairs to the total "affect community."

43. Constantly redefine your "affect community" as your unit's activities broaden.

44. Prepare and keep current a list of all individuals, organizations, and government agencies you wish to inform and educate.

45. Purchase goods and services locally whenever possible.

46. Make sure that your unit's facilities are clean and attractive and that they fit into the surrounding environs.

47. Make a concerted effort to adjust to your community's traffic patterns without disrupting them unduly.

48. Handle all complaints quickly and courteously.

49. Participate in community service activities and encourage other unit employees to do likewise.

50. Investigate the possibility of your unit's facilities being used in the case of emergencies or disasters.

51. Be at all times a good corporate citizen and a concerned neighbor.

52. Communicate your unit's performance to the division and corporate executives promptly and effectively for inclusion in communications with the company's publics.

53. Treat calls and visits from stockholders or members of the financial community courteously but carefully.

54. Supply stockholders, investors, analysts, and so forth with any information that has been published or approved on the corporate level.

55. Refer to corporate headquarters all questions that you are not able to answer or requests for information you are not in a position to reveal.

56. Participate in industry groups.

57. Establish your unit's executives (including yourself) as effective spokespeople for your segment of the industry.

58. Participate in activities to further the objectives of the industry even if there appears to be no direct benefit for your company.

59. Keep your primary customers, suppliers, and industry peers informed of your unit's activities.

60. Make your speakers' bureau an active part of your public relations program.

61. Prepare yourself and other unit executives to be knowledgeable spokespeople even in the course of personal contacts.

62. Merchandise the results of your public relations efforts.

63. Make suggestions regarding the advertising programs based on your own knowledge and on comments you get from customers, suppliers, and so forth.

64. Alert sales personnel, customers, suppliers, employees, and other interested people when a story on your unit is to appear or an executive is to be interviewed on radio or television.

65. Be equipped to interpret and explain employee benefits.

66. Establish a reputation as a fair and concerned representative of management in your relations with your unit's employees.

67. Make yourself available, within the limitations of your work schedule, to listen to employee grievances that are outside the regular structure.

68. Cooperate in the gathering and preparation of material for the internal house organ, if you have one.

69. Use the house organ as an important employee relations tool.

■ DO NOT DO THE FOLLOWING

1. Do not comment on political or economic issues except within the bounds of published or stated company positions.

2. Do not disclose corporate figures, divisional results, or other such information unless it has already been released or unless you have prior approval from corporate headquarters.

3. Do not comment on corporate activity of the company without corporate approval.

4. Do not presume, comment on, or explain any position of the company relative to laws, regulations, economic issues, or government policy.

5. Do not disclose details of internal operations, contents of internal memoranda, advisories, instructions, or other matters.

6. Do not discuss new services, installations, or possible acquisitions without prior clearance from corporate headquarters.

7. Do not discuss matters relating to burglaries, thefts, embezzlements, accidents, disturbances, or other matters (local or corporate) that may have a bearing on the corporate image or that may involve legal questions or insurance claims.

8. Do not discuss company investment policies or philosophies.

9. Do not comment on pending or threatened litigation or other legal proceedings involving your company without prior clearance from corporate headquarters.

10. Do not alter the corporate identity logo, trademark, or colors in any way for any purpose.

11. Do not say anything to a media person anywhere, at any time, on any subject that is "off the record."

12. Do not suggest an exclusive feature to a second reporter before it is definitely refused by the first person you pitched it to.

13. Do not become a pest by calling a publication too frequently to find out if a story has been accepted.

14. Do not invent reasons to call an editor or reporter.

15. Do not pressure a reporter or editor.

16. Do not mention that your company "advertises in the paper."

17. Do not insist on name identification in a story—no matter what its content.

18. Do not ask a reporter if he is going to use a story. It is not his decision.

19. Do not ask to read a story before it is used.

20. Do not send out a story you know to be dull or unimportant or a picture you know to be bad.

21. Do not attempt to service the financial news wires (Dow-Jones and Reuters) without coordinating your efforts with corporate public relations, if it exists in your company.

22. Do not schedule press conferences in any but the most unusual circumstances, and then only after prior discussion with the office of the chief executive officer.

23. Do not call a reporter or editor when he or she is on deadline unless you have important news developments.

24. Do not use fee-charging services such as public relations news wires; mat services; feature, news, or picture services; or public relations mailing houses without prior discussion with corporate headquarters.

25. Do not make any statement to government or community agencies regarding corporate positions or activities unless previously published.

26. Do not take stands on local issues without prior approval of corporate headquarters.

27. Do not make promises of financial or other types of aid on behalf of your unit, division, or company without prior approval.

28. Do not pledge your unit's facilities for any purpose without prior approval.

29. Do not spread yourself too thin in your community service activities.

30. Do not make personal commitments you cannot fulfill.

31. Do not give any information to a shareholder or member of the financial community unless it is already public knowledge.

32. Do not seek to communicate directly with or influence shareholders or the financial community.

33. Do not reveal any corporate, division, or unit activity that is not public knowledge either to your industry, employees, or personal contacts.

34. Do not become involved in labor negotiations unless they are your responsibility.

35. Do not become involved in the formal, established grievance procedure in your unit unless that is your responsibility.

36. Do not make any statement, comment, or analysis of corporate or division policy, activity, plans or philosophy to any individual or group unless the material has already been made public or unless you have prior approval.

INDEX